The
STAFFS
of
LIFE

Books by E. J. Kahn, Jr.

The Staffs of Life
Jock: The Life and Times of John Hay Whitney
Far-flung and Footloose: Pieces from The New Yorker,
1937–1978
About The New Yorker *and Me*
Georgia: From Rabun Gap to Tybee Light
The American People
The China Hands
Fraud
The Boston Underground Gourmet (with Joseph P. Kahn)
The First Decade
Harvard: Through Change and Through Storm
The Separated People
A Reporter in Micronesia
The World of Swope
The Stragglers
A Reporter Here and There
The Big Drink
The Merry Partners
The Peculiar War
Who, Me?
The Voice
McNair: Educator of an Army
G.I. Jungle
The Army Life

E. J. KAHN, JR.

The STAFFS *of* LIFE

Little, Brown and Company
BOSTON   TORONTO

FIRST EDITION

Most of this book originally appeared, in somewhat different
form, in *The New Yorker*.

LIBRARY OF CONGRESS CATALOGING IN PUBLICATION DATA

Kahn, E. J. (Ely Jacques), 1916–
The staffs of life.

Includes index.
1. Food crops.   I. Title.
SB175.K34   1985   338.1'9   84-26177
ISBN 0-316-48192-0

VB

DESIGNED BY JEANNE F. ABBOUD

*Published simultaneously in Canada
by Little, Brown & Company (Canada) Limited*

PRINTED IN THE UNITED STATES OF AMERICA

CONTENTS

PREFACE

I N THE SPRING of 1981, my wife Eleanor Munro and I were riding along a country road in India, in a chauffeured car. The car broke down. It was getting on toward dusk; our driver had barely enough light to inspect the parts of the engine he was trying to put back together again — using, as I recall, both of his shoelaces and one of mine. While he was struggling away, Ellie and I debarked. Across the road was a rice paddy, and in the paddy were a few women planting or replanting rice (I forget which), assisted more or less by a single water buffalo with a small boy perched on its back. The women were still there, bent over — by now it was nearly pitch-dark — when our driver finished his resurrective work and we took our carefree departure from the scene. But not before Ellie — whose wish, happily, is as often as not my command — took one last look at her sisters in the field and said to me, "*That's the sort of stuff you ought to be writing about.*"

Ellie and I had, by then, traveled throughout much of the world, including several trips to Asia and to Africa. Between us we had visited, briefly or for fairly protracted stays, some thirty or forty of the places that are often called, in the jargon of the day, "LDCs" — least-developed countries. (People who are comparatively optimistic about their future call them "developing.") As we made our way around the globe with our hired cars and credit cards, she and I had often been embarrassingly struck by the staggering differences between our fortunate standard of living and that of so much of the rest of the earth. We had become increasingly aware of how much our standard was characterized by what we ate, and how widely remote our diet (one of choice) was from that of most human beings, who, like the Indians across the road, were obliged to subsist largely on what they could grow — if they were lucky enough to grow enough of it to survive.

When we got home, I thought about all this some more, and I concluded that there was indeed something I should write about the subject. But what, and how? Thousands of books have been written about food or the scarcity of it. Relatively few of the ones I looked into, though, had sought to trace and report on the history — the biographies, if you like — of the astonishingly few plants that since the onset of civilization have succored the majority of the human race, and that will continue to do so until people fall heir — if that day ever arrives — to the synthetic fruits that microbiologists and other miracle workers are beginning to coax from their laboratory test-tubes. We take our staple plant foods far too much for granted — perhaps, in part, because they are not particularly mobile and are thus far less likely to be ennobled in television documentaries than, say, whales or butterflies. Among nature's splendid creations, however, these quiet, undemanding staffs of life rate unchallengeably high; and until something better comes along, all men and women have good cause to be grateful for their existence and to hope that their graceful stalks will wave forever.

AUTHOR'S NOTE

I AM NOT an academician (nor a farmer, an agronomist, a geneticist, or an economist) and therefore am not citing, outside of the text, the literally hundreds of books, pamphlets, and articles I have consulted in the course of my research. Without the admirable collections of many institutions I would have been helpless. Principal among them are the Harvard University Botanical Museum, the New York Public Library, the National Agricultural Library, and the libraries of the United Nations Food and Agricultural Organization, at Rome; the International Potato Center, at Lima, Peru; the International Center for Tropical Agriculture, at Cali, Colombia; the International Center for the Improvement of Maize and Wheat, in Mexico; and the International Rice Research Institute, at Los Baños, the Philippines.

I am no less indebted to these printed sources than to the hundreds of individuals who in one way or another have led me from sowing to harvest: Barbara Agostini, Dwayne Andreas,

E. A. Asselbergs, William Thomas Atkinson, Martin Baron, Tony Bellotti, Lawrence Bogorad, Robert Booth, Norman E. Borlaug, Nyle C. Brady, Michael Brandon, Havelock Brewster, William L. Brown, James Bryan, Richard E. Burket, Derek Byerlee, Robert F. Chandler, Jr., R. P. Chatelanat, Jay Cole-brook, Marie-Christine Comte, James M. Cornick, J. Cortés, Dennis Craig, Byrd Curtis, Michael B. Dale, Dana G. Dalrymple, Olivia Dent, B. C. Dutia, Peter T. Furst, Gene Futrell, Walton C. Galinat, Armando Samper Gnecco, J. Gonzalez, David Green, Lyn Gurley, Patti Hagan, Richard F. Hancock, Robert D. Havener, E. Thomas Hughes II, Clive James, Parviz Jatala, James E. Johnston, Barbara Jordan, Peter Keane, Haile-Michael Kidane, Uwe Kracht, Fritz Kramer, Loren Kruse, Douglas Laing, A. G. Leeks, Tony Loftas, Carlos Lozano, John Lynan, Fred MacMaster, Patricio Malagamba, Sat Pal Malhotra, Paul C. Mangelsdorf, Dan Miller, Fernando Mora, Derek Morgan, Amir Muhammed, Bill Murray, Gustavo Nores, Carlos Ochoa, John J. Odell, James O'Hagan, Orville Page, Julien Pélissé, Donald Plucknett, Susan V. Poats, P. A. Putnam, Chet Randolph, Robert Rhoades, Ray Roberts, Garry Robertson, Anna Curtenius Roosevelt, Wilbert A. Russell, Gideon W. Schaeffer, Lieselotte Schilde, Peter Schmiediche, Richard Evans Schultes, William Shawn, Robert J. Snyder, Loren Soth, Dan and Diana Stadtmueller, M. S. Swaminathan, Leslie Swindale, Alberto Valdés, José Valle-Riestra, B. Van de Walle, Maurice Van Nostrand, Aarte von Schoonhoven, Chris Wheatley, H. Garrison Wilkes, J. Trevor Williams, Wesley Wong, and L. Steven Young.

I

CORN
The Golden Thread

Wheat is the corn of history
Poverty's corn is rye
Rice is the corn of the Orient
But the New World's hunger cry
Was stilled by maize, the Indian corn
The Redman's gift to man.

Oats is the corn of hardy men
And barley the brewer's corn
Sorghum the corn of Africa
But nations, westward born
Fed man and beast on Indian corn
The Redman's gift to man.

— J. C. CUNNINGHAM

WHEN the New England farmer and botanist Edward Lewis Sturtevant retired, in 1887, as head of the New York Agricultural Experiment Station, in Geneva, he left behind a bulky manuscript that was published in 1919, twenty-one years after his death, as *Sturtevant's Notes on Edible Plants.* Dr. Sturtevant, who was also a graduate of the Harvard Medical School but never practiced medicine, had scoured the world's botanical literature for mentions of all the plants that human beings were known to have eaten (he did not count tree bark, which in times of famine was often one of them), and had come up with, among more than 300,000 known plant species, 2,897 edibles. (Latter-day scientists believe he may have missed as many more.) But, of all these, only 150 or so have ever been widely enough consumed to figure in commerce, and of those a mere handful have been of any real consequence.

The arboreal ancestors of human beings were, as most monkeys still are, primarily vegetarian. When primitive man descended to ground level and stood upright, he subsisted for aeons as a hunter of wild game and a gatherer of wild fruits and nuts. When he began domesticating plants and, in turn, became himself domesticated, he reverted in considerable measure to his inherited, largely herbivorous habits. Ever since (aside from the few hundred million inhabitants of the so-called Western world who are, or aspire to be, meat eaters), human beings — of whom there are today, of course, close to five billion — have relied for their principal sustenance on the produce of the soil. The chief plants that nourish them are wheat, rice, maize (what Americans call corn), barley, rye, oats, potatoes, sweet potatoes (a separate species), cassava, common beans, soybeans, peanuts, sorghum, millet, sugarcane, sugar beets, bananas, and coconuts. "These plants," a National Academy of Sciences publication declared in 1975, "are the main bulwark between mankind and starvation. It is a very small bastion." Among the relative handful of staples, the cereals and root crops are paramount. Although, according to one agricultural analyst, "people worldwide eat meat and various fruits when they can . . . and cereals and tubers only when they must," and although the surface of the earth is 70 percent ocean (and 24 percent more is untillable mountains, deserts, and tundra), land-grown plants constitute 93 percent of the globe's diet. Seafood accounts for a mere 1 percent. The very few plants that qualify as staples by the definition of the United Nations Food and Agriculture Organization (FAO), which deploys nearly four thousand people at its vast Rome citadel to ponder and articulate such concerns ("A food is known as a staple food when it is eaten regularly, and in large enough quantities to furnish a substantial proportion of the total energy supply"), provide, on average, about two-thirds of all the protein and two-thirds of all the calories consumed on earth. These plants are, as they always have been, the staffs of human life, and the disappearance of wheat or rice or corn — they are all annuals, not perennials — would be a catastrophe as devastating and annihilating as a nuclear holocaust.

Sturtevant gave most of the plants he cited just a few lines. To *Zea mays* (the name that Carolus Linnaeus conferred on corn in 1737), he devoted eleven and a half pages — in the view of many observers of the American scene, justifiably. "The history of the development of maize," it was asserted in the *Proceedings of the American Philosophical Society* for 1926, "is inseparable from the history of the origin and development of civilization on the American continent." The eminent corn breeder Paul Christoph Mangelsdorf — who remarked in 1983, after a more than sixty-year apprenticeship to and romance with *Zea mays,* "I'd rather talk about corn than anything else" — said years before that, "No civilization worthy of the name has ever been founded on any agricultural basis other than the cereals." And years before *that,* Mangelsdorf, now a Harvard professor emeritus (a chair has been endowed in his name at Harvard with the proceeds from a corn-breeding patent of which he was a designee), had acclaimed corn as "a cereal treasure of immensely greater value than the spices which Columbus traveled so far to seek in his search for a westward route to India." It is not Americans alone who have held corn in such lofty esteem. The English agricultural writer P. L. Simmonds — who was proud to be identified as a Knight of the Legion of Honour, a Knight of the Crown of Italy, and an Honourary and Corresponding Member of the Imperial Austrian Agricultural Society — had declared in 1889 that three successive corn-crop failures would bankrupt the United States. "It is the plant of the country," Simmonds said, "and the olive branch might with propriety be taken from the claw of the national emblem, and the Indian corn grass substituted in its place. . . . Indian corn is one of the most important and healthful articles of human food that a beneficent Providence has bestowed upon man; and to its high nutritive value is due in a large degree the strength and vigour of the race of men who laid the foundation of the great American Republic."

On November 5, 1492, two of Christopher Columbus's crewmen, Roderigo de Jerez and Luiz Torres, returned to their littoral command post from a trip to the Cuban interior and presented their leader with, as one commentator subsequently recorded, "a sort of grain they [the indigenes] call maiz which was well tasted, bak'd, dry'd and made into flour." Until then, with the possible exception, nearly five centuries earlier, of some Vikings exploring the coast of what would become Massachusetts, no white man was known ever to have seen a cornstalk or gnawed on a cob. What the Spanish at first also called *panizo* (panic grass) — a name that in the fifteenth century they bestowed haphazardly on several grains — was a widespread plant and, it is generally agreed, an authentically American one, having originated in southern Mexico or Central America and migrated to the rest of Latin America and the Caribbean. De Soto came across it in Florida, Cortés in Mexico, Pizarro in the Andes. It has been around, in one guise or another, for perhaps seven thousand years; and according to the American Society of Agronomy it is "a golden thread that stretches through human history."

Contemporary scientific journals will not usually accept papers about corn unless it is called "maize," its by now internationally adopted designation. (Some Americans seemingly find this hard to grasp. An official high in the state government of Kentucky came home from a 1983 business trip to South

Africa — whose first-rate corn crop has long succored the in-habitants of nearby lands who otherwise regard that nation with distaste — and on being asked to recount what he had learned said, "They grow maize, which is a sort of corn.") No-body called maize plain "corn" when Columbus brought it back to Europe, because that word had been much in use from biblical days on as a general description for such well-known grains as wheat and barley. Ruth did not stand in a field of alien maize; there wasn't any in Judah. The celebrated British Corn Laws had nothing to do with maize; "corn" meant "wheat" in England and "oats" in Scotland. The "kafir corn" of South Africa is a sorghum. It is strange, considering that in some old American Indian languages the word for corn also stood for "that which gives us life" (the Cherokees called the moon Mother of the Corn), how irreverently the nurturing plant has been treated by subsequent American linguists. "Comin' thro' the rye"* and "feeling one's oats" have pleasant connotations, and Wheaties is a breakfast food boastfully associated with champions. "Corny" and "cornball," on the other hand, are unarguably pejorative. "Corny" is said to derive from "corn-fed," an adjective disparagingly applied by itinerant performing troupes both to the audiences in the hick towns they played and to the kind of material those audiences relished. As for the word "corn," it was once used for any small particle of grain, or, by extension, any small round object — a node on the foot,

* Perhaps, "Rye." The Rye River of Scotland, which probably got its name because it irrigated fields of grain, was shallow. When young women waded across it, they would hold up their petticoats, and with their hands thus engaged, young men had a splendid opportunity to try to snatch a kiss from them without reprisals. The Jenny immortalized in the folk song as always wet and seldom dry was exceptionally pretty and a prime osculatory target; her plight resulted from her constantly having to drop her skirts and slap away at assailants.

for instance. (Corned beef got its name from the pellets of salt flung on meat when it was cured in brine.) During the Civil War, when partisans of the North wanted to mock their opponents they sometimes referred to them as Cornfederates. ("We coulda whipped them Yankees with cornstalks," one Johnny Reb purportedly retorted. "Trouble was, we couldn't get 'em to fight with cornstalks.") The most scathing appellation the inventive cartoonist Al Capp could conjure up for a Southerner of egregious imbecility was Jubilation T. Cornpone.

Until Linnaeus and succeeding botanists got almost everybody more or less straightened out with *Zea mays* (to the ancient Greeks, *zeia* stood for several kinds of wheat, and for rice and sorghum as well), maize bore a variety of names in Europe, where it spread rapidly after 1492. According to the German herbalist Leonhard Fuchs, by 1542 it was "growing in all gardens." Fuchs thought the ubiquitous plant might have originated in Greece, or in Asia. Quite a few other European scholars long believed, without too much evidence (indeed, not much has subsequently come to light), that maize — henceforth, in this nonscientific treatise, "corn" — was an Asian import. The late-sixteenth-century English herbalist John Gerard conjectured that it might have originated in both East and West; even after concluding that it had originated in America, he called it Turkey Corn and Turkey Wheat. Sweden went along with the latter — *Turkiskt hvete.* (Did not the tufts at the tips of the plant's ears, people who cared about all this reminded one another, strikingly resemble Turks' beards?) The Turks called it Egyptian corn, and the Egyptians, who were sometimes dubiously credited by others with having engendered the plant themselves, called it Syrian corn. Some Germans hedged; they called it *Welschkorn* — "strange grain."

Ardent Sinophiles have long contended that corn's geographical roots were in China. A late-sixteenth-century Chinese ideograph depicted something very much like a cornstalk with a cornlike ear emerging from its top. In March 1908, the Office of Foreign Seed and Plant Introduction of the United States Department of Agriculture received a packet of shelled corn from a Presbyterian missionary in Shanghai. He knew corn, and these kernels had looked peculiar to him — markedly different from those he was familiar with at home. Could this be testimony, he asked, to the Chinese birth of corn? The plant had certainly been prominent there for a long time, he pointed out. Why, back in 1575, he'd been reliably told, one Chinese emperor had received thirty million bushels of it in tribute from his subjects. None of that was compelling proof of anything, but what was one to make of a singular lacuna in a pre-Christian-era book, *Treatise of Mountains and Seas,* which, a Chinese botanist reported to a Harvard colleague in 1924, suggested that the Chinese were familiar with corn as far back as 400 B.C.? It was especially significant, the Chinese scientist said, that his forebears had always meticulously recorded the introduction into their region of new plants — for instance, cotton, tobacco, the grape, the opium poppy — but that there was no such provenance for corn. The inference was plain: corn hadn't had to be introduced into China because it had been there all along. He conveniently skirted what might have been another awkward omission to explain — the fact that the five "sacred grains" of Chinese antiquity are rice, millet, sorghum, soybeans, and wheat. (Confucius once said, "If you don't know the five grains, you don't know anything.") American corn experts were interested in such hypotheses but unimpressed. They thought it most likely that corn got to China when Portuguese seafarers, who habitually carried seeds on their global peregrinations, stopped by there early in the sixteenth century. At a 1906 session, in Quebec, of the Congrès International des Américanistes, one authority argued that the Portuguese, while deserving their full measure of credit, did not take corn *directly* to China but, rather, to India, whence it drifted onward via Sikkim, Bhutan, and Tibet. The protagonist of that theory went on to assert:

The history of maize is an instructive historical example which might be fruitfully applied to the prehistoric dissemination of ancient cereals, giving an idea, at least, of how cereals might have travelled in prehistoric days. Of all the manifold gifts of the New World, maize spread the most rapidly . . . with much greater speed than the ships of the European nations which then shared in the universal trade, for, long before the arrival of Europeans in China, maize was known there as an overland arrival . . . and, last but not least, it is worthwhile adding that maize travelled even faster than syphilis, which, after the discovery of America, so quickly spread in Europe.

Wherever it hailed from, *Zea mays* — "a wonder of bioengineering efficiency for transforming the energy of the sun into the energy of food, as well as a great staff of life for all of mankind," in the glowing words of the American corn geneticist Walton C. Galinat, who is sometimes fondly accused by his confreres of chatting with the plants he breeds — has made itself thumpingly manifest. In 1980, according to the FAO, it was grown on 323,543,000 acres, from which rose enough cornstalks to produce a crop of 392,249,000 metric tons — or, roughly, fifteen billion bushels. That came to more than three bushels, or nearly two hundred pounds, of corn for every human being then alive. Corn — a $40-billion worldwide business (few Arabs, oddly, command more than a pittance of it) — is now the staple food of more than 200 million people in eighteen nations in Latin America and Africa: Costa Rica, El Salvador, Ecuador, Guatemala, Haiti, Honduras, Mexico, Nicaragua, Paraguay, Venezuela, Benin, Kenya, Malawi, Somalia, South Africa, Tanzania, Zambia, and Zimbabwe. The United States grows about eight billion bushels a year. If spread evenly across Manhattan Island, somebody once took the trouble to calculate, they would reach a height of sixteen feet. Only a tenth of the American crop is directly ingested by the home folks, but their per-capita consumption of corn or food derived from corn — in the form of meat, milk, butter, cheese, and poultry — comes to more than three pounds a day. One-third of the globe's current annual output of all cereals — nearly two billion tons — is converted into food by being first funneled through livestock. This catalytic process, however, is prevalent mostly among developed nations. In developing nations, where, it is projected, by the year 2000, 60 percent of the world population will live, or hope to get enough to eat to live, no more than 3 percent of available cereal grains goes into animal feed. Today, just about the same amount of grains are fed to animals in developed countries as are eaten by human beings in China and India combined. Within the next year or two, it has been surmised by Montague Yudelman, who retired in 1984 as director of the Agricultural and Rural Development Department of the World Bank, animals worldwide will consume more of the precious grain available than human beings will. Some nutritionists — vegetarians of course prominent among them — take a dim view of this prospect, pointing out that to consume scarce food by way of animals is inefficient utilization: two pounds of grain produces one pound of poultry, and for other intermediaries the ratios are worse — four to one for pork, and seven or eight to one for beef.

Most Americans are unconcerned about such proportions. It seems not to bother them that of every ton of corn each of them consumes, 1,850 pounds has gone into another creature first. They have good reason to feel at ease. Since the beginning of history, there have been untold famines in other parts of the world. China alone had some eighteen hundred recorded famines between 100 B.C. and A.D. 1910; in 1943, another famine there was responsible for three million deaths. There is and probably always will be hunger in North America, the distributional journey from farm to stomach being long and arduous and costly, but never — not even in 1970, when an onslaught of southern-corn-leaf blight raised havoc with that year's crop — has there been what could be termed a famine in the United States. It is no wonder that in 1893 some grateful Americans — conceivably influenced by P. L. Simmonds's proposal, four years earlier, about putting the olive branch to pasture — convened a symposium to discuss the topic "Should maize be the national flower?" (Corn has been enshrined on the capitals of columns, designed by Benjamin Latrobe, that grace the Senate side of the Capitol in Washington, D.C.) Corn comes in many colors — white, yellow, red, black, blue — and it was long one of the nagging ambitions of Walton Galinat (who had already, by genetic manipulation, produced a square cob) to create a special breed with the hues of the Stars and Stripes on every kernel. It turned out to be simply a matter of time, genes, and patriotic patience before he came up with a corn bearing on each of its kernels red-and-white stripes and blue dots.

Corn, often dubbed by its loyalists King Corn or Queen Corn, now reigns over 25 percent of all American cropland. An Iowa farmer exulted not long ago that, on a summer drive from Des Moines to the border of Nova Scotia, from the crest of every hill he passed that afforded a reasonably sweeping view he had never once failed to spot at least a patch of growing corn. About one-third of all American corn is exported. The uses to which the rest is put — ears, leaves, stalks — are staggering. In bygone days, corn was optimistically believed to have singular curative powers. One mid-sixteenth-century German thought that the juice from its leaves vanquished erysipelas, and mid-nineteenth-century Americans prescribed cornmeal porridge for sufferers from a vast number of ailments. More recently, one part or another of the versatile crop has been implanted in — along with such routine products as corn syrup, corn oil, cornmeal, and corncob pipes — automobile paint, potato chips, plastics, ice cream, tires, leather, chewing gum, textiles, library paste, clam chowder, dog biscuits, spaghetti sauce, table mats, salad dressing, sausages, foot powder, gunpowder, face powder, table salt, mincemeat, mustard, mayonnaise, ketchup, peanut butter, dice, licorice, oilcloth, sandpaper, soap, drinking straws, surgical dressings, insecticides, boot polish, children's dolls (the "corn dollies" of English harvest festivals, however, were mostly fashioned out of wheat), lactic acid, jelly, candy (in 1915, the American Manufacturers' Association of Products from Corn persuaded a physician to write a brochure entitled *Candies Good for Children*), artificial silk, embalming fluid, scratchless polishers for jewelry and ball bearings, nail-polish remover, hair tonic, rubbing alcohol, ether, deodorants, mattresses, varnish, hydraulic-brake fluid, gasohol, adhesive tape, fireworks, film, safety glass, and — of all things — agricultural poisons.

The December 16, 1928, edition of the Danville, Illinois, *Sunday Commercial-News* was printed on paper made of cornstalks. "NEW EPOCH IN PAPER INDUSTRY ARRIVES," a banner headline proclaimed. (In fact, researchers had already been working on corn newsprint pulp for at least eighteen years.) In smaller type the editors noted that the first sheet of the newfangled paper had been processed by the Cornstalk Products Company, a local concern, on the preceding October 19, and they instructed their readers to "mark the date for it will be historic." Although one whole book also appears to have been printed on cornstalk paper, it could not compete in price with conventional newsprint, and in less than a year the experiment was abandoned. The Hungarian chemist responsible for the novelty, Dr. Bela Dorner, at least had the satisfaction of learning that that 1928 edition had been delivered to the Smithsonian Institution (which had earlier gone astray by exhibiting for years a hoary "fossil ear" of corn from Cuzco, Peru, that turned out to be a child's toy made of clay). Otherwise the episode was one of very few in which corn has let its country down. Fifty-five years after that abortive attempt to turn food into newsprint, microbiologists who were worried about the scarcity of nutriments in the future were talking cheerfully about converting newsprint, along with crude oil and automobile tires, into food.

In parts of Central America, corn grows twenty feet tall and is harvested on horseback. Cortés's mounted troops had trouble riding through it. Cornstalks have been used there to build fences, roofs, and whole houses; the corn plant is so tough that, in 1930, some scientists at Iowa State College, in Ames, were inspired to concoct from it a product called maizolith, which was as hard as stone and stronger than wood. Dr. Harvey W. Wiley, who was head of the Bureau of Chemistry of the Department of Agriculture in 1898, once declared, "The inner portion of the stalk — the pith — possesses remarkable properties as an obturator in the manufacture of battleships. It possesses a high degree of resilience and porosity, and when perforated by a shot or shell it instantly closes the aperture made by the projectile, and thus prevents the entrance of water into the vessel." The Navy is not believed to have acted on that proposal, although anything that that formidable chemist advocated was not to be taken lightly. A noted connoisseur of wines until he abandoned bachelorhood to wed a Prohibitionist, Dr. Wiley, who died three years before Repeal, came to conclude, or was nagged into concluding, that the only liquid suitable for human beings to imbibe was water. He considered the makers and purveyors of all drinks containing a trace of caffeine to be dope peddlers, and was an unrelenting foe of the Coca-Cola Company. He was the man chiefly responsible for the passage, in 1906, of the Pure Food and Drug Act, and his first son was known in the press as the Pure Food Baby. When Dr. Wiley gave his imprimatur to any potable or edible, it was much appreciated, if for no other reason than that his opprobrium was a nuisance. (He dragged Coca-Cola into nine years of skirmishing in the federal courts.) He had unfailingly good things to say about corn, which he once described as "this great cereal." On another occasion, he asserted: "In Europe, primarily in Great Britain, Indian corn is not considered fit for the manufacture of bread for the use of man. This prejudice seems quite baseless when we consider the very extensive use of this material for bread making in this country and the high nutritive properties which it possesses. With a diet of Indian-corn bread and pork the workmen of this country are capable of enduring the greatest fatigue and performing the greatest amount of physical labor." Wiley, who measured food values in terms not of proteins or calories but, rather, of oil or fat, digestible carbohydrates, crude carbohydrates, albuminoids, and ash, acclaimed corn as "of superior value to any of the other cereals produced in the United States." It can only be guessed how he would have felt about the use, long after he passed on, of its fructose content as a sweetener in the brewing of Coke. (It is known how the Iowa Corn Promotion Board felt; at a 1983 meeting in their state of regional soft-drink bottlers, they nettled the Pepsi people in attendance, who weren't yet much using corn sweeteners, by presenting an award for exemplary conduct to the Coca-Cola Company.) Once Wiley became a benedict, he must surely have frowned on the national penchant for corn liquor (not to mention beer and bourbon), which came into vogue as an American staple of sorts because when United States frontiersmen moved west toward what is now the Corn Belt it proved too expensive to transport rum out to them to slake their thirst. Corn liquor inspired the poet William James Lampton to describe the subject of his "Kentucky" as "where the corn is full of kernels, / and the colonels full of corn," and provoked the prose writer Irvin S. Cobb into coming up with an acerbic definition of the old distillation: "It smells like gangrene starting in a mildewed silo, it tastes like the wrath to come, and when you absorb a deep swig of it you have all the sensations of having swallowed a lighted kerosene lamp. A sudden, violent jolt of it has been known to stop the victim's watch, snap his suspenders and crack his glass eye right across."

If the geographical origins of corn have been somewhat tangled, its botanical origins have been an all but impenetrable jungle of confusion and controversy. In his *Indian Corn,* published in 1879, the hard-digging Dr. Sturtevant said:

The interest which surrounds an investigation into the history of a cultivated plant increases with the importance of the uses to which the vegetable is applied, and the obscurity which prevails over the origin. There is a delight in probing within mysteries, and in the following out of clues which trace to mythology and the beginnings of things, especially when the value of the production lends a factitious dignity to everything connected with the investigation, and the fancy can play without the appearance of triviality, or the accusation of idle research.

Twenty-four years earlier, the French botanist Alphonse de Candolle had written, in his book *Origin of Cultivated Plants:*

I dare not hope that maize will be found wild, although its habitation before it was cultivated was probably so small that botanists have perhaps not yet come across it. The species is so distinct from all others, and so striking [corn is unique among cereals in that its grains are encased in a protective husk, and in that its staminate (male) flowers are separated from its pistillate (female) ones], that natives or unscientific colonists would have noticed and spoken of it. The certainty as to its origin will probably come rather from archeological discoveries.

Archeology has been helpful, although some archeologists with slight botanical bent are rumored to throw away almost everything they discover that is not identifiable as pottery shards or statuary ears and noses. In 1948, a Harvard expedition to New Mexico, which included a botanist, found in the debris of caves there that had been inhabited from about 2500 B.C. to A.D. 1000 hundreds of shelled cobs, kernels, and other fragments of ancient corn plants. Subsequently, such refined analytic tools as radiocarbon testing and the electron microscope have made it possible for concerned scientists to examine timeworn trash in consummate detail — to deduce from the bones of skeletons from A.D. 400 unearthed in the Orinoco region of South America, for instance, that people then alive relied on corn for 80 percent of their sustenance. The teeth were ground down, apparently because those Indians ate their corn mixed with grit eroded from their grinding stones. The seemingly most venerable evidence to date of the existence of some sort of corn makes the plant emphatically prehistoric. In 1950, a few eighty-thousand-year-old grains of a fossilized cornlike pollen were excavated from two-hundred-odd feet below ground level while foundation cores were being drilled for a skyscraper in Mexico City.

No one has been more deeply immersed in the long, spirited, often acrimonious, and as yet not fully resolved debate about corn's origins than Paul Mangelsdorf. He was born in 1899 in Atchison, Kansas, a community on the Missouri River whose inhabitants, then numbering about sixteen thousand, hoped would get much bigger when, or if, a projected rail terminal was emplaced there. Atchison didn't get it, though its name was eventually immortalized with Topeka and Santa Fe; it lost out to Kansas City, farther along the stream. Mangelsdorf's father ran a seed-and-greenhouse business. He exhibited his prize botanical wares at Atchison's turn-of-the-century annual corn carnival, in the merry course of which the revelers, in lieu of confetti, flung kernels at one another. At one celebration in the 1890s, young Mangelsdorf later heard with awe, some townsfolk had constructed a fifty-foot phallus made entirely of ears of corn.

As a boy, Paul was already fascinated by corn, because it was so radically different from any other plant of his acquaintance. (He was an admirer of corn silk even before he was old enough to smoke it.) His first job was to remove suckers from corn stems; his father thought this was necessary for their vigorous growth. Later in life, Paul learned that their removal was not only unnecessary but deleterious. His knowledge of all plants was, for a youngster, encyclopedic: most summer Sunday afternoons, Mangelsdorf *père* would take his children (Paul's older brother Albert became a sugarcane breeder) on nature walks, identifying for them each cultivated plant or weed they passed. "I suppose you might say I had a precocious affinity for plants," Mangelsdorf told a friend long after Paul turned eighty. Entering Kansas State Agricultural College, in Manhattan, he studied for four years under the agronomist John H. Parker, and after graduating, in 1921, he got a job as an assistant geneticist at the Connecticut Agricultural Experiment Station, in New Haven — one of a nationwide network of such centers established by Congress in 1887 and put under the aegis of the Department of Agriculture. He stayed on there, part-time, until 1927, shuttling between the station and Cambridge, Massachusetts, for six months each year to do graduate work at Harvard. In both Connecticut and Massachusetts, he was apprenticed to established corn breeders — Donald F. Jones and Edward Murray East, respectively. They were authors of an influential work on hybrid corn called *Inbreeding and Outbreeding*. East, a biologist and geneticist, was on the Harvard faculty from 1909 until his death, in 1938. He had started off in potatoes; his doctoral dissertation at the University of Illinois was "A Study of the Factors Influencing the Improvement of the Potato." Dr. East spent a couple of diligent years in Connecticut breeding potatoes, but he abandoned them in dismay and disarray in 1908, after a fire destroyed just about all his research findings. He switched to corn, which he was soon hailing as "the prince of grasses." In 1923, while Mangelsdorf was one of his students, East wrote *Mankind at the Crossroads,* in which he predicted — sixty years later it was devoutly to be hoped he was wrong — that "under the most optimistic assumptions as to production and distribution of food that it is reasonable to make, the world can support but 5,200 millions of people." Even earlier, another titan in the pantheon of corn geneticists, George Harrison

Shull, was probing, on Long Island, into the effects of inbreeding on the inheritance of numbers of rows of kernels on corn ears. A professor of botany and genetics at Princeton from 1915 to 1942, and the founder, in 1916, of the magazine *Genetics,* Shull liked to refer to what he was up to with corn not as hybridization but as "pure-line breeding." *His* earliest work had been with the evening primrose, but he had turned to corn in 1905, painstakingly counting the individual kernels on ears he obtained from a horse-feed merchant, and breeding these to grains from cobs with differing totals. But not long afterward he had forsaken corn for his longer-cherished evening primrose.

At Harvard — where he roomed for a while with yet another corn statesman, Edgar Anderson, who later wrote *Plants, Man, and Life,* and became the director of the Missouri Botanical Garden, in Saint Louis — Mangelsdorf evinced interest almost exclusively in corn, from that time on his one true vegetable love, though he had scholarly flirtations, afterward, with wheat, barley, rice, oats, sorghum, millet, and potatoes. (One of the library books he fondly perused in Cambridge was the esoteric *Flour for Pretzels.*) In 1927, Sci.D. well in hand, he won an appointment as Agronomist in Charge of Corn and Small Grain Investigations at the Texas Agricultural Experiment Station, in College Station, the seat of Texas A&M. The only place he and his wife of four years could find to rent had scorpions proliferating not only on its walls but inside them, too. That did not exactly enchant Mrs. Mangelsdorf, but her husband found it scientifically stimulating. Mangelsdorf remained in Texas, breeding plants furiously, for thirteen years, and then was invited to return to Harvard as a professor of botany and assistant director of the Botanical Museum. He was forty-one, and had never taught, but he was encouraged to do so by the museum's director, Oakes Ames, who was also the university's senior botanist.

Some slaughterhouse workers, understandably, cannot stomach beef. Mangelsdorf loved to eat corn. On dining at a New England restaurant in 1949 and being served some sweet corn — its popularity, according to Walton Galinat, who was for a while president of the National Sweet Corn Breeders Association, derives from "man's instinctive desire to eat directly with his bare hands" — that didn't meet his exacting standard, Mangelsdorf teamed up with Karl Sax, the director of Harvard's Arnold Arboretum, to breed a succulent variety, which they loyally dubbed Harvard Hybrid. In Texas, Mangelsdorf had done much the same thing on his own, at that time coming up with a sweet corn he called Honey June, which achieved a great vogue — in no small part, he suspected, because of its name. Its popularity far eclipsed that of, for instance, Shoe Peg.

In 1945, Mangelsdorf succeeded Ames as director of the museum, which was, and is, the repository of Harvard's famous glass flowers. Visitors who travel by the thousands to gawk at them have since 1946 also been able to gaze at an oil portrait of Mangelsdorf by Blanche Ames, his predecessor's wife. She portrayed him holding in his hands — much in the manner of bygone Aztec brides during their wedding ceremonies — a half-shucked ear of corn. The Mangelsdorfs sometimes spent summer holidays in a guesthouse on the Ames estate, at Gloucester. Returning there once in the early forties from a graminological safari to Mexico, Mangelsdorf was presented by his wife with a homecoming gift she'd found in a nearby antique shop — a bracelet with square dangles, each bearing the embossed image of an ear of corn. That was the forerunner of a formidable trove of four or five hundred *objets de maïs* that the Mangelsdorfs accumulated over the next thirty years. They combed New England stores and yard sales for their specialty, and never once did they fail to spot something with an appropriate motif. "My wife and I developed a nose for corn objects,"

Mangelsdorf would say in later years. They had cornhusk fans, cob-shaped whiskey bottles, a plastic harmonica in the guise of an ear of corn, and Meissen-china cobs. "Being stylistic," Mangelsdorf once said, "the designers of most of the things we acquired missed one of the most important botanical characterizations of corn; namely, that the kernels invariably come in pairs of rows." Their pièce de résistance was a sixteenth-century Chinese ivory ear of corn — a remarkable item, Mangelsdorf liked to point out, because in his view corn had barely got to China when the object was carved. He had pounced on that one in a boutique in a Boston hotel lobby. The proprietor said he'd obtained it from a Philadelphia dealer a year or so earlier, telling his Pennsylvania counterpart, who had long stocked it unpurchased, "Give it to me. I can sell anything in Boston." His confidence had begun to flag when Mangelsdorf materialized.

Mangelsdorf became emeritus at Harvard in 1967, and moved to Chapel Hill, North Carolina, where he was eventually given a research professorship at the University of North Carolina. After his wife's death, in 1979, he agreed to have the bulk of their corn collection put on permanent display at North Carolina State University, in Raleigh. He kept for his own lifetime use and enjoyment, among a few other particularly cherished memorabilia, a brass corncob door-knocker, which he believed might be a true copy of an ancient Mexican Indian door-knocker. But in 1983, at eighty-four, he was still so busy breeding corn and speculating about its genesis that he hadn't found time to try to authenticate the knocker's provenance. At his first Chapel Hill home, he had converted a sun parlor into a sort of greenhouse, and had also had a modest outdoor garden, measuring ten by fifteen feet. It was large enough, however, to accommodate seventy-five cornstalks.

Mangelsdorf liked to tell people who asked about his practically nonstop corn-growing that he had two things in common with Gregor Mendel, whose own experimental plot was a tiny patch of soil alongside a monastery wall: a little garden and big ideas. "You can do a lot of work in a small area if you know what you're concentrating on," Mangelsdorf would say.

Mangelsdorf's 1940 appointment to the Harvard faculty had been prompted in part by the attention he received the year before, when, with Robert Reeves, he enunciated a novel theory about the origin of corn — a topic that, they wrote in the May 1939 issue of the *Bulletin* of the Texas Agricultural Experiment Station, was "one of the most intriguing puzzles of modern times." They said that "a solution of this problem may throw revealing light upon evolutionary processes in general and expand still further our knowledge and understanding of the corn plant." (They also took occasion to state that "all the great civilizations of all time have been based upon the culture of cereals; and some authorities consider it an axiom that no advanced civilization can develop without cereal culture.") They spent one summer apprenticed to Barbara McClintock, who had stopped off at Cornell on her long road to the Nobel Prize. In 1927, they had begun experimentally hybridizing corn with a perennial wild grass of the genus *Tripsacum*. After nine or so years of study and reflection, they had concluded — as Edgar Anderson had hypothesized to Mangelsdorf several years earlier — that in bygone days some wild corn or relative of corn, so far undetected by modern man, had mated with *Tripsacum* and produced a cousin of corn's called teosinte. This conclusion — which Mangelsdorf in time came regretfully to amend — was known in corn circles as the tripartite theory. Mangelsdorf and Reeves did not proffer it dogmatically. "If we have made any contribution toward the solution of the problem," they wrote, "it has been primarily one of realigning the parts of a puzzle so that many which previously failed to fit have now fallen into place to present a picture which, though far from clear and revealing because many segments are still missing, is at least visible in outline and is suggestive of many new points of experimental attack on the problem."

The tripartite theory ran directly counter to a belief of other experts that corn was not an ancestor of teosinte but, rather, that teosinte was the ancestor of corn. Teosinte, generally an annual, has foliage strikingly resembling corn's, except that a number of stalks sprout from a single base; corn usually has just one stalk. Whereas all the kernels on a cob of contemporary corn are snugly wrapped in a single protective husk, each of teosinte's is encased in a hard, bony shell of its own. (The shell drops off easily, however; thus teosinte can readily regenerate itself. The kernels of cultivated corn cling tightly to their cobs and therefore have to be planted by man or machine.) Early in the twentieth century, Luther Burbank buoyed the contentions of the teosinte-first boosters by proclaiming, with considerable fanfare, that after an eighteen-generation breeding marathon he had succeeded in producing corn from teosinte; but then it turned out that his parental teosinte had itself been a corn-teosinte hybrid. The pro-teosinte partisans nevertheless marshaled strong debating points on their behalf. Teosinte grows wild. Nearly all domesticated plants have been ascertained to have wild progenitors that still exist. Corn had so far been found to have none. Did not the Aztec name for teosinte — *teocentli* — mean "God's ear of corn"? Had not the Spanish conquerors of Mexico, presumably getting the idea from their victims, called teosinte "*madre de maiz*"? How could all that not be meaningful? To this Mangelsdorf replied that there was no reason to infer that there had never been a wild corn simply because none had yet been found. After all, he said, the piscine coelacanth had been discovered swimming animatedly off the coast of Madagascar sixty million years after its supposed extinction. "Regardless of the validity of the hypotheses which have been, and may be, put forward to replace it," Mangelsdorf wrote in *Advances in Genetics* in 1947, "the hypothesis that teosinte is the progenitor of maize is definitely no longer tenable." Twenty-six years later, he was still declaring flatly: "The ancestor of cultivated corn was corn."

The anti-Mangelsdorf forces in what some botanists took to calling the Corn War (to chronicle each of its skirmishes would require a whole book, and, indeed, it has been the central theme of many lengthy publications) were a well-armed array. Paul W. Weatherwax, the author of a much-respected 1954 volume titled *Indian Corn in Old America*, was one of the warriors. Their field commander off and on was the redoubtable geneticist George W. Beadle, who, soon after the Mangelsdorf-Reeves tripartite theory was made public, fired a broadside at it that went, in part, "The fragmentary circumstantial evidence offered in favor of this interpretation cannot be regarded as convincing."

Born in Wahoo, Nebraska, in 1903, and thus four years Mangelsdorf's junior, Beadle had done his graduate work in genetics at Cornell (crossbreeding corn and teosinte was one of his activities there), had been on the faculties of several other universities, and had settled down at the University of Chicago. (He served as its president from 1961 to 1968.) Once, he got to wondering whether pre-Columbian Indians might not, about eight thousand years ago, have fed themselves by cracking dried teosinte seeds. He borrowed some eight-thousand-year-old grinding stones from the Field Museum of Natural History, in

Chicago, and got down to work. "I concluded that in a day an energetic person motivated by sufficient hunger could separate enough partially shell-free teosinte meal from the ground shell-kernel mixture by a simple water-flotation method to feed a small family for a day or more," Beadle wrote. In the most laudable scientific tradition, he proceeded forthwith to feed himself — it turned out, adequately — on teosinte for four days. Moreover, in 1939, brooding about the possible edibility of teosinte, it occurred to him to heat some of its tough kernels. (As a normal American boy, he had been fond of popcorn.) When the kernels "exploded out of their fruit cases," he recalled forty-one years afterward, they were "indistinguishable from popped corn." So it seemed likely to him that prehistoric man had made the same discovery, probably by accident, and that that had led to the cultivation of teosinte and to its evolution — conceivably, again by chance — into corn. Accidental popping — by lightning or campfire embers or whatever — might indeed have revealed to long-ago human beings the nutritive appeal and value of certain grains, Mangelsdorf conceded, but he thought that what had popped was probably not teosinte but some ancient popcorn.

During the 1936–37 academic year, Beadle had been briefly on the Harvard faculty himself, as an assistant professor of genetics. He had left Cambridge (this was before Mangelsdorf joined the Harvard faculty) when it began to appear unlikely that he would be granted tenure — classroom lectures were not his forte (years later, when he shared the 1958 Nobel Prize in Medicine and Physiology for his explorations into the role of genes in regulating biochemical reactions, some of his erstwhile students were chagrined that they had booed and hissed at him) — and moved on to Stanford. Ever afterward, he seemed cool toward Harvard, where Mangelsdorf was so warmly embraced. In 1961, the archeologist Richard S. MacNeish, who had been digging in Mexico since 1945, found in a cave there some tiny, half-inch cobs seventy-two hundred years old. Eventually, he accumulated around twenty-five thousand specimens of ancient corn, some of which looked to Mangelsdorf's delighted eye like wild corn, and delivered them to the Botanical Museum at Harvard for researchers to scrutinize. These were still being pored over in 1969, by which time Mangelsdorf had departed for North Carolina. His successor as director of the museum, the botanist Richard Evans Schultes (by 1984, he had had more than a half century's affiliation with Harvard, during which he spent fourteen years prowling the Amazon jungles; the year before, he had had conferred on him by the president of Colombia that nation's most prestigious decoration, the Cross of Boyacá), deemed the specimens to belong to Mexico and expected to have them duly returned when his associates completed their leisurely assessment. That year, though, an American scientist who was a staunch Beadle fan hinted darkly to the Mexican government's Department of Pre-History that Harvard had stolen Mexico's corn treasures, or, at any rate, had accessioned the specimens — put numbers on them, that is, as possessive evidence. Schultes denied it; he said that the relics had been stored separately from any permanent acquisitions, and that Mexico was welcome to retrieve any of them it needed at any time. By then, things had got out of hand, and the Mexican government demanded *all* the specimens back, immediately. In 1972, accordingly (such matters take time), they were all handed over, though in Mangelsdorf's view Harvard could have spent another profitable decade examining them had it not been for anti-Harvard, anti-Mangelsdorf, and pro-Beadle interference. MacNeish, who during the fracas had become persona non grata in Mexico, transferred his digging to

Peru. Beadle had pretty much retired from corn-and-teosinte research in 1939 — though while president at Chicago he had a half-acre growing plot conveniently close to his campus headquarters — and had been devoting himself to fruit flies and bread mold. He harvested a bushel of honorary degrees over the years, three of them from Ivy League institutions, but he was never thus singled out by Harvard. Harvard did, however, bestow such an accolade on Mangelsdorf in 1977.

The Corn War was waged, in a sporadic but animated fashion, for decades. One of the participants, a sometime collaborator with Mangelsdorf who ended up in the Beadle camp, was Walton Galinat, whose efforts to replicate the Stars and Stripes on a single kernel were regarded by both sides as exemplary and neutral. In 1983, Galinat told a visitor to his research base at the Suburban Experiment Station, at the University of Massachusetts, in Waltham, where he had worked for twenty years (he countenanced no nameplate on his office door but only a large, emphatic "CORN"), "Corn is my religion, and this laboratory is my church." When Galinat went outdoors in cool weather to inspect his nearby stands of corn, he wore a wool hat that had been knitted in a kernel pattern, and when he got more fancily dressed up he was apt to sport a corn-decorated necktie. At Christmastime, the wreaths he favored featured a cornhusk doll and a corncob with a star on its summit — his version of the Madonna and the Star of Bethlehem. Galinat, who won first prize in a longest-ear-breeding contest in Columbus, Ohio, in 1978 (his entry measured close to two feet), and also bred a slender sweet corn called Candy Stick, which could be eaten in more polite fashion than the run-of-the-mill cob, usually designed his own Christmas cards. The sentiments they conveyed were all corn-oriented. His 1980 card was another sort of nativity scene, depicting three cobs and four stalks, and bearing the legend "The birth of maize — a rebirth for man." By 1983, he had made so many drawings of the various parts of the corn plant during nearly fifty years' adoration at its altar that, he claimed, once he put pencil to paper the rendition finished itself all but automatically, as if some corn spirit were guiding his hand. Once, to portray graphically his version of the origin of maize, he traced his own hand. His little finger represented teosinte, and then there was a thousand-year gap between digits until — presto! — his thumb stood for a plump ear of present-day corn.

"Teosinte is the wild progenitor of maize," Galinat felt it imperative to state in his otherwise matter-of-fact curriculum vitae. A man of gentle disposition, Galinat fought his battles in the Corn War with gloves on. In a couple of reviews of books by Mangelsdorf about corn's origin, he took sharp issue with the author's central hypotheses, but he nonetheless pronounced the texts "beautiful," "valuable," and "monumental." Other corn men have fought bare-knuckled; botanists are a scrappy bunch. One of them had a long-standing, acerbic feud over some abstruse scientific matter with a zoologist; the zoologist got so mad at one point that he conferred his adversary's name upon a previously unidentified species he discovered — a louse that lived on a skunk. One fairly hard-hitting Mangelsdorf ally in the origin-of-corn contretemps was H. Garrison Wilkes, a graduate student of his at Harvard. Wilkes discovered botany as a boy in Southern California. While his contemporaries were engrossed in such books as *Tarzan of the Apes,* he chose to read Anderson's *Plants, Man, and Life.* "Hey, this is really hot stuff," Wilkes recalls saying to himself. He became further impressed by the importance of plants to the life of man some years afterward, when he was teaching a summer course at the University of Wisconsin on plants and human affairs. One of his students came into his classroom, ashen-faced, the morning after a severe hailstorm, and said, "The oats lodged last night, and there went my fall tuition." Wilkes, who, like Galinat, found a permanent academic niche at the University of Massachusetts — in Wilkes's case, its Boston branch — shared his colleague's ardent feelings for corn. "When you're working with a wheat plant, who cares?" he said once. "But when you're dealing with a corn plant, it's different. It's of human height, and you can look it in the eye. It's one on one. I was once watching some Mexicans harvesting a crop, and every time they picked an ear they would cry '*Elote!*' — 'Ear of corn!' — just before they plucked it off, as if this would somehow excuse them from the onus of killing it. Much the same sort of thing was done in the Middle Ages, when to pull up a mandrake plant you'd tie it to a rope around a dog's neck. Then you'd kick the dog, and it would run, uprooting the plant. The dog would probably choke itself to death in so doing, but at least no human being could be directly charged with the crime." A similar note was struck in a *Royal Dream Book* circulated in nineteenth-century England: if in a dream you picked an ear of corn, that meant you had a secret enemy.

Wilkes's doctoral dissertation, prepared under Mangelsdorf's tutelage, was about teosinte and applied the words "crude" and "myth" to Beadle's concept of corn's origins. Beadle read the paper in 1967, and although he had retired from the fray, and from full-time corn work, nearly thirty years earlier, he was not at all pleased and girded up for further action. The following year, after relinquishing his University of Chicago presidency, he returned, with vigor, to the Corn War. He was sixty-five. Other corn men were not surprised at his reappearance on the field of combat; in their view he was like a widower being happily reunited, after a long interlude, with his high-school sweetheart. Beadle and Wilkes got on reasonably well despite their doctrinal differences (Beadle had come back out swinging, with statements like "If corn could have given rise to teosinte, the reverse must also be possible, and I would say much more probable, for teosinte is a highly successful wild plant and corn is not"), and soon took off for Mexico in joint search of some wild plants that might throw fresh light on the old controversy.

In 1969, in an attempt to resolve the matter, an Origin of Corn Conference was held on the Urbana campus of the University of Illinois. The meeting produced such lack of unanimity that its proceedings were never published — a rare debacle for a scholarly conclave. All the antagonists were present — Beadle, Mangelsdorf, Galinat, Wilkes, and also Jack R. Harlan, a professor of plant genetics at the Crop Evolution Laboratory in the Department of Agronomy of the host institution, who, it seemed, had botany in his own genes. His father, Harry, was, according to an anonymous introduction to a posthumously published Harry Harlan memoir, "the only man in the history of the world who devoted his entire life to the study of barley." (That was perhaps a slight exaggeration, the writer having failed to take into account England's E. S. Beaven, who studied barley from 1878 to his death, in 1941, and who wrote in the preface to his own, also posthumous, reminiscences that "one species of cereal provides more than enough material for a lifelong study.") Most of the participants in that Origin of Corn Conference — there was yet another scrappy one, at the Harvard Botanical Museum, in 1972 — were natives of the American Midwest. An exception was the botanist and taxonomist Hugh H. Iltis, born in Czechoslovakia, who delivered so uncompromising a putdown of the Mangelsdorf-Reeves tripartite theory that, it was later reported, Mangelsdorf walked out.

(Mangelsdorf said he might have felt like doing so but didn't.) Iltis, a professor at the University of Wisconsin at Madison and the director of its herbarium, had a prose style befitting a man who proclaimed himself a disciple of the goddess Flora. He was fond of phrases like "in awe and profound botanical satisfaction" and "dreaming botanical dreams." He once began a paper, titled, pointedly, "From Teosinte to Maize — The Incredible Transformation," with "The evolution of maize, like a suspenseful historical epic, has all the good themes — suppression and reactivation, multiplication and condensation, sex and transformation, wild and tame species — all orchestrated towards that most drastic of structural revolutions, the climactic ascendancy to absolute apical dominance of the FE-MALE POLYSTICHOUS EAR." In that polysyllabic treatise, he referred to, by name, virtually every corn scientist anybody had ever heard of — except Mangelsdorf. In a 1969 lecture, "The Maize Mystique," Iltis dismissed as a blind alley the *Tripsacum* research in which Mangelsdorf had so energetically engaged. (Mangelsdorf himself partially concurred with Iltis in subsequent years, but not without coming up with a modified tripartite theory and saying of his original one that it was "still of historical interest because of the extensive research that it has stimulated.") "The domestication of corn is no mystery, and needs no mystique, nor elaborate reconstruction of ancestors now extinct, nor ingenious genetic nor difficult morphological hypotheses," Iltis said.

Like Galinat, Iltis was partial to corn-embellished greeting cards of his own design. At New Year's time in 1976, he sent one such to a Mexican botany professor, Maria Luz Puga, at the University of Guadalajara. On it Iltis had drawn an imaginary *Zea perennis* and had noted that it was "extinct in the wild." Not long after Doctora Puga received the card, one of her botany students, Rafael Guzmán, made a startling discovery in the hills near Jalisco: a thitherto unknown wild, perennial teosinte. Perennial teosintes had been found before, but they were tetraploids — that is, they had forty chromosomes. Guzmán's was a diploid; like corn, it had only twenty chromosomes. Its genes could thus be transposed far more easily into another diploid plant than could those of a tetraploid. It could readily be crossbred with corn, and, for all anybody knew, that could have happened ages ago. The new discovery might, indeed, have been an ancestor of corn. When some sample seeds of the Guzmán teosinte were sent to Iltis, he christened it *Zea diploperennis* and wrote about it for the January 1979 issue of *Science*. It was acclaimed as the botanical breakthrough of the twentieth century. That a perennial teosinte chromosomally homogeneous with corn had positively once existed — and, wonder of wonders, was not extinct but still thriving — was consequential indeed. And *Zea diploperennis* turned out to have all sorts of useful traits. It was immune to several scourges that had long plagued corn in one or another part of the world, among them the maize chlorotic dwarf virus of the United States and the maize streak virus of Africa. By crossing *Zea diploperennis* with *Zea mays,* breeders soon discovered, they might within a few generations produce a plant that was also resistant to such other corn predators as earworms, rootworms, and stalk borers. And they could produce a perennial corn — a phenomenon that has proved to be of more interest to the breeders than to large-scale corn producers, because so much of the plant's energy has to go into its roots to enable it to regenerate that its yields of useful grain are puny. (Whether there was ever a naturally propagated perennial corn is moot. The Bororo Indians of Brazil seem to have thought there was. In *From Honey to Ashes,* Claude Lévi-Strauss recounted a Bororo legend about one

Bopé-joku, a supernatural creature who planted some corn. When it was ready for the neighborhood women to harvest, Bopé-joku reappeared and hung around, whistling. One Indian woman was so rattled by the noise that she cut herself on a cob, and she took him to task. That hurt his feelings, and he immediately caused all the ears to wither on their stalks. Never again, the legend had it, was there any perennial corn.)

Mangelsdorf, in Chapel Hill, had missed that issue of *Science*. He did not learn of the Guzmán-Iltis treasure until Garrison Wilkes, who was off hunting plants in the Himalayas, wrote to him urging him to investigate it. Iltis was in Mexico. Mangelsdorf managed to get a packet of *Zea diploperennis* seeds from John Doebley, an Iltis associate at Wisconsin. The retired Harvard professor was eighty and could only with some difficulty perform the plant breeder's routine crouch and stoop. Nonetheless, he at once began crossing the seeds — first in North Carolina and then, when the temperature dropped there, in Florida and Argentina — with some primitive Mexican popcorns, which he believed might have been in Jalisco centuries before. Some of the offspring he coaxed forth looked very much like the teosinte that Beadle, Iltis, et al. had pronounced the legitimate progenitor of cultivated corn. Mangelsdorf's experiments with those seeds revealed, as he and a collaborator wrote afterward, that "there was a merging of two streams of germ plasm that produced a gene pool so extensive and so rich in variation that almost any kind of corn could evolve from it through natural and artificial selection." They continued, "This concept of *Zea diploperennis* as coequal with *Zea mays* as one of the ancestors of cultivated corn appears to us to be simple, plausible, comparable with the history of Old World cereals, consistent with the paleobotanical and archaeological evidence, and in many of its aspects experimentally testable."

And in 1983 Mangelsdorf would on his own sportingly assert that the Jalisco find "may well be the most important botanical discovery of the decade of the seventies."

"Too many people have made too much of a fuss over the Mangelsdorf-Beadle Corn War," Garrison Wilkes told a visitor to his Boston laboratory in 1983. "There are more similarities than differences between the two points of view. Everybody agrees that domestic corn began about ten thousand years ago and that the place was Mexico. The monster that is present-day corn came, one way or another, from the interbreeding of teosinte and maize. What the argument boils down to is that Beadle thinks that the original plant was a teosinte, and Mangelsdorf, recent developments notwithstanding, thinks that it was a protomaize. There is really no definite answer yet to the question of origin. What's happened in the last thirty years is that we've substantiated the path of corn's evolution. Who the ancestor was is not as important as the path. We've traced that back eight thousand years now; in twenty years we may get back two thousand more. In the 1930s, after all, we didn't know the history of corn as of even two thousand years ago. People were throwing darts at a blank wall then — making perceptive guesses. Now we're much more sophisticated."

Though, about that same time, Richard Schultes told a visitor to the Harvard Botanical Museum, "The origin of corn is still a mess," Mangelsdorf, for his part, appeared to believe that the emergence of *Zea diploperennis* had tidied things up considerably; and perhaps, after all he had been through, he deserved the last word. In 1979, after his wife's death, he moved to a Chapel Hill retirement home, where in suitable weather he daily tended a crop of corn in a ten-by-twenty-foot garden, and where visitors to his quarters could not sit on his couch, because it was littered with corn cobs he had reared outside. In a scholarly paper he wrote that year, he said, "The long-debated question 'Which is the ancestor of cultivated corn — teosinte or wild corn?' is no longer relevant. Both are!"

The pre-Columbians who first populated the Americas — descendants of the pioneers from Asia who walked across the Bering Strait thirty thousand years ago or so — are not known to have concerned themselves with the genetic couplings and mutations of corn and other plants. Most of them were probably quite satisfied with their understanding of how such nourishing fruits of the soil had come to hand: gods had given them to mankind. Latter-day scientists, of course, generally scoff at such primitive perceptions, but only up to a point. The molecular biologist Lawrence Bogorad, for instance, whose studies of corn genes are too complex for some of his Harvard faculty colleagues to grasp, keeps on his office wall, just in case he might be on the wrong track, a photograph of an ancient Honduran corn god. "You can't take chances," Bogorad explains to nonscientists who stop by.

The supernatural bestowers of corn upon man took on all sorts of guises. One of the favorite myths of the Apinayé Indians, living southeast of the Amazon River, had to do with a widower who became enamored of a star. The star obligingly came down to earth, in various forms — as a frog, an opossum, a woman. She introduced the widower, who was seemingly starved for both sustenance and sex, to some corn growing on a hardwood tree and taught him and his fellow tribesmen how to plant it in the ground. (A hardwood maize tree occurs in several other old Indian legends.) The Kraho Indians, living farther southeast, also venerated a star-woman, who had blessed them not only with instructions for the use of corn — which, curiously, they had cultivated for a time merely as an ornamental plant while ingesting ant heaps and rotten wood — but with cassava, rice, potatoes, groundnuts, and, for dessert, watermelon. The Mundurucú, to the west of the Apinayé, believed that corn — and cassava, too — sprang from the grave of an old woman who, immediately after instructing a man about growing food plants, had herself buried in what quickly proved to be a prodigal garden. Such myths seem to be universal. One that long persisted in Indonesia had a bountiful woman's corpse giving birth to rice. Elsewhere, it was cassava, or manioc, alone that thus mysteriously emerged from a tomb, and the body inside was that of a one-year-old girl. In this version, the infant's mother, the supposedly virgin daughter of an Indian chief, had been unaccountably impregnated and had given birth to a white child. Her father wanted to kill her, but spared her when the only white man in the neighborhood swore she was an innocent victim of circumstances he could not elaborate on. (In bygone days, nonwhites would take white men's words for almost anything.) The infant had been named Mani, and was regarded as divine until she died. Thus, after her grave burst into useful bloom, the name "manioc." Another notable virgin of lore was a Javanese maid who attracted the eye of a god named Batara Goeroe. The god was married, and the young woman wanted no part of his advances, finally informing him that she would yield only when he could perform three tasks, which she had every reason to assume were impossible — one of them being to furnish her people with "a food of which, no matter how often one eats it, one does not tire." Batara Goeroe could not manage that and, in his frustration, tried to rape her. She died in his unwelcome arms. Forty days after her mourning relatives entombed her, there rose from her grave a galaxy of novel foodstuffs — rice from her navel, a coconut tree from her brow, and corn from her teeth.

The Aztecs of Mexico sometimes credited their bounty of corn to a pair of ants — a black one and a yellow one. The Pipil Indians of Central America believed that the red ant had brought corn to man. Charles Darwin, who encountered corn in South America when his *Beagle* anchored off Peru in 1846, told the Linnaean Society in London fifteen years later that he'd been informed by a doctor in Texas of a local superstition: that ants were the original sowers and reapers of grain. (Darwin may or may not have known that it had been the practice in rural India to employ ants to identify witches. If a woman was suspected of sorcery, some rice would be put in a cloth bundle with her name written on it, and the cloth would be put on a heap of voracious white ants. If the ants clawed through the bundle, that was proof of the accused's guilt.) Ants have been credited with extraordinary feats. One ant, color unspecified, allegedly revealed to an elderly Tacuna Indian woman, in South America, the nourishing existence of cassava, which the woman, unacquainted with fire, cooked by warming it in her armpits. Then a swallow brought her fire. When her fellow tribesmen asked how she'd heated the cassava, she said that the sun had done it. The swallow, still hanging around, laughed at her deception, and as it did flames shot out of its mouth. The other Indians then forced the bird's mouth open and took the flames, and that was how mankind came to have fire.

There has scarcely ever been a religion, or a language, in which the staple food plants have not played a significant role. (In parts of Asia, rice was long thought to have a soul — and why not, inasmuch as rice and man were deemed all but indivisible?) King Charles I of Spain, when his settlers went to South America, urged them to plant wheat there, whether or not the climate was right for it, because it was "the historic Eu-

charist bread of the Lord." Jesuit missionaries from Portugal
tried their best to plant wheat for Communion wafers in inhospitable Brazil. Monks at an Ecuadorian monastery, on the other
hand, still venerate an earthen pot because it was the receptacle
in which a missionary transported the first grains of corn that
grateful neighborhood had ever seen. Corn was introduced to
Guam, in the seventeenth century, by other missionaries; tor-
tillas have been popular there ever since.

A few lines from an Aztec poem expressed succinctly what
corn meant to the Aztecs:

> *I am a tender ear of corn.*
> *From your mountains I come to see you —*
> *I, your god.*

Many ancient theocracies boasted an imposing number of
agricultural deities. The Romans had separate gods for planting, harrowing, and weeding. Corn — real corn, not the "corn"
that was wheat or barley — does not figure in the Old Testa-
ment, of course, but Orthodox Jews, whose one God is emphatically nonvegetable, ritually hang husked ears in their
tabernacles at Sukkoth, their harvest festival. The Aztecs had
both male and female corn gods. One was sometimes called
"the long-haired mother," and when the plants under her aegis
were approaching harvest time the women tending them
would let their hair down, so the corn silks would grow longer.
Because of the accepted influence of spiritual forces on crops,
old-time Mexicans had a host of placatory ceremonies — some
of hope, some of fear, some of gratitude, and quite a few involving far more physical alterations than letting down one's
hair. A cherished rite of the Aztecs, who believed the corn ear
to be a phallic fertility symbol (so, presumably, did William
Faulkner, for he used one in a rape scene in *Sanctuary*), was to

sacrifice a young man. They would select an especially handsome one, rename him Tezcatlipoca — a one-footed god sometimes known, because he sported a fire-starting prosthesis, as Smoking Mirror — and treat him lavishly for a whole year. He wore a wreath of roasted corn ears, and turquoise earrings, and golden leg ornaments. He smoked the finest cigars. Twenty days before his scheduled death, he was given four wives — one was known as the Young Corn Goddess — and a packet of flutes. On his final day, he was escorted to a lofty temple, and as he moved up its steps he had to break a flute at each landing. When he reached the top, some waiting priests leaped upon him, tore out his heart, and offered it to their supervisory corn goddess. The tearing out of the heart was symbolically related to the husking of corn. A green jewel, representing corn, was embedded in the chests of some Aztec statues of their gods, consonant with a song dedicated to the god Xipe that went:

> It may be that I shall fade, fade and die,
> I the young cornstalk.
> A green jewel is my heart,
> But I will see gold,
> I will be content once it has grown ripe;
> The warrior chief is born.

During Montezuma's reign, the Aztecs customarily paid him an annual tribute of 300,000 bushels of corn. The Aztecs liked to describe themselves as "corn eaters," and they looked down upon their uncouth enemies, some of whom were fond of meat, as "suckers of blood." Nevertheless, it was another habit of the Aztecs, in the course of offering corn to one god or another, to slash their own bodies — tongues, ears, genitals — with stone knives, let their blood flow onto ears of corn, and then eat these in autoanthropophagistic piety. Convinced as they were of the efficacy of human sacrifice, before starting to consume any year's harvest they would routinely put to death a young girl — after stripping her and painting her face with the colors of a corn plant — and reverently place *her* torn-out heart upon a corn goddess's altar. Virgins assigned to the temple of the god of war, who were recognizable by their popcorn head-dresses, were exempt.

Among pre-Columbians, corn inspired numerous other beliefs and practices. Some tribes countenanced the consumption of corn bread at cannibal banquets; some forbade it at all festive meals, and some at any repast within five days of a king's death. The number seven was more often related to corn: here one couldn't bed down with one's wife for seven days before planting; there not for seven days afterward, either. It was a popular belief in parts of Nicaragua that a crop could be imbued with extra vigor if at the very instant that corn seeds were planted in the ground the men in the vicinity ejaculated their own seed. (At Truk, in Micronesia, where taro is a staple crop, it used to be that sex was taboo for seven days before planting; hot-blooded, easygoing Trukese found that an intolerable spell of abstinence, and persuaded their chiefs to shorten the period of interdiction to one night.) The Aztecs developed calendars not so much because they wanted to know when it was Tuesday as because they wanted to keep track of when it was time to plant or pick. They could also tell that planting time was near when the leaves of white oaks reached the size of a squirrel's foot, and this reminder was somehow eventually wafted all the way to Cape Cod: Champlain heard there in 1605 that the best time for putting down the first corn seed was when a white-oak leaf approximated a red squirrel's footprint, or — as a double check on the dimensions — when it was the size of a mouse's ear.

Corn was also a dominant crop when the Mayan and Incan empires flourished. That it could be grown relatively easily in the Central American and Andean hills gave the people it sustained plenty of leisure in which to construct the monuments for which they are principally remembered. Even without the help of irrigation, a family of three could grow enough corn in 120 days to sustain them for an entire year. The Mayans, who sometimes thought it helpful during sacrifices to their corn gods to flay young girls alive, enhanced routine burials by putting ground corn in the mouths of the dead to succor them in the hereafter. It was held by some Mayans that mankind had evolved from a botched experiment conducted by some of their deities — from, that is, a human body the gods had created out of corn after first trying unavailingly to fashion one out of clay and then out of wood. (How people came to the planet may not have been entirely clear to the Cañari Indians, of Ecuador, but they knew perfectly well how corn had originated: Two brothers hustled to the top of a mountain during a terrible flood that destroyed everyone else around. As the brothers were wondering what would happen to them, two parrots mercifully arrived, bearing food and drink. Next, one of the parrots even more obligingly turned itself into a woman. She not only gave the brothers corn seed to plant but invited them to plant their own seed in her, accordingly becoming the lifesaving mother of their threatened race.) In the ninth century, the Mayans, scholars have determined, abruptly abandoned hundreds of ceremonial centers they had laboriously built and hundreds of thousands of acres they had sedulously cultivated. They had worshiped at those shrines and tilled that land for ten centuries. They moved away. Why the sudden change? As good a guess as any was that the corn on which they were dependent had forsaken them, perhaps having succcumbed to an onslaught of maize mosaic virus transmitted from the Caribbean by windborne leafhoppers. Without agriculture, the Mayans had no culture. A European who spent forty years with the Mayans said of the typical Mayan afterward, "He does not raise corn to live; he lives to raise corn."

At Cuzco, Peru, near which corn-fed Indians — who also thrived on potatoes — erected Machu Picchu and other architectural marvels, one temple housed life-size corn plants fashioned of silver and gold. In a garden outside, real corn plants grew and were tended and harvested exclusively with gold and silver implements. The building blocks of some structures were put together in the pattern of kernels on a cob. In their prime, the Incas grew three hundred varieties of corn — among these one still obtainable in Peru: *choclo,* a short-stemmed breed with squat cobs and fat white kernels that all but fall off into one's mouth. The most revered variety was cultivated on a sacred island, Titicaca, at an altitude of more than twelve thousand feet. When the Titicaca crop was harvested each year, the kernels were distributed among various temples, for planting in their gardens. Anyone lucky enough to get a single kernel for himself was presumed to have been delivered from hunger forever. Not that malnutrition was much of a problem. The Incas had granaries accommodating several years' supply of corn. (The dilemma of the twentieth century is how to insure the availability of the right amount of staple foods in the right place at the right moment.) At planting time, the august Inca himself would turn over the first lump of soil, with a golden pickax. He would also pick the first ear at harvest time. In between, there were all sorts of corn rituals to be carefully observed. There were loaves of sacred bread to be baked from a mixture of cornmeal and llama blood. There was *sancu,* a corn gruel, to be spread on thresholds, on public fountains, on faces, and on mummies' faces. The fields under cultivation were to be sprinkled with *chicha,* the Incas' favorite alcoholic drink, which was concocted from corn that had been thoroughly chewed and expectorated by women renowned for their salivary skills; it was believed that the older the women were, the stronger and tastier the *chicha* would be. The Incas had their glorious era, and Peru has never been quite the same since; today, about half its rural inhabitants are judged by prevailing nutritional criteria to be undernourished.

In a paper he submitted to a botanical symposium in Sydney, Australia, in 1981, Walton Galinat wrote: "The hand of the American Indian must have directed the sequence of intermediate steps that eventually set the ear of maize apart from the female spike of teosinte. Starting with a profusely tillered wild grass he came to recognize as 'God's Corn' or teosinte, man selected for a condensation of its tiny scattered spikes into clusters, then into small ears, and finally into huge magnificent ears bearing hundreds of giant kernels all wrapped in a green mantle of husk leaves." Most North American Indians, like their counterparts to the south, gave credit to outside forces rather than themselves for the happy arrival and survival of the corn plant. Among the Great Lakes Indians, as Longfellow attested exhaustively in "Hiawatha," the corn plant was the embodiment of the great god Mondamin:

> *All around the happy village*
> *Stood the maize fields, green and shining,*
> *Waved the green plumes of Mondamin,*
> *Waved his soft and sunny tresses,*
> *Filling all the land with plenty.*

For all his powers, Mondamin sometimes needed assistance. Thus, Hiawatha felt obliged to tell his obedient wife Minnehaha to get up in the middle of the night, strip, and walk around their fields, in order to dispel "blast of mildew" and "blight of insect." Crows and ravens ogled, and while they were thus provocatively distracted, Hiawatha ambushed them with snares and decimated them. Such ornithocidal behavior would have horrified some Rhode Island Indians, who were firmly convinced that a crow had brought them corn, and wouldn't have dreamed of killing one. Navajos, on the other hand, thought that the credit belonged to a turkey hen, which, flying toward them in a straight line from the morning star, shook an ear of blue corn out of its feathers. (For some Indians, blue corn became the only corn suitable for the brewing of beer.) The Shawnees had one chief with the incontestably honorific name of Cornstalk.

Hiawatha and his fellow tribesmen considered the harvest to be a friendly wrestling match with Mondamin. When they shucked an ear that was bent or crooked, they would all dance around, laughing and singing; and any single girl lucky enough to find a red ear was sure to find herself a handsome husband soon. Sexuality figured importantly in myths handed down through generations of American Indians, who also deemed it prudent from time to time to sacrifice virgins to their demanding corn gods. (Later, they substituted rabbits.) One long-cherished legend dealt with a young man who had never experienced the warmth either of lovemaking or of fire. A beautiful girl appeared before him one day. First, she taught him how to make fire by rubbing sticks together. The fire he made spread to a field, causing it to burn off. When that cooled down, she invited him to drag her by the hair across the field; once he'd done that, she said, he'd be able to enjoy her, or whatever succulent crop emerged from the swath of her body, from that time on. The Zuñis of the American Southwest, whose young men were counseled by their elders to "love and cherish your corn as you love and cherish your women," were so often afflicted by droughts that they built dams to conserve what little rainfall they received, and kept a two-year supply of corn in rat-proof storehouses. It was Zuñi corn that fed the United States troops who in the 1850s came through that region to establish Fort Defiance and other usurpatory outposts. Had the Indians known what all that would lead to, they might have thought better of selling their produce to the outlanders. The anthropologist Frank Hamilton Cushing wrote an entire book about Zuñis and their corn, about which still another anthropologist, Joan Mark, has observed that " 'Zuñi Breadstuff' is a tour de force of what can be learned of a society from a study of its food habits." The Zuñis, who had a corn song for almost every occasion, also had a sort of town crier who would alert all hands when rain was imminent. (The Omaha Indians sought to avert drought by dancing around a water vessel, then spilling its contents on the ground and lapping up mud. This was, on the whole, less taxing than the antidrought practices of some Asian Indians, who would make naked women hitch themselves to a plow and drag it across a field at night — men were not supposed to look — or of some Russians, who would instruct their women to seize any passing stranger and throw him into a river.) In one Zuñi corn-grinding song, when the sky darkened it was corn itself that sounded the tocsin:

> *Lovely! See the cloud, the cloud appear!*
> *Lovely! See the rain, the rain draw near!*
> *Who spoke?*
> *It was the little corn ear*
> *High on the tip of the stalk.*

When the *Mayflower* sailed into Provincetown harbor, in November of 1620 — a month before it approached Plymouth

Rock — the ship's stores were lamentably depleted. There were some wheat seeds on board, but they would be of little worth until after they were planted. There was nothing to be found directly ashore. Captain Miles Standish set off with a few men of the company on a search for food. They marched for what they thought was ten miles up then heavily forested Cape Cod (William Bradford himself, foraging closer to the anchorage, got caught in an Indian deer trap), and at Truro, on a bayside cliff that is now called Corn Hill, they came upon what appeared to be freshly made graves. They dug. They unearthed several baskets, each with a capacity of three or four bushels, containing corn — yellow, red, and blue — that the Pamet Indians had cached there. It was "a very goodly sight," Bradford observed in his journal when the party returned. That corn — some at once cooked and eaten, some saved to be sown once they had staked out a settlement — kept the Pilgrims going. Bradford thanked God for having guided Standish to the hoard, but his God was not consistently merciful. During their first winter in Plymouth, half the Pilgrims died; the survivors planted wheat across their cemetery, so that the not yet fully trusted Indians in the vicinity wouldn't know how few of them were still alive. When spring came, though, an unexceptionably amicable Indian, Squanto, taught the Pilgrims how best to plant their corn — in little hillocks fertilized with fish, four kernels to a mound, in deferential keeping with an old chant that went, "One for the squirrel, one for the crow, one for the cutworm, and one to grow." (Some 360-odd years later, Squanto was posthumously inducted into an Agricultural Hall of Fame at Bonner Springs, Kansas — at the same time as Andrew J. Volstead, who not only gave the United States Prohibition but also helped frame the legislation that led to the establishment of American farm cooperatives.) Once the Pilgrims had harvested sufficient grain for their own sustenance, they sent a boat back to Cape Cod and returned to the Indians the same quantity of corn they had stolen to tide them over. (They were probably unaware that in Mexico an old law required farmers to plant some of their corn near the edge of a road, so that hungry wayfarers could help themselves to it. There was a caveat, however: seven ears was the allowable limit, and anyone caught taking more, who couldn't plead the excuse of poverty, was likely to be hanged.) By then, too, the Pilgrims had enough corn to be able to follow the Plymouth Indians' custom of hanging spare ears at the entrances to their homes in November, as symbols of a welcome harvest. In 1624, only four years after their arrival, Edward Winslow, in his *Good News from New England*, gratefully eulogized corn as "the staff of life." More than three centuries later, Paul Mangelsdorf repeated a celebrated observation of the archeologist Arthur C. Parker concerning the Pilgrims and other English settlers and their hard early days: "And thus it is that the maize plant was the bridge over which English civilization crept, tremblingly and uncertainly at first, then boldly and surely, to a foothold and a permanent occupation of America."

The Pilgrims were relatively unfamiliar with corn when they arrived, because, for one thing, few of them had had much experience farming in England, and, for another, the plant had not attained the sort of foothold in Northern Europe that it had farther south. And where it was known in the north it wasn't universally admired. One sixteenth-century English historian, reflecting on corn, had written, "The bread that is made thereof is drye and hard, having very small fatnesse or moysture, wherefore men may easily judge, that it nourisheth but little, and is evill of digestion, nothing comparable to the bread made of Wheat, as some have falsely affirmed." In Sweden, as late as 1748, Linnaeus, who wanted to know more than he did about corn, sent a thirty-two-year-old disciple, Peter Kalm, off to North America to look into it. In Maryland, Kalm reported on his return, the rich served bread made from both wheat and corn, but they ate only the corn bread themselves. That was the only kind of bread that Kalm — and his manservant, too — subsisted on for an entire winter, and, he was glad to say, the two of them had never felt better. (There may have been moments, though, when the master, at least, felt terrible; for he also told Linnaeus that cornmeal was effective against swellings, boils, and toothaches.) Kalm was so impressed by the ratio of corn seeds harvested to seeds sown — three hundred to one, he calculated with awe — that he called the plant, meaning no disparagement, "the lazy man's grain."

During his trip, Kalm had an enlightening talk with the protean Benjamin Franklin, one of whose concerns was agriculture. Franklin grew corn, and also oats, on a three-hundred-acre farm in Burlington, New Jersey. He related to Kalm how the colony of Pennsylvania had almost gone broke because of squirrels' fondness for corn; there was a three-penny bounty for squirrel heads, and in just one year so many of them had been turned in that Pennsylvania had had to pay out eight thousand pounds. It had to cut the bounty in half to stay solvent. In New England, contemporaneously, some towns offered rewards for shooting another predator, the blackbird. By the summer of 1749, blackbirds were almost extinct, and grassworms, which they had habitually devoured along with the corn, were multiplying at a horrifying rate. The authorities who had initiated the bonus arrangement for blackbirds canceled it, and expressed their contrition at having thus upset nature's delicate balance. American Indians, Kalm was informed along the way, had a more sensible method of dealing with blackbirds. Before planting corn, they would soak it in liquid resulting from boiling a root called veratrum. That had no malign effect on the corn, but it caused dizzy spells among blackbirds — and porcupines, too — that attempted to molest it.

Franklin's interest in plants went back a long way. In 1725, at nineteen, returning home from a journey to Europe, he had brought with him the Colonies' first broomcorn — a sorghum from which whisk brooms are made. Even earlier, he had been an unbending vegetarian. He changed when he watched a cod's belly being sliced open one day and saw a smaller fish inside; if he was going to have to live in a dog-eat-dog world, he ruefully concluded, he might as well eat meat. He never really cared much about any food; he would assert in adulthood that a few hours after dinner he couldn't remember what he'd dined on. But as a young man he'd had strong views about other people's dietary habits. In his *Autobiography,* he recounted how detestable he had found it, when he was eighteen and was working in a London printing house, that a fellow employee not only drank six pints of strong beer every day but also maintained that he did so because it gave him the energy to perform his duties. "I endeavour'd to convince him," Franklin wrote, "that the Bodily Strength afforded by Beer could only be in proportion to the Grain or Flour of the Barley dissolved in the Water of which it was made; that there was more Flour in a Pennyworth of Bread, and therefore if he would eat that with a Pint of Water, it would give him more Strength than a Quart of Beer."

Most Americans in Revolutionary days were at least parttime farmers — George Washington and Thomas Jefferson prominent among them. Both Washington and Jefferson grew corn. Washington, a gentleman farmer who seriously cared about seed quality, crop rotation, soil conservation, and erosion control, wrote to his estate manager at Mount Vernon about his crops every week, even while he was president. Washington was partial to alternating rows of the corn he grew with potatoes. He corresponded with Jefferson about that. They both rated potatoes above corn as a staple. When Jefferson remarked of the nation, in 1788, that "the introduction of anything which will divert our attention from agriculture must be extremely prejudicial if not ruinous to us," Washington heartily concurred. As president, he hoped that Congress would establish a Department of Agriculture, but not until Lincoln's administration did that come to pass. (The department's official seal sports a shock of corn.) Jefferson, who stepped down as secretary of state in 1793 to immerse himself in agriculture almost exclusively for three years at his Virginia plantation, once described himself as "the most ardent farmer in the state." He possessed ten thousand acres, only a portion of which was under cultivation. He shared Washington's view that corn, however highly others might regard it, was in the long run detrimental to the soil it grew in — an opinion that Jefferson may have arrived at because he didn't much like to eat corn. He raised it, nonetheless, to feed his animals and farmhands. Of the many notable comments uttered by Jefferson, none is more revered by botanists than his assertion that "the greatest service which can be rendered any country is to add a useful plant to its culture, especially a bread grain."

The prickly agricultural scientist William Cobbett (1763–1835), who wrote *Rural Rides* and was better known by his pen name Peter Porcupine, disagreed vehemently with Washington and Jefferson about the comparative merits of corn and potatoes. Of the latter, Cobbett wrote that "it was the greatest villain on earth who first brought the root into England." In

1822 — twenty-three years before the Irish potato famine — he said that if the English ever began to eat potatoes ("this root of wretchedness") on a large scale they might be reduced to "the state of the Irish whose mode of living, as to food, is but one remove from that of the pig, and of the ill-fed pig, too." Some Englishmen were highly suspicious of corn. They thought that it was the source of pellagra, an affliction that was sometimes called, in nonmedical circles, "the plague of corn." (People who subsist almost entirely on corn, which is low in some essential proteins, can and do get pellagra, but the corn is less to blame than their inability to supplement it with other foods.) Cobbett would have no part of such aspersions. He acclaimed corn unequivocally as "the greatest blessing God ever gave to man." Like Peter Kalm before him, he spent some time in America, and on his return to England he brought with him two prized trophies. One consisted of the bones of Thomas Paine, who had died ten years earlier. (After Cobbett's own death, his executors came upon the bones among his possessions and judged them to be worthless; they haven't been seen since.) The other treasure was some corn, which Cobbett planted in Kensington. "It will and must drive the accursed soul-degrading potato out of that land, into which it never ought to have come," he declared. But the English climate, as others had realized before him, was inhospitable to *Zea mays.*

Cobbett's advocacy of corn was enthusiastically seconded by a contemporary — John S. Bartlett, the editor of the *New York Albion* and the author of *Maize, or Indian Corn; Its Advantages as a Cheap and Nutritious Article of Food for the Poor and Labouring Classes of Great Britain and Ireland,* which he dedicated to Bickham Escott, Esq., M.P., "the first public man in England who stepped forward to call for the free admission of a new, cheap, and wholesome article of food, for the use of your poor and suffering countrymen." Bartlett, a physician, had been in charge of a prison camp near Halifax, Nova Scotia, where American soldiers captured in Canada during the War of 1812 were interned. He had been touched by their dietary demands. "Their cry for *'mush and milk'* was incessant," he wrote. He had procured some corn for them, and noted, "I soon placed before the poor sufferers the object of their longings." Dr. Bartlett believed that if England imported substantial amounts of corn from the United States it would "put forth another ligament for unifying the two countries" — would "enlist a large mass of the agricultural people of this country in favour of a continuance of peace, and tend to dissipate the clouds that now overshadow the pacific relations of England and America." He appended recipes for, among other corn-based delicacies he hoped the British would or could take to, egg pone, Virginia cakes, johnnycake, Indian mush, and artificial oysters ("1 pint grated green corn, 1 egg, 1 tablespoonful wheat flour, 1 spoonful butter — Fry them brown"). Bartlett's proposal bore some fruit. P. L. Simmonds wrote in 1854, after the Irish famine, when some corn had been shipped to Ireland: "Like the gold discoveries, the potato rot may be regarded as a providential means of effecting a great change in the condition of society. Those discoveries are not without their influence in the East, and, combined with the potato rot, they have rapidly increased the commerce between the East and West of Europe, while they are spreading broad paths between all Europe and the lands in the Southern Ocean."

In 1842, in the course of urging Queen Victoria's Special Minister Plenipotentiary for the United States to persuade his government to authorize the importation of corn, Dr. Bartlett felt constrained to allude to "the natural repugnance which all mankind feel to the use of a new and comparatively unknown description of food." He sensed what many others, before and after him, have resignedly come to perceive: it is hard to impose changes on the eating habits of people, even when they are desperately hungry. Rudyard Kipling, in India at the turn of the century, is said to have seen rice-eating indigenes starve rather than sample wheat that the British sent to succor them. Solomon Islanders working at a Lever Brothers plantation in 1933, whose conventional diet consisted largely of taro, breadfruit, yams, coconuts, and a little rice, refused to go to work when their employers tried to replace a substantial amount of that fare with corn. During the First World War, when Herbert Hoover was in charge of sending emergency food to the Allies in Europe, he wrote articles for the *National Geographic* entitled "The Food Armies of Liberty" and "The Weapon of Food." Hoover called corn "delectable" and noted that firemen in Washington, D.C., were growing it patriotically in vacant lots next to their firehouses. "If we cannot maintain our Allies in their necessities, we cannot expect them to remain constant in war," he said, but he had to concede, regretfully, that although it would be a splendid idea to send corn across the Atlantic, it probably wouldn't do much good, because few Europeans had ever learned how to eat it. He had already discovered that most Belgians, even after adequate instruction, simply weren't interested in corn. Off New Guinea, during the Second World War, an American naval vessel drew alongside a British warship that hadn't been provisioned in a long time. Its crew was jolly hungry. The American captain shouted across that he had some corn aboard that he'd be glad to spare. The megaphoned response was a contemptuously snorted *"Corn!"* William Bradford and William Cobbett, if they could have heard the colloquy, would have been mightily aggrieved.

In the United States today, the growing and marketing of corn is a $25-billion business. Among the principal American cash crops, corn ranks an unchallenged first, followed, not always in the same order, by soybeans, wheat, and — a staff of life to its own faithful legions — marijuana. Early in the nineteenth century, the two major corn-growing states were Virginia and North Carolina, which were joined by Kentucky and Tennessee. In the 1850s, as the railroads opened up the Middle West, corn pushed out with them into the states that soon became known as the Corn Belt: Illinois, Indiana, Iowa, Kansas, Michigan, Minnesota, Missouri, Nebraska, Ohio, South Dakota, and Wisconsin. The acres given over to corn peaked in 1932, at 113 million; if, a half century later, the total has dwindled a bit, to about 80 million acres, corn still occupies an impressive one-quarter of all the cropland in the nation. The prominence — if not preeminence — of corn over so vast an expanse has been consecrated by shrines even more splendid than the giant phallus of Atchison, Kansas. The cob-coated Corn Palace of Mitchell, South Dakota, is a sine qua non on many a tourist's itinerary. Mitchell has had three such bizarre edifices. The first, erected in 1892, was rebuilt on a grander scale in 1905 (its exterior design in that incarnation featured a big swastika, an emblem that was not yet in disrepute) and further enlarged in 1921. It has to be reshingled — with two or three thousand bushels of corn — every summer. During a Corn Palace Festival in Mitchell in 1952, Guy Lombardo's orchestra — its reputation for corniness was unimpeachable — gleaned thirty thousand dollars for a single week's engagement, then approximately the wholesale value of twenty thousand bushels of corn.

In Sioux City, Iowa — inhabitants of the state sometimes proudly call themselves Cornlanders — there is another corn palace, with a cob-sheathed tower more than 150 feet high. The rich soil of Iowa makes farmers from less fertile regions envious — as Robert Frost once wrote, "it looks good enough to eat without putting it through vegetables." From that nourishing bed springs 20 percent of all the corn grown in America and almost 10 percent of the global output. According to the 1980 census, Iowa had the largest agricultural population of any state — 391,070, or 13.4 percent of its inhabitants. Its Fourth Congressional District has been represented for more than twenty-five years by a Des Moines attorney, Neal Smith, whose political fortunes have not been hindered by the fact that he is a onetime cornhusking champion. One of Iowa's popular early-morning television programs is called "Ag Day." A popular TV standard, "Market to Market" — its regular host, Chet Randolph, doubles as a commodities-futures broker — has as its slogan "Food is everybody's business." A farmer being interviewed on that show confessed, in an intensely introspective moment, "One spring, we were planting corn and I didn't care whether I planted it or not — and that's awful." Of Iowa's total of 117,000 farmers, 87 percent grow corn. Some of them call their cornfields "corn factories." Some call corn "yellow gold." Some have private airplanes. Iowa's chief resident poet, Paul Engle, has published a collection of his work titled *Corn,* which includes the lines "Golden like nothing in the English earth, / Sweet with the rain and yellow with the sun." In the 1970s, Miss Iowa in the Miss America contest would bring along, to distribute among their fellow aspirants, jars of corncob jelly.

Most Iowans, like their midwestern neighbors, used to be basically isolationist in outlook. No longer. One-third of all corn grown in the United States is exported. Earl O. Heady, Iowa State University's first Distinguished Professor of Agriculture, in 1957 founded the Center for Agriculture and Rural Development there, and in the ensuing twenty-five years traveled tutorially to fifty nations and welcomed to his campus two hundred students from sixty countries. Iowa farmers are gravely concerned nowadays with deficits in Mexico and droughts in Australia; late in 1982, they were collecting money so they could send a million bushels of corn as feed for hardpressed Polish poultrymen. "It's difficult to imagine that a chicken . . . more or less . . . might shape the fate of an entire nation," one fund-raising brochure said. "But to the people of Poland, this lost poultry production means a reduction of almost three pounds of meat per person per month." Iowa farmers, sometimes wearing caps emblazoned "I'm an Iowa Corngrower," have become globe-trotters; the news notes in their trade journals are apt to say, in covering the annual meeting of a cooperative society, "Bud Gallagher of Lake Mills was on hand to discuss his recent trip to Thailand." At home, they entertain a stream of visitors from abroad, chatting with them equably about the exchange of millions of bushels. In the 1970s, when Nigeria was riding the crest of the oil boom and wanted to create a flock of new rural communities, it turned for counsel to a West Des Moines organization called Agri Industries, which is owned by 135,000 farm families in the Corn Belt. Agri put out feelers to ascertain whether it could recruit any Iowans to go to Nigeria for ninety days and help that country build roads and schools and sewers and set up local governments. The response was so strong that Agri was able to inform a visiting Nigerian delegation that whenever their countrymen were ready to proceed (they didn't; the boom busted) it could provide a thousand knowledgeable advisers.

Before mechanical corn harvesters made handpicking obsolete, anyone who could pluck and shuck a hundred bushels a day (there are two hundred or more ears to a bushel) was considered a husking paragon. "Rip of the fingers, snap of the wrist, crash on the wagon bangboard" was the way Paul Engle described it in one of his corn poems. By 1983, an Iowa corn grower might remark offhandedly to a visitor that he and his wife, just the two of them, working together with their machines, had harvested ten thousand bushels — about thirty thousand dollars' worth — the day before. Husking contests are still held in the Corn Belt, but mainly out of nostalgia. Once, they were a sport of immense popularity. The national finals would attract up to 150,000 spectators, and enough pickpockets so that policemen on muleback were detailed to thwart them. The winners' pickings in prizes were slim — a hundred dollars and a trophy, perhaps, for the grand champion — and to stand much of a chance one had to account for at least an ear a second for eighty nonstop, grueling minutes. The gold medalist in 1935 was credited with 41.52 bushels over that stretch — 2,325 pounds, or about 8,300 ears, or nearly 2 ears a second. Some buffs considered cornhusking the toughest sport on earth. Franklin D. Roosevelt's third-term vice-president, Henry Agard Wallace, a native Iowan who loomed large in corndom, once said, "We hope to see the day when farm people will get as much enjoyment out of watching cornhuskers competing for a record as the people of the cities now get out of watching track athletes in their efforts to do unusually well in running and jumping." He added that a first-rate cornhusker "is entitled to more fame than the man who made the touchdown for Iowa against Yale." (In 1922, thanks to the heroics of Leland Parkin, Iowa beat Yale at football, 6–0, in what Iowans to this day call the "corn over culture" game.) Wallace, who died in 1965, would surely have been pleased to read, in a November 1977 story in the *Des Moines Register*, "Tony Polich husks corn with the graceful ease of an Olympic swimmer."

As in Japan the *Asahi Shimbun* long sponsored rice-yield contests — the winners got to meet the emperor — so did the Des Moines paper put up an Iowa Corn King Trophy. (When a corn growers' convention was in town, the paper fancied larksome headlines like "ALL EARS ON CORN.") For a while, another Iowa daily, the *Washington Evening Journal,* sponsored an annual tallest-corn contest. The all-time Iowa record — the Caribbean has claimed 30 feet — was set in 1944: 28 feet 5¼ inches. Although dwarfism has been the goal of most contemporary food-plant breeders (according to Norman E. Borlaug, the Iowan who won the Nobel Peace Prize in 1970 for, among other things, dwarfing wheat, the ideal corn plant would be 6 feet tall and diseaseproof, insectproof, and droughtproof), some Iowans still like to call their home the Tall Corn State. Lofty plants were regularly a much-admired exhibit at Iowa state fairs. The I'm-from-Missouri school thought that ridiculous. "The money or premiums given for the 'longest ear of corn,' the 'tallest stalk of corn,' the 'biggest ear of corn,' 'the most wonderful freak,' are wasted," the *Missouri State Board of Agriculture Monthly Bulletin* sputtered in 1916. "It would be just as wise to offer a prize for the largest horse. He might be blind, knock-kneed, sweenied, spavined, ring-boned, have the heaves and be balky, yet win the prize — and many 'big' ears of corn show just as little quality!"

Expositions featuring corn were then common throughout the United States. In 1899, people from Sioux City had sent a corn exhibit as their contribution to the festivities attending President Benjamin Harrison's inauguration. Forty years after that, in Chicago, where trading in corn futures had become and continues to be a major enterprise, there was an International Corn Show in honor of "the king of all farm crops." There were shows in Europe, too — for instance, in Paris in 1852 (corn from Algeria, Australia, Canada, Hungary, Portugal,

Syria), in London in 1862 (two hundred varieties from all over the globe), in Paris again in 1900. The last had an American pavilion displaying cornhusks used in mattresses and bourbon, and its kitchen offered passersby free tastes of hominy grits, fritters, muffins, popcorn, and corn soup. In December 1908, at a ten-day-long Second Annual National Corn Exposition, in Omaha, 43,056 ears of corn were on view, and all but 3,056 of them were sold to breeders, who coveted their kernels. Delegations came from twenty-nine states and also from Canada, China, Cuba, England, Germany, Hungary, and the Philippines. At the New York exhibit, a sign was posted reading· "GO EAST, YOUNG MAN, AND OWN YOUR OWN FARM." William Jennings Bryan delivered an oration. "When I attend an exposition and see the biggest ear of corn that can be produced," he declaimed, "I find myself asking the question: 'Are not these things intended to raise our people to a higher standard and to a better civilization and citizenship; and after all are not manhood and womanhood the greatest products of this or any country?' " He continued, "I think that it is a reflection on this country, which is the greatest agricultural country in the world, that the money spent on agriculture is so small in comparison with the expense of other departments of government; that we spend more than forty times as much in preparation for war as we do in developing the things the farmers are interested in."

In corn circles, the 1893 World's Columbian Exposition in Chicago has particular historical significance, because it was there that most people became aware of a variety called Reid's Yellow Dent. (Most corns are either flints or dents. Flints have rounder kernels than dents; dents' kernels are dented.) Reid's Yellow Dent, which, after winning a prize at Chicago, also became known as World's Fair Corn, was born, in 1847, of an accidental cross — on the farm of Robert Reid, in Tazewell County, Illinois — of a Gordon Hopkins Red, which Reid had brought west from Ohio, and a local brand called Little Yellow. Reid's son James took over the new breed and for half a century nurtured and improved it. Breeders of pedigreed dogs sometimes take their best-looking pups to bed with them; James Reid kept his handsomest ears of Yellow Dent between two mattresses, to forestall mice and other intruders. By the start of the twentieth century, Reid's Yellow Dent had spread from Illinois into Iowa and Indiana. It was the favorite corn of that era, and one of its offspring, Doerr's Yellow Dent (its other parent was Mammoth Johnson), achieved almost equal popularity. An entry of Doerr's Yellow Dent in one corn show won a fifteen-year-old, third-generation Doerr a Deere cultivator. Breeders were proud of their varieties: one illustrated his seed catalogue with a photograph of an infant grandchild wearing little but a top hat and sitting on a pile of corncobs; the caption was "Grandpa's Big Ears."

Many teenage exhibitors at corn shows were members of corn clubs. Corn-state agricultural agencies put out bulletins addressed specifically to them. So did the federal Department of Agriculture, which had corn-club directors in nearly every state. State governors conferred certificates, attesting to their prowess, on all young men and women who had harvested at least a hundred bushels an acre at a production cost of no more than thirty cents a bushel. (There was interstate commerce, of sorts. The governor of Virginia once invited all the corn-club members of the Agricultural High School of Driver, Pennsylvania, to visit his executive mansion. So many of them turned up that when it was time for what in later days would be called a photo opportunity the picture had to be taken outdoors.) In 1911, when James Wilson, of Iowa, was secretary of agriculture, he not only gave out citations to corn-club luminaries but invited the stars of every state to Washington to meet President Taft. The year before, a *Farmers' Bulletin* issued by Wilson's department had said, "Many a boy and girl — and teachers, too — have dwelt in the presence of cornfields for a considerable part of their lives without appreciating the many features of interest which the structure and functions of this plant have to offer to the inquisitive students." The public-school system of Illinois published a *Corn Day Annual.* It urged parents to drop everything else and help their children observe Corn Day, and it urged teachers to suggest appropriate essay themes to their pupils: "What I Think Is a Good Ear of Corn," "Why Corn Should Be Our Emblem," and (no answers were suggested) "Why I Think Corn and Boys are Similar." Corn Day should culminate, the *Annual* dictated, in a patriotic feast, the organizers of which would "use every device to make it a corn dinner," and the counsel continued, "If the number of people is not too large, a splendid lesson in art would be the making of place cards and decorating them with some corn design. . . . Be sure to include the local editor in the list of invitations."

Corn shows were as popular in the Corn Belt at the turn of the twentieth century as tulip shows were in Holland in the seventeenth. Among the curios on display in Walton Galinat's cluttered office museum in Waltham is an ear that won a thousand-dollar prize in 1909. The entries in such contests — normally ten ears of each type of corn submitted — were judged chiefly on appearance. Among the criteria were length, weight, circumference, uniformity, color, tips, butts, shape of ears, and space between rows. A *Manual of Corn Judging* was published in Illinois in 1902 and had a brisk sale. Ideal dimensions, Henry Wallace reported in *Corn and Corn Growing,* a book published in 1923 on which he collaborated, were 10½ inches in length and 7½ inches in circumference. Twenty or twenty-two straight rows of kernels were preferred; so was a "well-rounded butt." There were professional judges; the Illinois College of Agriculture conducted classes for them. Different states had different value systems. Iowa and Illinois arbiters tended to be more influenced by the contours of the rear ends of corncobs than did those from Indiana. In Iowa contests, 10 points out of a possible 100 were generally awarded for shape of ear but only 5 for tips; in Indiana, precisely the reverse prevailed. Officials had to be alert. Unscrupulous competitors were known to cheat. They would soak ears in the hope of adding a quarter of an inch to their length. They would run a thin metal rod through an ear to make it heftier. To obtain a prize for a freak, odd-numbered cob, they would perform surgery on an immature ear while it was still ripening. A thirteen-year-old farm boy who won a prize for an untainted seven-row ear in 1909 at an Iowa state fair was still celebrated for that feat sixty years afterward, at which time he told a respectful interviewer, "To me, a hill of corn is prettier than a flower." (He was not pressed to respond to the obvious follow-up question: How did he rate a single ear of corn against a rose garden?) Corn Belt students still take part in contests, but the squareoffs are less spirited. The students are asked, say, to write essays in an American Society of Agronomy competition on topics like the identification and control of iron-deficiency chlorosis in soybeans.

A Mexican farmer who handed out one trophy after the judges had rendered their verdicts at the 1908 Omaha exposition said in his presentation speech: "In Mexico, when I have urged the possibility of changing the size of ears of corn and tried to introduce new methods of farming, I have met many men who thought I had 'wheels in my head,' and go so far as to urge that it is profane to change the old ways of farming and correct the work of God. Some say that science and agriculture are two things that never match." By contrast, many American farmers, eager to increase their yields per acre, were not at all averse to learning about superior varieties. The railroads had largely been responsible for making Corn Belt agriculture possible to begin with. Now, at the start of the century, the railroads made agriculture more sophisticated. Word about Reid's Yellow Dent and other promising varieties was in large measure passed around by speakers on the rear platforms of what were sometimes called Seed Corn Gospel Trains, which huffed and puffed about, often making seventeen exhortatory stops a day, during which seed samples and instructional literature were lavishly dispensed. The railroad companies were delighted to indulge the corn missionaries aboard: the more corn the region's farmers grew, the more would ultimately be transported by freight car.

Unarguably, the star performer on the corn-train circuit was an orator almost as silver-tongued as Bryan. He was Perry Greeley Holden, a professor at Iowa State College, and the co-author of *Corn — America's Greatest Crop.* Holden found it difficult to refer to corn — "king of all farm crops" — without indulging in hyperbole. After a visit to the 1908 Omaha show, he declared, "I have never seen anything like it." He had been lured away from Illinois to Iowa in 1902 by the proprietor of the weekly *Wallaces' Farmer,* Henry Wallace, whose son and grandson would both become secretaries of agriculture. The aval Wallace, a United Presbyterian minister, himself moved from Illinois to Iowa in 1862 and settled in Adair County, some hundred miles west of Des Moines. By 1885, his health had become frail. He therefore quit preaching for the notoriously less onerous task of editing, and launched a magazine that was first called *Wallaces' Farm & Dairy* and soon afterward *Wallaces' Farmer*. Its masthead bore a legend consonant with his calling: "Good Farming . . . Clean Living . . . Right Thinking." *Wallaces' Farmer* was known and admired as a sponsor of both corn trains and corn contests; its founder was known as Uncle Henry. His son Henry Cantwell Wallace was Warren Harding's secretary of agriculture, then Calvin Coolidge's. Uncle Henry's grandson Henry Agard Wallace, who was born in 1888, held that post during Franklin Roosevelt's first two terms, until he was elected vice-president, in 1940. (In Washington, he lived at the Wardman Park Hotel and grew corn — and also strawberries — in a little garden at the nearby Swiss Embassy.) Henry Agard Wallace ran for president himself in 1948, on a third-party ticket. As a cabinet member, he had been largely responsible for the New Deal's agricultural policies and had probably done more than anyone else to help the American farm population achieve a semblance of parity with the rest of the nation. (In 1932, the per-capital income of farmers was about one-third that of nonfarmers; today it is more than three-quarters.) All that progress got Wallace nowhere when he became the short-lived Progressive party's standard-bearer. He received 2.8 percent of the vote nationally and under 1.2 percent of the Iowa vote. He was his home state's second presidential hopeful. The first was James B. Weaver, who ran on the Greenback slate in 1880 and the Populist one in 1892. Weaver advocated a progressive income tax, a low tariff, and a flexible monetary policy — concepts that were then considered heretical, if not downright subversive. He didn't get to the White House, either.

Brought up on a corn-growing farm, Wallace matriculated in 1906 at Iowa State, which was then, as it is now, a stronghold of agricultural research. Contemporary students in its agronomy department engage in an annual long-distance race that they call an agronathon. (In 1983, a bulletin board in the school's Department of Seed and Weed Sciences displayed a photograph of a weed towering menacingly over a man's head. A reassuring caption read, "Fortunately this picture was not taken in Iowa.") Though Wallace had been initiated into the study of genetics as a boy by George Washington Carver, the peanut man, he was not distracted from his dedication to corn. Returning to Iowa State after he became secretary of agriculture, he told an audience: "Of all the annual crops, corn is one of the most efficient in transforming sun energy, soil fertility, and man labor into a maximum of food suitable for animals and human beings. It is to be regretted that so few of the millions whose prosperity rests on the corn plant should have . . . appreciation or knowledge of it. Even those who work most with corn display little of the genuine reverence for it which characterized the majority of the corn-growing Indians up until this century." In 1956, after he had extricated himself from the maelstrom of politics, he reiterated, in *Corn and Its Early Fathers,* a book of which he was co-author, his unswerving affection: "We can safely say that if a corn breeder has a real love for his plants and stays close to them in the field, his net result, in the long run, may be a scientific triumph, the source of which will never be revealed in any statistical array of tables and cold figures."

By the same time Wallace graduated from the School of Agriculture, in 1910, he was a veteran exhibitor at corn shows. As early as 1904, when he was sixteen, he had concluded that the way they were run was nonsensical. He thought that corn should be honored for its yield, not for its attractiveness. "Looks mean nothing to a hog," he continually pointed out.

Perry Holden was a show judge that year. Wallace received from him samples of seeds from the varieties that Holden had rated among the top twenty-five and the bottom twenty-five. Henry's father gave him three acres to plant them on. Not only did the prettiest specimens not produce better than their dowdier sisters; they did worse. On leaving college, Wallace went to work for the family publication, but he continued breeding corn in his spare time, and he focused on productivity. By 1919, he was so confident that corn's beauty was irrelevant to its value that in the Christmas issue of the *Farmer* he issued a yield challenge to the most recent corn winner at the International Livestock Exposition, in Chicago: he proposed a showdown between that variety and one of his own, all expenses to be underwritten by the magazine. The glove he threw down was not picked up.

Most crossings of corn had traditionally been made through open pollination — that is, by planting two varieties side by side and letting one, through airborne dissemination of its pollen, fertilize the other — rather than by hybridization. Open pollination was chancy; hybridization could produce a stable, unvarying seed. In 1919, Wallace moved seriously into hybrids. He was by no means the first person to do this; Edward East, George Shull, and Donald Jones, among others, had long preceded him. (As a college senior, Wallace had read about Shull's research, and in 1926 he would be invited by East to participate in a round table on population at the Institute of Politics, in Massachusetts — probably his first foray into national affairs.) Yet though he was no trailblazer in corn hybridization, he emerged as one of its major figures — a distinction he was rightly proud of. "We hear a great deal these days about atomic energy," he said in 1955. "Yet I am convinced that historians will rank the harnessing of hybrid power as equally significant." By the early 1920s, he had proposed a new kind of competition at Ames — the Iowa Corn Yield Contest (later, Iowa Corn Yield Test). In 1924, he entered one of his progeny, called Copper Cross. It won a gold medal, though some old-school corn judges could barely bring themselves to glance at it; the ear was twisted and gnarled and was a hideous red in hue. (One of its parents went by the name of Bloody Butcher.) That was the first time a hybrid had ever outshone an open-pollinated corn. By 1925, Wallace hybrids were winning so many prizes all over Iowa that an Illinois corn grower, Lester Pfister, made a pilgrimage to Des Moines to learn about them. He listened to Wallace extol their virtues and resolved that he, too, would concentrate on raising hybrids. Eventually, these made Pfister wealthy, but first he suffered through exceedingly lean years, in the course of which some of his farmer neighbors jeered at him for his outlandish notions, and his wife and children lived on corn mush in a house heated mainly by cob fires.

The first fifteen bushels of Copper Cross seed that Wallace put on sale were marketed by the Iowa Seed Company. The response was heartening enough to encourage him, in 1926, to found his own firm, the Hi-Bred Company. (Its name was changed in 1935 — by which time Wallace was in Washington — to the Pioneer Hi-Bred Corn Company.) It grew slowly. Its big break — a break for all the hybrid-seed distributors then on the scene — came in 1936, when a howling wind flattened the open-pollinated corn in a field in Hartwick, Iowa; the hybrid corn in a nearby stand, according to the *Des Moines Register,* stood up "straight as a ramrod." Today, Pioneer Hi-Bred is a far-ranging entity with annual sales of more than half a billion dollars. In the main lobby of its corporate headquarters, in Des Moines, a place of honor has been accorded a portrait of Wallace done by another esteemed Iowan, Grant Wood. Although no post-Columbian artist has done for corn what van Gogh did for potatoes and their eaters, *Zea mays* has covered its fair share of canvas; Alfred Montgomery, a Tulsa, Oklahoma, artist, who painted *Just Corn* in 1921, sometimes seemed to find hardly any other subject to his taste. The critics said he portrayed corn so realistically that horses and chickens would try to nibble at his finished work. How they got close enough to do so was never explained.

What made the hybrids attractive to farmers was something they could observe with real appreciation: a substantial increase in yield per acre. (Luther Burbank once wrote that if anybody could create a kind of corn that, in mass production, could result in just one more kernel per ear than the average of its forerunners, it would mean an annual addition of over five million bushels to the output of the United States alone.) The per-acre yield of corn had been astonishingly steady, if not stagnant. Before the white man moved into and settled what became the United States, all the Indians together who were resident here are thought to have cultivated about fifteen thousand acres of corn, and to have harvested about 300,000 bushels — 20 to the acre. In 1936, although the countrywide average had previously climbed somewhat higher, it was only 18.6. (That, to be sure, was a drought year.) In 1937, when the average for Iowa, an exceptionally high-yield area, was just over 40, that state's much-praised champion attained 120.7. But in 1982 the *national* average — a figure that included much marginal land — was 114.5; it was as if any high-school athlete who made even a halfhearted attempt could come close to matching an Olympic record. The new hybrids were the reason. In 1933, fewer than 1 percent of all Corn Belt acres were planted to them. Ten years later, 78 percent were. Between 1942 and 1945, the cumulative increase in the value of the American corn crop was greater than $2 billion. And soon after the war ended, hybrids spread worldwide. The FAO persuaded Hungarian corn growers, for instance, to switch to them, and between 1957 and 1964 the percentage of planting of hybrid seeds jumped in Hungary from 3 to 100 — a reflection in part, of course, of how swiftly changes can occur in a controlled society. Yields in Chile averaged under 20 bushels an acre in 1960, when hybrids were introduced there. Twenty years later, the figure was 70, and chicken — largely corn-fed poultry — which had formerly been a luxury food, was to be found on many a middle-class dinner table.

Pioneer Hi-Bred has happily ridden the crest of the hybrid wave. It sells its corn in units — 80,000 seeds to a unit. In 1936, it disposed of 75,000 units; in 1982, nearly 7.5 million — almost 600 billion kernels — which constituted more than 35 percent of all American corn-seed sales. Among Pioneer's competitors are not only other big grain companies but also multinational corporations like Royal Dutch/Shell, Occidental Petroleum, and Ciba-Geigy, which from time to time are accused of ulterior motives — of, say, marketing seeds that they have bred to be supinely dependent on fertilizers, pesticides, and herbicides that they also peddle. Pioneer is by now a multinational itself, operating in some ninety countries, and it spends close to $20 million a year on research — two-thirds of that allocated to seed corn. It releases from 7 to 10 new corn hybrids a year (by 1981, American farmers had a choice of some 450), but only after testing 15,000 possibilities in 300,000 yield plots on 250 scattered sites. As Philip Morris has extracurricularly sponsored art, and Mobil music, so has Pioneer been a patron of literature; among the publications it has underwritten is *Maize in the Great Herbals.*

Pioneer's course was long steered by William L. Brown, a geneticist from West Virginia. His academic specialty had been Kentucky bluegrass until, as a graduate student in Missouri, he came under the wing of Edgar Anderson, who nudged him toward *Zea mays*. Brown joined Pioneer in 1945, at thirty-one. He went on to become its president and board chairman, and, en route, collaborated with Henry Wallace on *Corn and Its Early Fathers*. "No plant has changed so fast in so short a time as has corn, in the hands of the white man," they wrote. In 1983, at seventy, Brown was delighted to be able to give up most of his executive responsibilities and address himself to serious contemplation of the evolution of some Cherokee Indian corn he had first come across in the mid-1940s on the Qualla Reservation, in North Carolina — a flour corn he'd never before heard about. He went back there forty years later, imagining that by then the Indians, like the vast majority of American corngrowers, had turned to some hybrid or other — perhaps even a Pioneer one. He was happy to discover that they had stuck to their indigenous variety. He borrowed some of their seed and began growing it himself. "This won't help anybody produce any better corn," he told an acquaintance, "but it's interesting."

In 1929, Henry Wallace made an agreement with a Coon Rapids, Iowa, real-estate man, Roswell Garst, who had a flair for salesmanship. On the basis of a handshake, Garst was granted the right to distribute Wallace's seeds in certain areas. (It was possible in 1929 to make deals with handshakes.) Garst, some Wallace seeds in hand, went into farming. Their casual arrangement was formalized in 1932 by a written contract between Hi-Bred and the firm of Garst & Thomas. A further contract, in 1940, extended the arrangement through 1955. After that, the two companies simply worked together on a basis of mutual understanding. In 1959, Garst, who was already well known in Iowa (his uncle Warren had been elected governor of the state in 1908), became internationally prominent when Nikita Khrushchev visited his corn-and-hog farm. Khrushchev had made a speech back at home in 1955 about the Soviet Union and livestock, and mentioned Iowa. The editorial-page editor of the *Register* and of the *Tribune*, Loren Soth, thereupon wrote a piece to the effect that Iowans would be glad to tell a Soviet delegation anything they wanted to know about raising and feeding animals if they cared to stop by. They did, although Secretary of State John Foster Dulles didn't think much of that notion. President Eisenhower, however, gave it his imprimatur. The Soviet leader himself arrived in Iowa in 1959, and he was impressed by, among other things, what he heard about hybrid corn, which nobody had previously dared pay much attention to in the U.S.S.R., because of the xenophobic atmosphere there in the forties and because Stalin's pet agronomist, Trofim Lysenko, had scoffed at it. The Russian diet before Khrushchev's trek to Coon Rapids had consisted in the main of potatoes, bread, cereals, and turnips. Khrushchev wanted a switch to more meat, milk, and eggs. For that to happen, he knew, he would need large quantities of feed grains. High-yielding corn, he decreed, would thenceforth be welcome in Russia.

The two seed companies became so lucrative that when the Garst family bought out the Thomases' half interest, in 1982 (Roswell Garst had died five years earlier), the price was $24.5 million. But before that the amicable relationship with Pioneer had turned sour. There had always been squabbles from time to time, to be sure, as there are in close-knit families. Once, for instance, Pioneer had introduced a gene into some of its hybrids that caused nick trouble. ("Nick" is the term for what happens when pollen doesn't land on corn silks at precisely the right moment; the kernels that emerge are apt to be misshapen.) The Garst people contended that because of unacceptable nicks in four hybrids alone they had suffered a loss of the revenue from about 175,000 bushels of seed corn in a single year. Nevertheless, everything had gone along smoothly enough until Pioneer decided that it wanted exclusivity in the selling of its seeds, and offered to buy out the Garsts. They declined. Pioneer thereupon notified them that they would receive no more Pioneer seeds after August 31, 1983. Garst took Pioneer to court. After one interim partial verdict in Pioneer's favor, a settlement was reached according to the terms of which Garst could peddle all the Pioneer seed it had in stock but could obtain no more. The settlement took so long that a lot of lawyers, who tend to disapprove of any understanding that is sealed by a mere handshake, no doubt ended up enjoying a fat share of the huge profits generated by hybrid corn.

Another lawsuit that involved Pioneer and Garst (and every other American seed company — about four hundred of them) also involved Paul Mangelsdorf and Donald Jones. In the breeding of hybrid seeds, some plants were arbitrarily designated males and the others females. The two sexes were planted in alternating strips, usually six female rows and then two male. One of the difficulties was that the female stalks — those, that is, which were marked for reproduction and also for emasculation — had to be carefully detasseled by hand. (A single, bisexual corn plant, left to its own reproductive devices, can scatter about twenty-five million grains of pollen.) The originator of detasseling is usually held to be James Logan, who in 1727 was one of William Penn's chief administrators of the Province of Pennsylvania. One year, Logan, who grew corn in his backyard, cut the tassels off some of his plants, covered the silks of others, and perceived that none of the mutilated stalks grew ears. Thus was revealed — to modern man, at least — the secret of corn sexuality. For hundreds of thousands of Corn Belt high-school students, detasseling jobs — with teachers often serving as supervisors — became an agreeable source of extra income each summer when the corn in their vicinity silked; during one recent vacation period, boys and girls in Iowa, North Carolina, Michigan, Indiana, and Illinois earned $9 million from such employment. Detasseling was one of many matters brought up in the Garst suit against Pioneer, and when the litigation was publicized it turned out that a lot of the teenagers had never known *why* they were detasseling; whatever sex education their teachers had conveyed to them evidently hadn't covered that.

Working in the 1930s, Mangelsdorf and Jones had discovered, jointly and separately, that by manipulating a gene in corn's cytoplasm — the liquid content of its cell — they could produce non-pollen-bearing tassels. This male-sterile variety could be used as the female in breeding, without recourse to the laborious, expensive ordeal of detasseling. There was a hitch, however: for the resulting hybrid to produce seed itself in the following generation, a fertility-restoring gene also had to be introduced into the cytoplasm. Jones and Mangelsdorf accomplished that, too. Their contribution to corn genetics became known as T-cytoplasm — the *T* for "Texas." They applied for a patent on their male-sterile innovation in 1948. The application was turned down. In 1950, Jones, acting alone, applied for one on the fertility-restoring development. It was granted in 1956. (The government does not give out patents on breeding materials per se — Jones got his for the method he had devised — but since 1970, when a Plant Variety Protection Act was passed, it has allocated "certificates of protection."

They are good for eighteen years, which is longer than the life span of most new plant varieties.) Early in their research, Jones and Mangelsdorf had agreed to share equally whatever income either of them might receive from any successful patent application. In 1948, they had turned over their patents-in-progress to a nonprofit organization called the Research Corporation, of New York, which handled patents and their protection for many academicians. The customary arrangement was that the inventor and his institution would get 60 percent of any proceeds. When it came to the Jones-Mangelsdorf patent, however, the Research Corporation was so dubious about its prospects that it agreed to allot to each man 10 percent of the after-expenses potential take and to each man's named institution — the Connecticut Agricultural Experiment Station for Jones, Harvard for Mangelsdorf — 28 percent of the remainder of the proceeds.

For a long while, there weren't any proceeds. The seed companies all gleefully incorporated the T-cytoplasmic gene into their hybrids, but they seemed to regard it as being in the public domain. By 1960, nearly all the corn grown in the United States was derived from the hybrid lines with T-cytoplasmic sterility and fertility in their genealogy, and high-school students had to look elsewhere for their summer employment. (Some found jobs searching cornfields for "rogues" — alien varieties that had somehow crept into a stand of uniform plants.) In 1963, the Research Corporation filed a class-action suit charging all the seed companies in the country not only with infringing on the patent but with conspiring to do so — an allegation that, if it should be sustained, would have tripled whatever damages might be assessed. The Research Corporation was lucky, because a Chicago patent lawyer it retained to press its case, Clyde Willian, happened as a teenager to have detasseled corn himself. Willian thus knew something about the issues at stake, whereas the lawyers opposing him had to start from scratch. This case was also settled out of court, in 1970; along the way, the conspiracy charges were dropped. The defending companies agreed to pay the Research Corporation a 5¼-cent royalty for every bushel of T-cytoplasmic seed corn they turned out between January 1, 1961, and July 10, 1973, when the patent would expire. The total reimbursement came to about $2.5 million. Harvard, which had known little about the convoluted goings on, was pleasantly surprised to come into a windfall of some $300,000 — enough money to initiate the endowment of a Mangelsdorf professorship.

In that same year of 1970, disaster struck. Corn, like all other plants, has its fierce, unrelenting natural enemies, underground and aboveground, before and after harvest. (A vivid example of the havoc that plant predators can cause was the Australian mouse plague of 1917, whose primary target was wheat. A newspaper in Victoria reported that so many mice were on the rampage that hawks and snakes wouldn't eat any more; they were stuffed. "The cats and dogs have become disgusted and nauseated at the sight of a mouse," the story went on. "The people are sleeping on tables to avoid the mice. The women are kept in a constant state of terror, and the men are kept busy preventing the mice from crawling down their coat collars." One gentleman, trying to get some sleep, covered his face with his top hat. Mice ate the hat. Broad fields of wheat were riddled with mouse holes, and prayers for relief from the hordes filled the churches. In two months, thirty-six million mice were trapped at 120 railroad stations; altogether, fifteen hundred tons of them were destroyed before the reign of terror abated.) Corn has been as subject to attack as any other staple. In Nepal, it is deemed a delicacy by bears, but bears, for all their agility, do not get around as frighteningly or damagingly as mice, or, worse yet, insects. Early in 1981, for instance, the larger grain borer, which can also bore its way through wood, and which had been thought to be confined mainly to Brazil, Colombia, Central America, and the American South, turned up in Tanzania. The mere mention of a migration of grasshoppers makes farmers the world over shudder as if they had been hit by an earthquake, and the outcome can be equally appalling. Grasshoppers are so voracious and so indomitable that, according to a legend long recounted in Canadian wheat circles, when an Edmonton farmer bought a flock of turkeys and turned them loose to dispose of the pests, the turkeys came squawking back to their pens three hours later with their feathers plucked clean. The disappointing gobblers were notably less efficacious than old-fashioned religion was in Minnesota a century ago. When grasshoppers descended en masse on that state in the spring of 1877, the govenor declared April 26 a day of prayer and fasting, and called upon his fellow citizens to "humbly invoke for the efforts we make in our defense the guidance of that hand which alone is adequate to stay 'the pestilence that walketh in darkness and the destruction that wasteth at noonday.' " Unlike chieftains of more ancient civilizations, he did not propose human sacrifices — or, at any rate, not public ones. Church bells pealed, businesses and stores were closed. On April 27, there was a bright, hot sun, the earth warmed, and grasshopper larvae emerged from their burrows and began crawling around. Then, all of a sudden, the temperature dipped, and a severe frost set in; the fledgling grasshoppers were caught above-ground and perished.

Some thirty insects range hungrily across the Corn Belt, among them the European corn borer, the Western corn rootworm, the corn-leaf aphid, the black cutworm, the corn earworm, the slender seed-corn beetle, the seed-corn maggot, the billbug, the armyworm, the flea beetle, the mite, the slug, and the thrip. In numerous research laboratories — in Mississippi, the Agricultural Research Service of the Department of Agriculture subsidizes a Corn Host Plant Resistance Research Team — entomologists spend their days, and often nights, breeding more of the pests, in the hope of figuring out ways of eradicating them. In China, there is a laboratory that rears colonies of hornets with a known appetite for corn borers; to unravel further secrets of that one insect's habits, Pioneer raises a million and a half corn-borer egg masses each year. An entomological enclave in Mexico breeds what are surely the world's most pampered corn earworms: they are fed a diet that might conceivably sustain a Bulgarian weightlifter, including, as it does, such fortifying delicacies as soybean meal, ground maize, yeast, wheat germ, sorbic acid, ascorbic acid, vitamins, Aureomycin, streptomycin, and corn-tassel powder. Uncooperative or shy female earworms nesting there are encouraged to lay fertile eggs by the presence in their cages of potted corn plants. The entomologists hovering over those insects do not know exactly why this works. The plants may act as an aphrodisiac, they think; and they liken its effect on the bemused worms to that of wine and music on human beings.

The major diseases that afflict corn are equally fearsome. Just a few of them are seed rot, seedling blight, helminthosporium leaf spot, crazy top, southern corn rust, diplodia stalk rot, gibberella stalk rot, and common smut. As soon as antidotes are found for old scourges, new ones turn up. Anthracnose invaded Iowa for the first time in 1980. Gray leaf spots and eyespot concurrently made a pernicious appearance there. Plant breeders hope at best, by making their new varieties increasingly resistant to plants' enemies, to attain a state of peaceful coexistence; they are gloomily aware that insects and diseases are able to mutate just as readily as plants, and to do so without human tinkering. It is almost axiomatic among geneticists that whenever you get a better plant you get a worse pest. Corn hybrids with T-cytoplasm in their parentage became enormously popular partly because they had a built-in resistance to southern-corn-leaf blight. But they could not withstand a new strain of that blight which was first spotted in the Philippines in 1961 and, after working its way unostentatiously across the Pacific, hit the United States like a rogue wave in 1970. Some 15 percent of the national corn crop succumbed to it; the loss to farmers was calculated at nearly a billion dollars. And at that the growers may have been fortunate. "Even slight changes in the virulence of the pathogen or in weather patterns could easily have led to total corn disaster," a National Academy of Sciences report subsequently stated. Some scientists at Iowa State called the 1970 blight analogous to the Irish potato famine. Pioneer had some seed that was free of T-cytoplasm and was unaffected by the inundation. Somebody hijacked a truck carrying six hundred bags of it. It was a precious haul. As quickly as seed companies could, they began breeding new varieties from which all traces of T-cytoplasm had been eliminated. After that epidemic, there were no more royalties to be paid to the Research Corporation on the Jones-Mangelsdorf patent; grateful high-schoolers refreshed their detasseling skills and went back to work.

In 1982, American farmers spent over $3.5 billion on insecticides, herbicides, and fungicides. It was a valiant effort — though scarcely such in the view of most ecologists — but that vast outlay produced no appreciable reduction in crop losses from the level of forty years before. (At a symposium on agricultural research in Beltsville, Maryland, in the spring of 1983,

James B. Kendrick, Jr., the vice-president for agriculture and natural resources of the University of California, proposed the establishment of a new profession: plant-health specialist, whose practitioners would dole out agricultural chemicals by, in effect, prescription.) By the 1980s, the subcategories of the plants that farmers were trying to protect from their rampant foes had become dangerously few in number. Varieties that fared well in one area, it had long been recognized, were not necessarily right for another, and once a variety disappeared (in those same forty years 95 percent of the wheats indigenous to Greece, for instance, had become extinct) it was irretrievably lost. And yet there was a global tendency for cultivators of all food plants to concentrate on just a few successful varieties — successful, that is, until some new predator evolved to demolish them. (Rice breeders were pleased by the introduction of a variety that was resistant to the brown plant hopper, which transmits grassy stunt; but almost before the producers of that variety had had time to sit back and properly congratulate themselves on their achievement, a new biotype of plant hopper had emerged to vex them.) Nearly 50 percent of the corn planted in the United States today stems from just a half-dozen major cultivars. Farmers who in the past reproduced their own varieties from their own hoarded seeds have become increasingly dependent on the output of the seed companies. The National Academy of Sciences has issued the stark reminder that "the key lesson of 1970 (year of the corn blight) is that genetic uniformity is the basis of vulnerability to epidemics." Henry Wallace, for all his devotion to hybridization and standardization, once warned, "Neither corn nor man was meant to be completely uniform." Uniformity could annihilate genes that, according to a 1981 report of the General Accounting Office, "are the basis for future intentional or evolutionary crop improvement and development, and the fundamental defense against natural and man-made threats to crop survival." California's Dr. Kendrick went on record in 1977 to the effect that "if we had to rely only on the genetic resources now available in the United States for the genes and gene recombinants needed to minimize genetic vulnerability of all crops into the future, we would soon experience losses equal to or greater than those caused by southern-corn-leaf blight several years ago — at a rapidly accelerating rate across the entire crop spectrum." Garrison Wilkes has put it more succinctly: "Quite literally, the genetic heritage of a millennium in a particular region can disappear in a single bowl of porridge." And Walton Galinat, for his part, has observed that unless genetic variability is treasured, and carefully preserved, "we and our mutually symbiotic food plants may vanish like the dodo."

At universities, and at national and international research centers, scientists far more acutely aware than most people of this peril to the human race plod on, trying both to make plants stronger and to weaken their aggressors. (In a laboratory at Cold Spring Harbor, on Long Island, the inimitable Barbara McClintock is in her fifth decade of corn breeding; she is not professionally interested in yields and resistances, of course, but in chromosome patterns.) One of the biggest challenges to corn breeders — and one whose successful outcome would be welcome news to sufferers from pellagra — has been to produce a successful plant embodying a sufficient content of lysine, one of the amino acids (the components of protein) in which corn is, for all its praiseworthy qualities, lamentably deficient. In Colombia, where a high-lysine cornmeal has lately been test-marketed, children who ate it were cured of kwashiorkor, and pigs that ate it fattened at three times their previous rate. In 1963, scientists at Purdue isolated a mutant gene called

Opaque-2, the incorporation of which into corn increases its lysine content. For quite a while after that, further research on what breeders began to call Quality Protein Maize was only desultory. Many of them gave up on it because the end product was discouragingly susceptible to a number of diseases, and because its yields were generally too low to appeal to farmers. Recently, however, researchers have found ways, not yet commercially exploited, of overcoming those and other detrimental traits. All along, moreover, there has been a steady, unwavering increase in the yields obtainable from conventional strains of corn. It was not beyond the realm of possibility to hope, corn enthusiasts were saying in the early 1980s, that by the year 2000 there might be varieties of high-lysine, high-protein corn that would yield a monumental six hundred bushels an acre. To the half-billion or so inhabitants of the earth who are less concerned with how or where corn originated than with how much additional nourishment they can obtain from it, that would indeed be a godsend.

II

POTATOES
Man Is What He Eats

Oh! There's not in the wide world a race that can beat us,
From Canada's cold hills to sultry Japan,
While we fatten and feast on the smiling potatoes
Of Erin's green valleys so friendly to man.

— Rev. John Graham, of Magilligan, County Derry,
who died in 1844, the year before the Irish famine

N ORMAN E. Borlaug, the onetime Iowa farm boy
who was awarded the Nobel Prize in 1970 for his role
in what was perhaps euphemistically called the Green
Revolution, won it for Peace, because the will of Alfred Nobel,
the munitions man, did not specify Agriculture as a deserving
category. The omission seems strange, inasmuch as food —
especially the handful of edible plants on which most of hu-
mankind has been all but totally dependent since it attained
what it likes to perceive as civilization — has figured as consequentially and decisively in most of history's lethal conflicts as
has firepower. That an army marches on its stomach, as Napoleon said, is not a mere cliché. During the First World War,
when Herbert Hoover was in charge of procuring emergency
rations for the Allies, a popular slogan in America was "Food
will win the war"; after the United States became an active
participant in the Second World War, Hoover declared: "The
first word in war is spoken by guns — but the last word

has always been spoken by bread." Back in the Middle Ages, there was sometimes a sort of gentleman's agreement that no wars were to be started at harvesttime; when crops were ready for picking during the Wars of the Roses, everybody stopped fighting and went off to tend to them. One of the causes of the American Revolution was the imposition by the British of binding restrictions on the trade of farm products in the colonies. Earlier, when white Americans were forcibly subjugating red ones, the destruction of Indians' corn was considered as strategic an objective as the destruction of people; a not very long-lasting agreement that those antagonists signed in 1831 was called the Corn Treaty. Twenty-five years before that, when the British had blockaded Europe and thus deprived it of the sugarcane that continent customarily imported from the West Indies, Napoleon offered a 10,000-franc reward to anybody who could devise an acceptable sweetener from indigenous sources. Soon glucose — sugar from starch — was in general use. When Napoleon marched east, he counted on Russian wheat to sustain his troops. It apparently didn't occur to him — any more than it would to the Nazis in their turn — that the Russians might burn their crops as they retreated. The Nazis, incidentally, believed that an addiction to white bread had sapped the fighting will of German soldiers in the First World War and that a switch to rye in the Second would give their troops "the strength and endurance of the Nibelungs," and they were glad to sign a pact with the Soviet Union in 1939 because, for one thing, it meant that Germany could obtain, via the Trans-Siberian railroad, all the protein-rich soybeans it also esteemed.

The naturalist Jean-Henri Fabre once wrote that history "celebrates the battlefields whereon we meet our death, but scorns to speak of the plowed fields whereby we thrive; it knows the names of the king's bastards, but cannot tell us the origin of wheat. That is the way of human folly." There is no staple food plant that has not affected the outcome of the strife on one battlefield or another. Genoa would probably have won the War of Chioggia in 1381 had not the contending Venetians foresightedly cached more than five hundred tons of millet. (Millet is the grain on which today, along with its cousin sorghum, several hundred million Asians and Africans inescapably rely.) When William D. (Big Bill) Haywood, of the Industrial Workers of the World, was indicted in 1917 for seditious conspiracy, one of the charges against him — a grave one, indeed, in time of war — was that he had threatened to burn American wheat fields. One of the nation's most ardent partisans of white bread was Harry Snyder, a frequent contributor to the *Northwestern Miller,* whose editor once said that because of Snyder's long-standing efforts "to defend and uphold the cause of honest, pure, white flour, assailed viciously and persistently by its enemies, the millers of the world owe him a lasting debt of gratitude." Snyder himself observed, in the January 4, 1919, edition of the *Miller,* that the American victory at Château-Thierry the year before had coincided meaningfully with the harvest at home of a splendid winter-wheat crop. "Great credit must be given wheat for its very efficient aid in helping to win the World War," he added. "No nation can wage and win a war without bread." The 1895 war between Japan and China, and the Russo-Japanese War a decade later, were both fought in no small measure for control of the soybeans of Manchuria, which was then sometimes called the Land of the Bean. The Russians there were amazed at the stamina of their Japanese opponents, who were on a soy-fortified diet; as soon as that war ended, Russia inaugurated an all-out soybean-research program, and by the time of the Revolution the soybean was known among those combatants with access to it as "our young Chinese ally." When General Sherman marched through Georgia during the Civil War, his men had standing orders to burn every corn shock they encountered. The North won that war because it had more bread than the South, and its bread was sometimes enviously described below the Mason-Dixon line as "Lincoln's cannonballs." (The story went that one Southern child, watching a wagon train of bread lumber by, asked a nearby Confederate soldier whether cannons really ate it. "No," the soldier replied, "the men do, but it amounts to just about the same thing.") Of the 173 million bushels of wheat that had been harvested in the United States in 1859, only 31 million were from the seceding states, which before the outbreak of hostilities had been buying another 10 million bushels from the North (where one variety was aptly named Pride of the North) to supplement their own meager stocks. Lincoln's 1861 blockade of the Confederacy put Great Britain on the spot. The South had a near-monopoly on worldwide cotton exports; it supplied close to 80 percent of Britain's cotton in 1860 — a year in which four million people there were dependent on that commodity for a living. British imports of cotton shrank from more than 2.5 million bales in 1860 to a mere 72,000 in 1862, and half a million textile workers were idled. That sorry circumstance might have made Britain side with the South, but it was no less dependent on Northern wheat than it was on Southern cotton. To make matters worse, from 1860 through 1862 the United Kingdom had below-average wheat crops of its own, and it couldn't obtain much wheat from Russia or Poland or France. Its only source of supply was the American North. You can't eat cotton. If the South had had both cotton *and* wheat, the Civil War might have seen some formidable intervention from abroad. As for rice, one of its chroniclers,

Edwin Bingham Copeland, who was also the author of the scholarly *The Coco-nut,* said in his 1924 book *Rice* that rice growers, because they are tied down to their fields, tend to be more peaceable than other mortals, and accordingly they more easily fall prey than most to marauding warriors. "No other human activity has held men fixed, and made them peaceful and conservative," Copeland wrote, "as rice culture has done. Industrial development may enable a people to levy on the produce of other lands, and develop a denser population than any agriculture will support, but there is no warrant in history for the expectation that any other means of livelihood will lead to the evolution of a human cultural system as permanent as that associated with the culture of paddy rice has proved to be." In 1941, when the Japanese invaded the province of Hunan in China just as its rice was ripe for harvest, the Chinese there resisted with exceptional vigor; they were fighting for their rice. Later, one of the much-quoted sayings of Chairman Mao Zedong was "To grow a single additional grain of rice is to produce one more bullet and kill one more enemy."

The FAO, whose proclamations from its massive base in Rome are universally listened to, if not always heeded, declared in 1981 that "by and large cereals and starchy roots and fruits have been the basis of human diets throughout recorded history, and this applies to the majority of human beings in the world today." Of all the plants to which men cling, sometimes precariously, for survival, the only one to have a war named after it is *Solanum tuberosum,* the common — and often termed lowly — potato. That war was the Kartoffelkrieg of 1778–79, also known as the War of the Bavarian Succession. Frederick the Great of Prussia, who believed that the best time for planting potatoes was at the dark of the moon, was at odds with Austria. The opposing armies vied strenuously in eating one another's potatoes. "They consumed the resources of the enemy's country till the cold weather set in and forced them to terminate," Redcliffe N. Salaman wrote in a monumental 1949 work titled *The History and Social Influence of the Potato.* Frederick came from a royal line whose sovereigns, unlike many of their European contemporaries, had long manifested an interest in potatoes. His great-grandfather, the Frederick who was called the Great Elector, had had them planted in 1651 — in the Berlin Lustgarten, because he found their flowers attractive. The Great Elector's grandson and the Great's father, Frederick William I, was so convinced of the nutritive value of potatoes that for a time he threatened to have the noses and ears cut off of any of his subjects who neglected to plant them. It can only be conjectured whether he was aware that among the means sometimes thought to have been used years earlier by the South American Indians to appease their potato gods was the mutilation of the noses and lips of unfortunates chosen for the pious rite.

Salaman, a British geneticist who died in 1955, at age eighty, likened primitive human beings' struggles with nature to warfare, and said, "How long that combat lasted we may never know, but when it was over, man had as his allies the manioc, the potato, and the maize." Salaman, a physician, became ill when he was twenty-nine. On recovering, in 1906, he decided to abandon medicine — he had independent means — and study evolution. He experimented for a while with butterflies, guinea pigs, and mice, but deemed their study insufficiently rewarding and switched to food plants. He confided his change of plans to his gardener, Evan Jones, who at once told him, "If you want to spend your spare time on vegetables, then you had better choose the potato, for I know more about the potato than any man living." Jones didn't. Salaman, who eventually became director of his government's Potato Virus Research Station, at Cambridge, spent five years breeding a couple of varieties before he learned that the gardener had given him the wrong names for them. When Jones steered him onto his solanaceous path, "I embarked on an enterprise which, after forty years, leaves more questions unsolved than were at that time thought to exist," Salaman wrote toward the end of his life. "Whether it was mere luck, or whether the potato and I were destined for a life partnership, I do not know, but from that moment my course was set, and I became ever more involved in problems associated directly or indirectly with a plant with which I then had no particular affinity, gustatory or romantic." He added that "there have not been wanting those who have regarded these activities with a shake of the head and an indulgent smile, indicating that nothing short of mental instability could excuse a lifelong attachment to the study of so banal a subject." By the time that attachment had become unbreakable, Salaman was calling the potato, which first flowered in the Andes, "the most important if less acclaimed of all the Spanish discoveries and conquests."

Of the 3.5 billion tons of food produced on earth each year — close to a ton per capita — more than three-quarters is of plant origin. Potatoes alone account for some 300 million tons, ranking in bulk just behind wheat, corn, and rice. Occupying nearly 50 million acres of land, potatoes have been a vital staple food in, among other Third World countries, Bolivia, Colombia, Ecuador, India, China, Guatemala, Kenya, Nepal, Peru, and Rwanda. The early-twentieth-century plant breeder Edward Murray East once wrote testimonially, "Either because it possesses no strong flavor to dull the appetite, or possibly on account of its antiscorbutic properties [potatoes have freed many a ship's crew from fear of scurvy], the common potato *Solanum tuberosum* has overcome seemingly insurmountable obstacles in its claim upon the public taste and has become a close rival to our cereal staff of life." The Soviet Union now produces about 25 percent of all the world's potatoes; China, 19 percent; Poland, 12 percent; the United States, 5 percent. (Even so, Idaho's yearly output is a robust 8.5 billion pounds of "spuds" — a nickname much used there, and one that is derived from an old-time potato-digging spade.) According to a 1982 calculation of per-capita potato consumption, East Germany, with a figure of 370 pounds, was the globe's pacesetter. (Belgium's tally was 290; Poland's, 270; the Soviet Union's, Ireland's, and Romania's, 210; and, in tenth place, the United States', 115.) In the last two decades, the world production of potatoes has increased at a more rapid rate than that of any other food — up 130 percent in the Near East, up 180 percent in the Far East, up 120 percent in Africa. For those regions, that should be beneficial. Potatoes — which can be eaten, though they are not fully mature, only two months after planting — provide, per unit of land and time, more calories and more protein than any other crop. Their yields — about five times greater, again per unit of land, than those of corn or wheat or soybeans — are prodigious. Even in the so-called developing countries, where agriculture is often hampered by limited irrigation and fertilizers, they come to ten thousand pounds an acre.

Potatoes are 80 percent water, but then so are human beings — and, as the nineteenth-century German philosopher Ludwig Andreas Feuerbach once said, "Man is what he eats." Of the remaining 20 percent, 85 percent is starch, 5 percent sugar, and the rest a mixed bag of fiber, mineral salts, and a dash of vitamins B_1, B_2, and C. Potato buffs like to stress their favorite food's "biological value" — a measure of the nitrogen retained in the body for its maintenance and growth. By that yardstick, eggs rate a 96, but the potato, at 73, outscores soybeans (72), corn (54), and wheat flour (53). People have been reported to have subsisted on nothing other than potatoes — with a bit of margarine added — for three hundred days at a stretch. (When the British settled the remote South Atlantic island of Tristan da Cunha in 1816 — they wanted to keep it out of American hands and also to prevent it from being used as a base for an expedition to rescue Napoleon from exile — a handful of colonists took up permanent residence. By 1949, there were two hundred of them. They ate mostly potatoes — about three or four pounds each a day. Even though toothbrushes were apparently alien to their culture, they had exceptionally fine teeth. Their potato diet seemed to be the most plausible reason for their dental health.) The 20 percent of dry matter contained in potatoes comprises more of the food consumed by human beings than — milk excluded — all meat and fish and fowl together. Tastes vary according to geography. In northern Bangladesh, farmers send the large, white-skinned varieties they produce to market; they keep smaller red- and purple-skinned ones, which they deem more flavorful, for their own tables. Venezuelans generally prefer white-skinned ones; Colombians, red-skinned. In Peru, the majority of the citizens lean toward mealy, yellow-fleshed, very dry, floury potatoes that stick to the roof of the mouth. Americans like french fries, and the French *pommes de terre soufflées,* which supposedly came into being when a chef at a railroad station, upon the late arrival of a train, tossed some already fried potatoes into hot oil to reheat them and, to his surprise and delight, they puffed up.

Potatoes, along with other roots and tubers, have long had to contend with the aspersions cast upon plants whose edible parts are not visible in their natural state. Emerson, Thoreau, and their fellow Transcendentalists, for instance, would have no truck with any food that grew below ground. Most civilizations that consider themselves advanced have been based on grains. Root crops have been described as "the inferior foods of inferior peoples." Yet to half a billion or so contemporary human beings such plants are truly buried treasure. Taro, the basis of Hawaiians' poi, is the staple of many other Pacific islanders. An old saying of the Palauans of Micronesia has it that "the taro swamp is the mother of life." (On the islands of Truk, not far away, it was long believed that any man foolish enough to insult the taro gods by indulging in sex immediately before standing in a taro patch was in grave danger of being stricken with elephantiasis of the scrotum for his indiscretion.)

And then, of course, there is the sweet potato — *Ipomoea batatas* — which belongs to an entirely different family from the ordinary potato — one that is related to the morning glory, whereas *Solanum tuberosum* numbers among its close botanical kin the deadly nightshade. The word "potato" derives from the South American Indian sweet-potato word "*batata*"; the Europeans who gave *Solanum tuberosum* — the Indians called it *papa* — its nonscientific name were unaware of the dissimilarities between the two plants. One of these is that the edible portion of the sweet potato is part of its root, while that of the plain potato is a tuber, attached to stolons, or stems, that emanate from its root. Almost any part of a potato plant, once duly interred, can produce more potatoes. (To encourage regeneration along acceptable lines, the Indians of pre-Columbian Peru would sometimes bury potato-shaped stones of their favorite colors in their potato fields.) Potatoes have traditionally been spawned from whole or sliced progenitors called seed tubers; the buds that mature into new plants grow out of the "eyes" with which potatoes' skins are marked. (The plant geneticist Edgar Anderson once wrote that his notion of a pleasant evening was to sit in an easy chair with a "succulent brown blob" in front of him and look it in the eye.) Recently, potato breeders around the world have been busying themselves developing "true potato seed" — that is, the seeds contained in the "berry" of the potato, which is a small, hard, green ball resembling an unripe tomato and is produced *above*ground. There are as many as two hundred seeds to a berry. Potatoes may never be grown on a large scale directly from TPS, as potato folk refer to true potato seed — although farmers have already begun doing that in, for instance, Sri Lanka, Western Samoa, Rwanda, and the Philippines; more likely, they will be grown from tubers derived from TPS seedlings. One advantage is that such plants can be disease-free for several generations. Another advantage that TPS has over seed tubers in general is that seeds can be transported much more easily to remote farms — in rural China, say, or Nepal — with poor links to sources of supply. Specialists in *Solanum tuberosum* like to point out to less knowledgeable acquaintances that seven hundred thousand potato seeds weigh only one pound, and that a small glass jar filled with TPS is the equivalent, in crop potential, of two tons of seed tubers.

Writing about nineteenth-century England, when wages were linked to the subsistence level, and for many workers potatoes were just about the cheapest food available, Redcliffe Salaman said in his potato history, "The potato can, and generally does, play a twofold part: that of a nutritious food, and that of a weapon ready forged for the exploitation of a weaker group in a mixed society." If the potato is, as it is often dubbed, "the poor man's staff of life," then cassava, the main sustenance today of some 500 million inhabitants of Africa, Asia, and South and Central America, is probably the poorest man's. (It may be illustrative of cassava's relatively low repute that when one of the leading researchers involved with it recently described a euphoric development in his work, he said he was "as happy as a potato.") "Cassava" is the informal name for *Manihot esculenta* most widely used in Thailand, Sri Lanka, and anglophone Africa; in francophone Africa, "manioc" is the word for it; in much of Latin America, "yuca"; in India and Malaysia it is "tapioca" — which in the United States, of course, connotes a dessert often inflicted on helpless children. Cassava can easily be grown on almost any kind of soil in warm climates. It is as easy to plant as a geranium; all that one has to do is chop off a piece of its stem and stick it in the ground. A single plant, once it has achieved its full subterranean spread, can produce fifty pounds of food — five tons of it (like the potato) an acre, on the worldwide average, or the equivalent in caloric value of six acres planted to, say, wheat. If left undisturbed underground, cassava can be dug up in mint condition as long as three years after it matures. It is mostly starch, to be sure, with a mere 1-percent content of protein, but, again like the potato, it constitutes an admirable source of energy. Yet it has one formidable drawback: unless eaten or processed quickly after it is harvested, it rots in a couple of days. In Paraguay, where the annual rural per-capita consumption of fresh cassava comes to nearly a pound a day (more than three times the rate for any other Latin-American country), fresh cassava provides more than 11 percent of the national caloric intake. Many Paraguayans, especially those in rural communities, eat a bowlful of boiled cassava in lieu of bread. An often-heard phrase there is "as Paraguayan as cassava." Eighty-two percent of Paraguayan farmers grow cassava, and whenever virgin land is settled the first order of business is to plant some of it. Photographs of Paraguayan migrants show them trudging along carrying their most essential belongings, and on top of many a pile of pots and pans are to be seen some stalks — called "stakes" — of cassava. Wherever those displaced persons ended up, they would at once plant their dependable, and perhaps livesaving, stakes.

In Brazil, which produces 19 percent of the world crop of cassava, most people use it in a roasted-flour form, generally complemented by rice and beans. Many Africans also sensibly eat the leaves, which are nutritious and taste not unlike spinach. Cassava, through now grown on nineteen million tropical African acres, is not native to that continent. The Portuguese took it there toward the end of the sixteenth century. They had judged that the Indians they subjugated in Brazil were, by their harsh criteria, unsatisfactory laborers; so they imported slaves from western Africa. Dried cassava was used as food on the ships sent over to fetch them, and there were also stakes on board, which were duly planted. Even earlier, at the same time that Columbus discovered corn in Cuba, he had found cassava; presumably it had been carried there from another Caribbean island, or directly from northeastern Brazil. Whatever the case, from then on Spanish missionaries — and Portuguese missionaries as well — began to take cassava with them in their evangelical peregrinations. The Spanish introduced cassava to the Philippines; the Portuguese, to Indonesia. Its emergence in Africa proved a boon to many people there who had previously subsisted, in stressful times, on, among other things, leaves, fungi, and dogs. By the nineteenth century, cassava was ubiquitous. Both Livingstone and Stanley, though they had trouble finding one another, found cassava — Livingstone, in 1854, in Angola; Stanley, two decades later, along the Congo River, where one regional king had long since made its cultivation compulsory for his subjects. (In Ghana, where chalk is hard to come by, contemporary schoolteachers sometimes use dried cassava chips for blackboard exercises.) Colonial nations had a high regard for cassava as an emergency food supply; when locusts gobbled up everything in sight, cassava was an estimable insurance against famine. Like all food plants, it had, and has, its rapacious predators of all sizes and types — from monkeys and wild pigs to mealybugs and green spider mites — but, snugly buried and long-lived underground, it was blessedly locustproof. For some colonies, moreover, it became a valuable export crop. By the middle of the nineteenth century, there was a thriving cassava-starch industry on the Malay Peninsula, and it flourished for fifty years — until rubber plantations were accorded a higher priority in international trade.

After the First World War, the Belgians, for their part, urged their new subjects in the former German colony of Ruanda-Urundi (it later became the independent nations of Rwanda and Burundi) to embrace the hardy crop. The tribal chiefs there at first demurred; they had plenty of potatoes. (There had been demurrers when *they* were introduced, by missionaries, around 1900; the chiefs had suggested that they would somehow poison cows' milk, and children who ate them on the sly were punished for their impudence.) But in 1924 Belgium issued a no-nonsense order to grow cassava; and within a few years, as sixty thousand porters carried five thousand tons of stakes around the region, they came to be greeted in village after village with dancing and speechmaking. In 1943, Ruanda-Urundi went through a near-famine; 250,000 tons of potatoes, the bulk of that year's crop, succumbed to the same blight that had laid Ireland low a century before. Cassava saved the day, and at get-togethers of cassava aficionados, who sometimes suspect that they are perceived as socially inferior to the potato elite, that episode is apt to be affectionately related. (Cassava saved a lot of lives, too, in eastern Nigeria during the Biafran war.) By the Second World War, the inhabitants of Ruanda-Urundi were not only indebted to cassava but thoroughly familiar with its peculiarities. In initially foisting it upon them, however, the Belgians had failed to warn all of them strongly enough that under no circumstances should cassava be ingested raw or half cooked. Its skin contains a stiff dose of cyanide, which deters many of its natural enemies from bothering it; and unless the prussic acid is neutralized by boiling, squeezing, leaching, or some other antidotal process, eating the root can aggravate nutritional imbalances that can lead to goiters, cretinism, and even — especially in the case of people with too little iodine in the rest of their fare — to death. In *Manioc in Africa* William O. Jones wrote, putting it mildly, that after the appearance of cassava on the Ruanda-Urundi scene "the usual accidents occurred."

Cassava will not normally prosper at more than five thousand feet above sea level. The potato, which Noah Webster once definitively characterized as one of "the greatest blessings bestowed on man by the Creator," is, unlike cassava, a temperate-climate crop, and it has done nicely at twice that altitude. The hub of the world's potato research is the International Potato Center, in Peru — hereinafter referred to by the initials of its name in Spanish, "CIP" — and scientists there are hoping to breed varieties that can tolerate jungle heat at altitudes of a thousand feet, or even lower. Given all the advances that have been made in the past few decades in plant genetics, botanists are already beginning to have some positive results. The implications could be profound for the needier nations of Latin America, Africa, and Asia, which by the year 2000 may harbor

90 percent of the global increase in population after 1980, and where food enough to maintain their already low standards of living will have to come from enhanced local production. The authors of a 1980 treatise in rice-dominated Bangladesh, where about half the population of 100 million has to make do with fewer than two thousand calories a day (about 80 percent of the generally accepted minimum for good health), asked: "Could not the potato be accepted by the poorer nations too as a staple or at least partly staple besides being used as a vegetable? Could it not contribute to the solution of food and nutritional problems faced by them?" The authors went on to express the hope that their readers would "look at the potato, from now onwards, with special admiration, that was not there so far, for this gift of God and a miracle food crop for the hungry billions, yet to be fully appreciated and exploited." The authors of that book would surely have been pleased by a later one, *Potatoes for the Developing World,* which CIP published in September 1984; it disclosed that potatoes were the most rapidly expanding major food crop in those areas, with consumption doubling about every dozen years.

It is fitting that CIP is located in Peru — it has its headquarters just outside Lima, and it operates three additional growing-and-research stations, at altitudes ranging up to 10,761 feet — because potatoes originated in that region and are known, from radiocarbon analysis of ancient trash, to have been there at least eight thousand years ago. (Peru, curiously, is one of the few inhabited places on earth where McDonald's french fries have yet to intrude.) Of 2,000 species in the botanical genus *Solanum,* about 170 are wild tuber-bearing species. Of the 8 cultivated species, only *S. tuberosum* is significant in the developed world. All 8, however, are to be found in the Andes. Some, impervious to cold, thrive where *S. tuberosum* would freeze. Among them, there are infinite permutations of shape, color, and taste. The Quechua language has a thousand words for different kinds of potatoes. The Incas, who often measured time by how long it took potatoes to cook, also used them for divination: finding an even number of potatoes in a pile was a promising omen; odd numbers meant trouble. Even today, in the Peruvian highlands, a meal without potatoes, no matter how many other comestibles it may contain, is considered incomplete. The Indians up there preserve some of their harvested potatoes by "freeze-drying" them. They spread them on the ground so that they are dried by the sun during the day and frozen at night. That breaks down their cell walls. Then the Indians stomp on them to reduce them to fragments. Next, the pieces are soaked in a running stream. Finally, they are sun-dried again. The end product is called *chuño*. "A stew without *chuño*," one of their hallowed sayings goes, "is comparable to life without love." Their ancestors offered occasional human sacrifices to potato gods — as also to even more demanding corn gods — and nowadays they reportedly still indulge in a much more moderate version of the ritual. If at harvest time a man finds a blood-red potato or a grotesquely malformed one, he chases a woman until he catches up with her and then touches her with it. If a woman finds one, she goes up to the nearest man, who is not allowed to run away, and clouts him with it.

CIP, which boasts the world's most extensive collection of potato cultivars — the germ plasm of fifty-five hundred tuber-bearing varieties — construes its mandate to be "to develop, adapt, and expand the research necessary for the technology to solve priority problems that limit potato production in developing countries." (Some malnourished children in those countries who cannot tolerate milk can digest potatoes, which scientists at CIP have credited with being able to furnish 75 percent of an infant's energy requirements.) Research alone, however, the Center believes, will not suffice. "The final evaluation of food production technology," it stated in a recent evaluation of its own potential, "is in a grower's field and on a consumer's plate." The Center has, among others on its staff of 350 professional men and women, several anthropologists. They not only conduct potato taste tests among Lima housewives — for whose schoolchildren CIP, supported by a grant from the Irish government, has processed a nutritious dry-food mix, three-tenths of which is dehydrated potatoes and the rest a jumble of rice, corn, oats, barley, and beans, plus a pinch of salt — but also look over consumers' shoulders and check out their china in, for instance, Bhutan. There rice — red rice, the highest-altitude rice on earth — is the staple, but potatoes have been part of the diet at least since 1774. The British East India Company sent George Bogle there that year. His principal assignment was to negotiate with the Bhutanese for a trade route to Lhasa, but he was also instructed to "plant a few potatoes at each camp and bring back two yaks, the giant Himalayan rhubarb (*Rheum nobile*), and any other curiosities." CIP has been heavily involved since 1980 in a National Potato Development Program in Bhutan funded by Switzerland. A popular potato variety that is known to most of the rest of the world by the beguiling name of Désirée is called Swiss Red in Bhutan. Susan V. Poats, a CIP anthropological emissary to Bhutan, was pleased to be told by one village woman that "even if we take rice, unless we also eat potato, we don't feel like we have eaten." Miss Poats also heard from a Drukpa farmer that whenever he and his neighbors overindulged in potatoes they got stomachaches, constipation, and diarrhea. She was relieved to learn that their travails might not be attributable after all to potatoes, for when those Bhutanese put them on their plates they also usually put on them generous helpings of hot chili peppers.

In 1982, when CIP celebrated its tenth anniversary, it convened a potato congress that was attended by about three hundred delegates from fifty-four countries. The president of Peru, Fernando Belaúnde Terry, stopped by to pay his respects, and his government issued a commemorative postage stamp to mark the occasion. CIP, for its part, put out a great many technical papers, and also distributed a book of recipes in Spanish and English, titled *International Potato Cookery.* Compiled by the CIP Women's Club, it does not include a recipe for something unappetizingly called Potato Mold, which — along with Chocolate Potato Cake and Potato-and-Nut Sausage — was touted in a 1918 United States Department of Agriculture circular that stated, "The potato has a place on our food list which no other vegetable occupies." Nor does it mention Poached Eggs in Potato Jackets with Lobster Sauce or Curried Potato and Shrimp Salad on Avocado, which *Town & Country* apostrophized in a March 1983 article called "The Lordly Spud." (Perhaps the lordliest of all recent self-proclaimed potato gourmets was Truman Capote, whose 1972 oeuvre included a foreword to *The Potato Book,* published to raise funds for a day school at Bridgehampton, Long Island. Capote was interested in the project because he had a house on the site of an old Sagaponack potato farm and because, he confessed, it was his wont to go out into nearby fields in October, after the commercial harvest was finished, and collect leftover potatoes. What he saved by not having to buy his own could hardly have covered the cost of the raw materials for *his* pet potato dish. He declared that there was only one way he could "bear to eat" potatoes — baked, covered with sour cream, heaped with the freshest, grayest, biggest-grained beluga caviar, and washed down with eighty-proof Russian vodka. There was no indication in *The Potato Book* of how many Bridgehampton tots had sought to emulate him.) The CIP cookbook did, however, contain some fairly esoteric entries: Spicy Orange Potato Doughnuts, from the United States; Pâté de Pommes de Terre, from, naturally, France; and Potato Pizza, from, of all places, Australia.

Peru's commemorative stamp depicted, along with two plump potatoes, CIP's institutional emblem: a skirted pre-Columbian deity holding in one hand a healthy potato (or, some ethnobotanists have contrarily argued, sweet potato) and in the other a plainly sick one. The diseases and pests that vex *Solanum tuberosum* and its close relatives also prey heavily on the thoughts and efforts of the CIP staff, at least one of whom cannot abide eating potatoes no matter how dolled up or disguised. The potato has more than 260 recognized scourges: 6 bacteria, 119 insects, 68 nematodes, 38 fungi, 1 viroid, and 23 viruses. And of just one of these species of fungi, over two thousand strains have already been isolated. Merely a few of the enemies against which CIP's researchers stand arrayed in grim and endless battle are early blight, late blight, leaf roll virus, rugose-mosaic virus, potato mop-top virus, tobacco rattle virus, purple top wilt, potato spindle tuber viroid, wart, stem canker, green peach aphid, black scurf, blackleg, black rot, brown rot, violet root rot, pink rot, pink eye, and — among nematodes — golden, root-knot, and false root-knot. (Sprout Nip is not among them; it is a commercial spray to protect stored potatoes.) The 68 species of potato-attacking nematodes — tiny worms that assault both the roots and the tubers of a potato plant — have their own foes. Using steamed rice as a bed, CIP grows fungi that attack *them*. Nematodes are suspected of traveling around to do their dirty work by attaching themselves to seagulls' feet. Some nematodes can remain viable in soil — even when there is no potential potato host in the vicinity — for twenty years. (So can the seeds of some weeds.) According to the Department of Agriculture, the ravages that all nematodes inflict on all food plants add up to a loss every year of 7 percent of all American crops — a $6-billion depradation.

To thwart yet another pest — the potato tuber moth, which can raise havoc in storage bins — researchers at CIP (and elsewhere, too) have lately been synthesizing pheromones. These replicate the scent exuded by female moths when they are in a mood to entice males. The male moths come flying in droves toward the fake perfume and flounder into traps. Other ingenious scientists in Peru, collaborating with colleagues at Cornell, have been crossbreeding cultivated varieties of *Solanum tuberosum* with a wild Bolivian species, *S. berthaultii,* which has gummy, glandular hairs on its stem and leaves. These, like flypaper, immobilize unsuspecting mites, thrips, leafhoppers, aphids, and flea beetles, and might even be effective against the dread Colorado potato beetle. That scourge was first discovered in the Rocky Mountains in 1824, where before it developed a fondness for potatoes it seemed content to feast on sand nettles, wild tomato plants, and buffalo bur weed. It soon began to move eastward, in a relentless sweep. It got to Nebraska in 1859, to Iowa in 1861, and it crossed the Mississippi River in 1864. By 1866 it was in Wisconsin, by 1867 in Indiana and Ohio, by 1870 in Canada, by 1873 across the whole Atlantic seacoast. It was crawling all over the streets of Saint Louis in 1871. It caused train wheels to slip because it had blanketed railroad tracks. It infests Long Island potato fields today. Along its destructive migratory trek, it mutated and eventually became resistant to DDT and other insecticides. It also became involved in human conflicts. Hitler's Ministry of Agriculture tried to arouse German farmers' wrath against the British even before the start of the Second World War by spreading the word that English planes had dropped the larvae of the Colorado potato beetle into areas where the Nazis had stored 53 million tons of potatoes. At the height of the cold war, the Soviet Union accused the United States of bombing East German, Czechoslovakian, and Polish farms with the beetle, which one Russian paper called "the six-legged ambassador of Wall Street." Actually, the bug had almost certainly got to Europe, with the best of American intentions, in food-relief shipments after the First World War.

No one member of the CIP hierarchy has been more resolute in searching for as yet unearthed wild potatoes (whose genes may help breeders neutralize the onslaughts of the potato's unrelenting tormentors) than the Peruvian taxonomist Carlos Ochoa, who was born and raised at Cuzco, near Machu Picchu. Ochoa began his professional career as a wheat breeder but switched to the potato early in the 1950s because it was, like him, native to Peru, and because no other Peruvians were then thus preoccupied. He has collected wild potatoes throughout the Western Hemisphere. "I would drop everything and go anywhere upon hearing that a new species might be there," he has said. He has also said that upon arriving at a promising location he could sniff out potatoes; he once flushed one that was hiding behind the six-foot spikes of a thirty-foot cactus plant. Ochoa found some especially rewarding specimens in the hills of Ecuador in 1980 — one of these, being immune to four debilitating potato viruses, has proved to be of immense value in CIP breeding programs — but then some xenophobic Ecuadoran law-enforcement operatives found him and, after relieving him of his field notes and photographic equipment, clapped him into prison; a week passed before he was able to get out. He is credited with the discovery of more than forty new wild-potato species. Ochoa has respectfully named a few of them in honor of such eminent patrons of the potato as W. Glynn Burton, a physiologist who wrote in the preface to his *The Potato,* following twenty-six years of intimate association with *Solanum tuberosum,* "No one man can be fully conversant with the results of all the work on the potato"; Donovan S. Correll, whose book *The Potato and Its Wild Relatives* is a classic in solanaceous literature; and Richard L. Sawyer, a past president of the Potato Association of America and CIP's director general since its launching, who gave an invocation to the four hundred or so delegates to the seventh triennial conference of the European Association for Potato Research, held at Warsaw in 1978, that went, in part, "Give us our daily potatoes." (During the Second World War, when Sawyer was a German prisoner in Poland, he had eked out his slim rations by stealing seed potatoes from the camp stores.) A Russian scientist, Professor Vadin Lecknovitch, named a potato for Ochoa, and so did a Peruvian scientist, Dr. César Vargas. Another Russian scientist, Serge Mikhailovich Bukasov, with a sack over his shoulder, prowled around Latin America in the 1920s to gather potatoes for the collection of the celebrated Nikolai Ivanovich Vavilov. Ochoa has memorialized Vavilov: the Peruvian's discovery, plucked from a moss-covered alpine rock in Bolivia in February 1983, is *S. neovavilovii.* Vavilov's 1926 pronouncements on the centers of the origins of all food plants — he believed that their domestication began in the area in which the largest number of their wild ancestors were to be found — are still regarded as near-gospel. Between 1921 and 1934, he had twenty thousand people working under him at four hundred installations, and he dispatched them worldwide on hunting expeditions. From

1923 to 1931, for example, they brought him twenty-six thousand strains of wheat alone. In 1930, he was moved to declare, according to Anna Louise Strong's *The Soviets Conquer Wheat:* "Agriculture, the basic industry of man, almost immobile for ages, is today entering upon a new phase." That was the same year in which the Soviet commissar of agriculture told the Sixteenth Congress of the Communist Party, "We have solved the grain problem." He noted that the United States was then reported to have a million tractors and the U.S.S.R. only seventy thousand. And in March 1931, he said, "In America this agricultural revolution is drawn out for decades, in a process of ruin for the majority of farmers and enrichment for the few at the top. . . . Our way means the betterment of life for the overwhelming majority of peasants. . . . We shall be able in a few years not only to solve our food problems . . . but in a very short time to satisfy the needs of the toiling people of the U.S.S.R. to an extent unknown in history." The Soviet Union today, of course, is one of American farmers' biggest customers. Vavilov, however, fell out of favor with Trofim Lysenko, and thus with Stalin; he died, in disrepute and, officially, of natural causes, at Saratov Prison, in 1943.

CIP's emissaries have been almost as peripatetic as Vavilov's were in his heyday. One of the first requests for outside assistance made by Zimbabwe after it became independent was to CIP, for help in setting up a national potato program. The Peruvian center has outposts in Brazil, Colombia, India, Kenya, the Philippines, Tunisia, and Egypt; and it had one in Pakistan, to serve that country along with Iran and Afghanistan, until the area became too volatile for serene research and culture. CIP has been working throughout the Middle East from its Cairo headquarters, particularly in seed production; and it has a solid working relationship with Vietnam and with China, where during rice shortages people sometimes fool themselves by chopping potatoes into tiny bits the size of rice grains. (A European noticed potatoes growing in Taiwan in 1650, and it seems likely that they got there from abroad, for the Chinese then called the plant *yang shu* — "foreign yam.") Vietnam, which first learned about potatoes from nineteenth-century French missionaries, got involved in modern potato-breeding in 1973, when Le Duc Tho, Hanoi's chief representative at the Paris peace talks, took time off from his negotiations with Henry Kissinger for an instructive visit to the Laboratory of Plant Morphogenesis at Orsay University; by 1981, Vietnamese breeders were working with fifty-two CIP cultivars. By February 1984, when CIP ran a workshop there on tissue culture — growing potatoes out of test tubes — Vietnam was producing 745,000 tons on 185,250 acres, and just twelve of its native farmers had raised, in small laboratories at their homes, 3 million seedlings for other farmers to plant. CIP also collaborates with the Soviet Union, which has employed a good deal of CIP germ plasm in potato-breeding programs. Potatoes were introduced to Russia, in the seventeenth century, by Peter the Great, who imported them from Holland as a delicacy for imperial banquets. Eighteenth-century Russian peasants, however, considered them unclean and unchristian, called them "Devil's apples," and even when they had scarcely anything else to eat, burned them at the stake. Nevertheless, by the twentieth century, potatoes were so essential to all walks of Soviet life that during the siege of Leningrad several scientists, though near starvation themselves, would not dip into a sack of precious seed potatoes they were guarding but, rather, burned furniture to keep their treasure from freezing. Carlos Ochoa has made a number of business trips to the Soviet Union. When he was in Leningrad in 1982, to inspect a potato collection at the

Komarov Botanical Gardens, and to visit the Vavilov Institute, he heard that the official version of Vavilov's death was imprecise: he had died in prison, all right — not from natural causes, however, but from hunger.

The Spanish conquistadores introduced potatoes to southern Europe not long after first encountering them, in 1536, in northern Ecuador and Colombia. Francisco Pizarro appraised them as "a tasty, mealy, truffle"; his countrymen at home, aware of the fondness of swine for truffles, fed most of the potatoes they proceeded to grow to their pigs. (At the end of the eighteenth century, when the American-born natural philosopher and inventor Count Rumford [Benjamin Thompson] — who gave the world the drip percolator and the sofa bed — ran a soup kitchen for the poor in Bavaria, some of the intended recipients wouldn't go near the place no matter how hungry they were, once they heard that what they were being offered, though it was tactfully called Rumford soup, was made of barley and potatoes.) Elsewhere in Europe, potato plants were valued solely as ornamentals; when in flower, they were a much-admired exhibit in, for instance, the Vienna gardens that the French botanist Jules Charles de l'Ecluse, better known as Carolus Clusius, tended for Maximilian II. In Japan, similarly, although the Dutch had brought potatoes there in the early seventeenth century, they were considered largely decorative until Commodore Perry persuaded the emperor to sample them.

Clusius, the author of *Rariorum Plantarum Historia,* had received *his* first potatoes through a papal legate who, the Frenchman wrote, "ate these tubers, prepared like chestnuts or carrots, in order to gain strength, as he was of delicate health." Few plants can match the reputation that the potato has acquired, over the years, as both a boon and a bane. It has been hailed as cure for gout, lumbago, drunkenness, black eyes, sunburn (when rubbed on the back), rheumatism (when carried in the pocket), sore throat (when sliced and put in a stocking tied around the neck), temper tantrums, and toothache. (The trick was to put a peeled potato in a pocket on the same side of one's body as the ailing tooth; by the time the potato decomposed, the pain would be gone. What happened meanwhile to the lining of the pocket is hard to imagine.) The Irish long believed that the water in which potatoes had been boiled could heal sprains, and even broken bones. In Holland, people who bathed in that sort of broth supposedly risked getting warts; any they got, though, they could remove by rubbing them with a potato — preferably a stolen one.

Bygone European physicians, on the other hand, blamed the potato for causing rickets, scrofula, flatulence, syphilis, and indigestion. Another Irish superstition was that if a pregnant woman ate potatoes at night she was apt to bear a macrocephalic child. An oft-repeated legend of dubious veracity has it that in the early seventeenth century a French provincial parliament went as far as to decree that "in view of the fact that the potato is a pernicious substance whose use can cause leprosy, it is hereby forbidden, under pain of a fine, to cultivate it." The leprosy scare lasted well into the eighteenth century, by which time the potato's singular alleged virulence had inspired some Sicilians to become convinced that if they wanted somebody to die all they had to do was write his name on a piece of paper and pin it to a potato; he'd be gone in a month.

In the second edition of the *Via Recta ad Vitam Longam* of the English herbalist William Salmon, published in 1622, he wrote that potatoes "do wonderfully comfort, nourish, and strengthen the bodie," and he added, in an amendment to his

1620 first edition, "that it incites to Venus." He called potatoes not only Diuretick and Stomatick but also Spermatogenetick, and said, "They nourish the whole Body, restore in Consumptions, and provoke Lust." Until the end of the nineteenth century, it was a widely held concept in much of Europe that the potato was a cure for impotence and an aphrodisiac. In *The Merry Wives of Windsor,* the raunchy Falstaff intones, "Let the sky rain potatoes . . . [and] hail kissing-comfits." (Some exegetes believe that Shakespeare was thinking of the sweet potato.) In *Don Juan,* Byron called propagation "that sad result of passions and potatoes." For proof of the erotic nature of potatoes, Englishmen pointed to Irish peasants, who ate a lot of them and also produced a lot of children. Because potatoes were often associated with sex, they were also associated with sin. They were shunned by many Scotsmen, who were constantly reminded by their clergymen that potatoes were nowhere mentioned in the Bible. In the eighteenth century, when the parishioners of Chauncey Goodrich, an irreproachably God-fearing minister in Massachusetts, learned that he had grown twenty bushels of potatoes behind his manse, they all but drove him from his pulpit. A century later, another East Coast reverend who was an inveterate potato breeder was regarded more tolerantly, but largely because he was raising them for an institution of which he was chaplain — the New York State Lunatic Asylum.

The potato began to attain respectability in continental Europe toward the end of the eighteenth century, and the man chiefly responsible was a French chemist, Antoine-Augustin Parmentier. A pharmacist in the French Army during the Seven Years' War, he was captured by Frederick the Great's troops and imprisoned for three years at Hanover. He subsisted largely on, and became exceedingly grateful to, what some Germans then still considered animal food — potatoes. Back home, he became an earnest, though for quite a while unheeded, proselytizer for potatoes. In 1771, a year after a severe famine, the Academy of Besançon offered a prize for the best "study of food substances capable of reducing the calamities of famine." Parmentier forthwith produced a pro-potato *Inquiry into Nourishing Vegetables That in Times of Necessity Could Be Substituted for Ordinary Food*. A copy of it ended up in the library of Thomas Jefferson, who may have got wind of it from Benjamin Franklin, for Franklin, while American commissioner to France, was reputedly one of the guests at a dinner given by Parmentier that, from soup to liqueur, consisted exclusively of potato courses. Elegant restaurants today that don't like the vulgar look of "Potato Soup" on their menus call it "Potage Parmentier."

Parmentier's diligence was rewarded on August 23, 1785. King Louis XVI — a decade after his ill-nourished subjects had looted the bakeries of Paris in what became known as the Flour War — was celebrating his birthday. Parmentier purportedly presented him with a basket of potatoes and a bouquet of potato flowers. The king pinned a sprig to his lapel and his consort stuck one in her hair. There were two aftermaths. All the ladies of the court made such haste to emulate Marie Antoinette's example (some outdid her and had potato blossoms painted on their best china) that Paris florists were able to charge outrageous prices for potato flowers. What mattered far more to Parmentier was that Louis, at the chemist's request, let him plant some potatoes at a field called Les Sablons just outside the city. To arouse curiosity about what he was up to, Parmentier, once his crop was ready for harvest, had it patrolled during the day by soldiers. They were removed at dusk. People in the neighborhood, under the impression that whatever merited that sort of protection had to be immensely valuable, sneaked in at night and stole potatoes — just what Parmentier had hoped they'd do. Eating potatoes became routine. The king later told Parmentier that "France will thank you someday for having found bread for the poor." He wasn't thanked much in his lifetime for having conferred a new source of nourishment on his compatriots (neither, of course, were Louis or Marie Antoinette); indeed, when during the Revolution of 1789 Parmentier was mentioned as a candidate for a municipal post, he was denied the nomination after a rival declared, "He will make us eat nothing but potatoes — he who invented them." Not long afterward, however, other Frenchmen, their fears of leprosy and other afflictions long dispersed, began to call the potato, in a backhandedly complimentary way, "the only substantial blessing which the inhabitants of Europe derived from the discovery of the continent of America."

After Parmentier's death, in 1813, his countrymen showed him greater respect. One of France's gastronomic societies, the Académie Parmentier, holds an annual banquet during which his acolytes, clad in ornate regalia, deferentially toast the potato and its patron. Every year, too, potatoes used to be planted at his grave in Paris. At least two statues honoring Parmentier have been erected — one at Montdidier, his birthplace, and the other behind the city hall of the Paris suburb of Neuilly-sur-Seine. The latter effigy was destroyed during the First World War, but inside the *hôtel de ville* a mural survives showing Parmentier welcoming Louis XVI to the well-secured potato patch at Les Sablons. *Solanum tuberosum,* on its own, has figured prominently in other works of art. The Louvre harbors Jean-François Millet's 1858 painting *The Angelus,* depicting a farm couple standing in prayer above a basket of potatoes. At a park in Alingsås, Sweden (potatoes arrived in that country about 1655, but it took a royal edict in 1764 to get people actually to cultivate them), the sculptor Dieter Matzner unveiled a fiberglass potato nineteen feet long in 1969, in tribute to a local potato pioneer named Jonas Alströmer; that one lasted only two years before vandals smashed it. Claes Oldenburg was inspired in 1965 to envision a huge baked-potato sculpture, which he never got around to executing, for display at the Hotel Plaza, in Manhattan. "The baked potato," he explained, "is an object which, in its structure, resembles the kind of sculpture I like to make. It's a soft sack that registers what is done to it, where it is placed. Its form can be molded and returned to its original position. . . . Butter also changes form and returns to its original form. The addition of butter to a slit baked potato creates a very suggestive drama which is constantly being recorded in the magazines. One can go pretty far in form with just a baked potato and a pat of butter." Seventeen years after that revelation, the Guggenheim Museum did prominently exhibit — on, fittingly, its ground floor — Giuseppe Penone's 1977 work *Potatoes,* a jumbled heap of genuine, unbaked, butterless tubers, some of them sprouting, with a handful of bronze potatoes strewn among them. And then, of course, there are the four potato canvases that Vincent van Gogh painted between 1883 and 1885, when he was at Nuenen, Holland. Concerning the most famous of these, *The Potato Eaters,* van Gogh later wrote his brother, "I have tried to make it clear how those people, eating their potatoes under the lamplight, have dug the earth with those very hands they put in the dish, and so it speaks of *manual labor,* and how they have honestly earned their food." In his potato still-lifes, the artist added, "I mean to express the material in such a way that they become heavy, solid lumps, which would hurt you if they were thrown at you."

For many years — until the Nazis had it razed, in 1939, because it memorialized an Englishman — one work of art with potato connections was a red sandstone statue put up in 1853 at Offenburg, in Baden-Württemberg, of Sir Francis Drake. He was depicted holding a potato plant, and was acclaimed in an inscription on the frieze as the person who, in 1580, had brought potatoes to northern Europe. A translation of part of the eulogy goes: "The blessing of millions of men who cultivate the globe of the earth is thy most imperishable glory; the precious gift of God as the help of the poor against need prevents bitter want." Its sculptor, Andreas Friedrich, had hoped initially to sell the piece to a citizen of Strassburg, where potatoes were said to have once inadvertently been the cause of an unusual scare. When they putrefy, they emit luminosity. The story went that a pile of them was stored in the cellar of a military barracks there, and when they rotted they gave off so much light that a sentry thought the building had caught fire, and sounded an all-quarters alarm. When the Strassburgher would not meet his price, the aggrieved sculptor gave his statue to nearby Offenburg. He stipulated, however, that when it was emplaced, Drake's back would have to be turned on Strassburg.

What, if anything, Drake had to do with bringing the potato and Europe together is moot. Legend has it that he gave some potatoes to a friend in England, or Ireland, who planted them in his garden. When they matured, the recipient mistakenly had their seed balls rather than their tubers sliced and fried. They tasted terrible. The friend forthwith had his gardener dig up all the plants and burn them. Later, the gardener happened to step on a couple of tubers that had been baked in the ashes. He broke one open and tasted it; it was delicious. Thus potatoes got a reprieve, and were under way. Very much the same story has been told, and retold, with Sir Walter Raleigh the protagonist instead of Drake. One of Raleigh's ship captains came upon *something* on Roanoke Island, off the North Carolina coast, in 1586, and had it sent back to Queen Elizabeth, but it is uncertain just what that was; it may have been a walnut-size root called *Apios tuberosa*. Sir Joseph Banks, in his 1912 essay "An Attempt to Ascertain the Time When the Potatoe *(Solanum tuberosum)* Was First Introduced into the United Kingdom," gave the nod to Raleigh, and pinpointed the historic moment as July 27, 1586; but he may have been confused, because he called the plant he had in mind the openawk, which is not a potato at all but a tuber-bearing climber of the bean family. Raleigh has even been credited by others with having put a dish of cooked potatoes on Elizabeth's table. In any event, the potato was well enough known by 1597 for the barber-surgeon John Gerard, when he then published his voluminous *Herball,* to choose for his frontispiece an illustration of himself holding a spray of its blossoms.

Gerard's testimonial notwithstanding, it took a long time for potatoes to catch on solidly in England. James I is said to have served some at court in 1619, and early in the 1660–1685 reign of Charles II numerous efforts were made to persuade the common folk to plant and eat them. In 1664, the *Gardener's Calendar* of the Royal Society, which evidently judged potatoes to be a crop of last resort but better than nothing, enjoined its readers to "plant potatoes in February in your worst ground." That same year, the Englishman John Forster published a book with the title *England's Happiness Increased* and with, as was the literary custom of the day, a much longer subtitle: *Or a Sure and Easie Remedy against all succeeding Dear Years; by a plantation of the roots called* POTATOES *whereof (with the addition of wheat flour) excellent, good and wholesome bread may be made every Year, Eight or Nine Months together, for half the Charge as formerly . . . Invented and Published for the Good of the Poorer Sort.* At one point, King Charles was urged by his counselors to grant potato-growing licenses to ten thousand of his subjects. It was estimated that each of them would net thirty pounds a year for his pains, out of which Charles, for his magnanimity, was to receive five. Not much happened, although some people did turn to potato starch as a hair powder in lieu of wheat flour, the use of which for that purpose Parliament, concerned about shortages of bread, had proscribed. During another stressful period when wheat was scarce, in 1795 and 1796, King George III announced that the royal bread — and that of his servants, too — would be made with rye and potatoes. He asked his subjects to follow suit. The clergy fell in line and, though in a few cases doubtless with lingering misgivings, preached compliance; and William Pitt wrote to the *Times* in praise of a corn-and-potato bread he had sampled; nonetheless, the English, by and large, shied away from potatoes. As late as 1829 — shortly before the feisty William Cobbett, who despised potatoes, had begun inveighing against them as suitable sustenance for the poor or anyone else ("Faith!" he sputtered in 1830. "Those old papas of ours [he meant fathers, not potatoes] would have burnt up not only the stacks, but the ground itself, rather than have lived upon miserable roots.") — the *Times* editorially pronounced potatoes acceptable for the well-to-do, but said that if the working classes ate too many of them Great Britain would become "a nation of miserable, turbulent drunkards."

As far back as 1776, in *The Wealth of Nations,* Adam Smith had said that "the very general use which is made of Potatoes in these kingdoms as food for man, is a convincing proof that the prejudices of a nation, with regard to diet, however deeply rooted [he may have been unaware of his play on words], are by no means unconquerable." It was not until the Victorian era, though, that the upper-class English, at least, truly began to take the potato to their hearts, and increasingly to their stomachs. A popular nineteenth-century variety was the Prince Albert. (There was also a British Queen, an Irish Queen, a Prince of Wales, and, later, a King Edward VII, a Red King

Edward, and a Purple-Eyed King Edward.) In 1863, a wealthy Irishman from Dundee named William Paterson brought forth the Victoria. He had got into serious potato culture in 1854, when he imported varieties, for his breeding stock, from Australia, India, South Africa, and the United States. In nine dedicated years, he spent seven thousand pounds on his quest for a first-rate new variety, and his perseverance made him the butt of many a joke. After his Victorias came along and proved popular, the queen ordered some for her own larder. People quickly stopped laughing at Paterson — "I would not give a farthing for any potato," a rival breeder declared toward the end of the century, "if I could not trace its descent from the Victoria" — and began calling him the savior of the British potato. (Her Majesty also had a wheat and an oat named after her. The Victoria oat, which was resistant to crown rust, was an ancestor of most of the oats that were raised in the United States until the middle of the twentieth century. But the Victoria's gene that defied that rust was nearly identical to a gene that was helpless against Victoria blight disease; and when that assailant sprang to the attack all the offspring of the Victoria oat were wiped out.) By 1898, the once derided potato was being characterized in the *Journal of the Royal Agricultural Society* as "the noble tuber." Five years after that, when there was a scarcity of potatoes, the demand for them reached such manic heights that single tubers of new or allegedly new varieties sold for hundreds of pounds apiece, the going price for shoots from prized specimens went as high as four pounds, and one entrepreneur purportedly sliced and sold a thousand cuttings from a single plant. Until the speculative bubble burst, potatoes were reputed to be worth more than their weight in gold.

However the potato (often called, of course, the Irish potato) got to Ireland — via Raleigh, via Drake, or, as has also been put forth, from plundered ships of the scattered Spanish Armada — it was unarguably there in 1663, when the Royal Society advocated its being planted as, ironically, a hedge against famine. For the following two hundred years the tuber was indispensable. Ludwig Feuerbach once said disparagingly of the Irish and their potatoes, vis-à-vis the English and their roast beef, "You cannot conquer, for your sustenance can only arouse a paralysing despair not a fiery enthusiasm. And only enthusiasm will be able to fight off the giant in whose veins flows the rich, powerful, deed-producing blood." But when Oliver Cromwell invaded Ireland in 1649, and in the fashion of so many other warriors had destroyed all the visible food that his soldiers could get their hands on, it had been potatoes that had succored the indigenes. "In the potato," Redcliffe Salaman once wrote, "people discovered a new weapon with which to withstand the oppression of their conquerors. In the great struggle which followed, it was, I believe, the potato which saved them from extermination and gave them the opportunity to effect a temporary recovery. From now on, it was to prove itself a shelter to the people against the economic weapons of their enemies." By 1780, the Irish were eating an average of eight pounds of potatoes apiece daily — a statistic that, since it included the children of all ages, meant that some adults were accounting for a dozen or more. (It was often considered good manners, before biting into any potato — which Oliver Goldsmith in his time would call "Thou source of all my bliss and all my woe, that found'st me poor at first, and keepst me so" — to point it toward a salt herring or bit of bacon hanging in front of a chimney.) There was an old saying that went, "While you're eating your first potato, peel the second, don't put down the third, and keep your eye on the fourth." An Englishman of that era was moved to exclaim, "What hope is there for a nation that lives on potatoes!" The Reverend Patrick Brontë, paterfamilias of the literary brood, demurred: he raised his daughters chiefly on potatoes because he was proud of his muscular physique and attributed it to the fact that he had eaten little else in his own childhood. Another old saying had it that in Ireland there were only two things too serious to jest about: marriage and potatoes. Some people jested anyway — one, for instance, defined an Irish "sauce" as a little potato to go along with a big one.

"If one may attempt to sum up in a sentence the influence of the potato on Irish history," Salaman wrote, "I would say that it played the part of the least common denominator in Irish economic life for close on three hundred years, with an efficiency as great as it was disastrous." It was the view of Robert McKay — an agricultural scientist specializing in potato diseases, who in 1961, on behalf of the Irish Potato Marketing Company, in Dublin, edited *An Anthology of the Potato* — that "the potato and the Irishman are often considered as somewhat synonymous." McKay put a good deal of verse into his book. One stanza, authorship undisclosed, went:

> *We praise all the flowers that we fancy,*
> *Sip the nectar of fruit ere they're peeled,*
> *Ignoring the common old tater*
> *When, in fact, he's King of the Field.*
> *Let us show the old boy we esteem him,*
> *Sort of dig him up out of the mud;*
> *Let us show him he shares our affections*
> *And crown him with glory — King Spud.*

Famines punctuated Irish history with doleful regularity. Between 1728 and 1845 there were twenty-four instances of crop failures, mainly attributable to unusually cold springs or wet summers. The loss of most of the expected 1739 potato harvest precipitated three hundred thousand deaths — one-fifth of the population. (An earlier famine, after the 1727 oat crop was decimated, had provoked Jonathan Swift into writing *A Modest Proposal for preventing the Children of Poor People from being a Burden to their Parents or the Country* — by feeding them to the rich.) But the Irish stuck with their potatoes. For one thing, many of them didn't know how to plant and nurture grains. They were root farmers, dependent on nature to do their work for them. And nature did it agreeably well: on a 1½-acre plot, enough potatoes could be grown to sustain a family of five or six for a year. By the 1840s, the population of Ireland had risen, periodic crop failures notwithstanding, to nine million; half that number rarely ate anything except potatoes. Cecil Woodham-Smith said in her book *The Great Hunger* that "the existence of the Irish people depended on the potato entirely and exclusively." It was not that other crops were unfamiliar to them. Thousands of Irish acres were planted to wheat, and to oats, and to barley. But these nourishing cereals were earmarked by their absentee proprietors for export to England or for feeding animals whose meat would also end up across the Irish Sea.

The outlook for the 1845 Irish potato crop was bright. There had been a warm enough spring, an only moderately rainy early summer. True, Sir Robert Peel, Queen Victoria's prime minister, had had a letter from the Isle of Wight disclosing inexplicable trouble there, but perhaps that was an isolated case. And, indeed, a part of the 1845 Irish crop survived. But 1846 was something else again. On July 27, a man traveling overland from Cork to Dublin was impressed by the fine look of the potato plants in the fields he passed. When he retraced his steps just one week later, the plants were drooping, and there was a foul stench in the air. At digging time, in October, most of the tubers were found to have rotted. Those that appeared to be healthy decomposed — like cassava — soon after they were unearthed. In London, a Committee on the Potato Disease was hastily formed. On October 31, it reported to Lord Heytesbury, the lord lieutenant of Ireland, on "the awful state the kingdom was likely to become reduced to, if the Government did not at once step in to prevent as far as possible, by all human means, the dreadful scourge of anticipated famine and pestilence." Upon receiving what they judged to be an unsatisfactory response from Heytesbury, the members of the committee resolved to meet daily, starting November 5. On November 7, their chairman, the Right the Honourable Lord Clonclurry, wrote to the prime minister, "We do wish to impress upon your mind the awful responsibility which, as Her Majesty's principal adviser, you incur, if our government hesitates to adopt the most speedy and extensive possible modes of alleviating the impending calamity. Whilst you hesitate, if hesitate you shall, the people of Ireland are about to perish in countless numbers." The committee recommended, inter alia, that Irish ports be opened up for duty-free food imports, that distilling be halted, that food-for-work programs be initiated in Ireland, and that English cavalry regiments cut down on their horses' consumption of oats. Peel replied that he would take the matter up with his colleagues in the cabinet. When he did, he suggested to them that they seek to repeal the Corn Laws, which imposed stiff tariffs on imports from abroad. The cabinet wouldn't go along with him. Repeal the Corn Laws? Let in alien grains? Wheat? Rice? The maize that those Americans perversely insisted on referring to as "corn"? Peel resigned. Victoria, even though she had yet to have her potato named after her, took his side, and reappointed him. He got the Corn Laws repealed in 1846. It was the end of protectionism, and also the end of Peel. London would soon be sending a half-million dollars' worth of American corn to Ireland, but there were not enough mills there to grind it (some hungry Irish ate it raw, and suffered indigestion), and many Irish were suspicious of the unfamiliar cereal. They called it Peel's brimstone. Irish peasant women had no idea how to cook it anyway. They didn't really know how to cook anything except potatoes, and knew very little about preparing *them* except by boiling. All the while, the traffic from Ireland to England of export commodities — wheat and barley, oats and oatmeal, cattle, pigs, eggs, butter — went routinely on. The farmers who handled those commodities felt they had no choice about that; they had to give them to their landlords as rent. And the landlords stolidly shipped them across to England, though now as they loaded their ships they had to have armed soldiers standing by to disperse hungry mobs. (There were plenty of fish offshore, but most of the commercial fishermen had long since pawned their gear to buy whatever food was obtainable.) England, all in all, did too little too late. When, for instance, it passed the Poor Relief (Ireland) Act, in 1847, the statute stipulated that anyone who owned more than a quarter of a British acre of land — the Irish dimensions were slightly different — would not be eligible for food relief unless he gave up his land.

The Irish famine was the worst European disaster since the Black Death of 1348–50. Before it ran its course, something like a million and a half Irish were dead, many of them from typhus or relapsing fever — after they'd been evicted, for nonpayment of rent, from their squalid homes into ditches or streets or open fields. A million and a quarter more had emigrated — most to the United States and Great Britain, and a few to Australia, where they had the distinction of being the first immigrants to that distant colony who had not come there from jail. The *Illustrated London News* saw fit to run a poem entitled "The Potato Crop, 1846":

> *Alas! The foul and fatal blight*
> *Infecting Raleigh's grateful root,*
> *Blasting the fields of verdure bright,*
> *That waves o'er Erin's favorite fruit.*
> *The peasant's cherished hope is gone,*
> *His little garden pride is o'er,*
> *Famine and plague now scowl upon*
> *Hibernia's fair and fertile shore.*

Redcliffe Salaman later wrote, much more soberly, "After proving itself the most perfect instrument for the maintenance of poverty and degradation amongst the native masses, the potato ended up wrecking both exploited and exploiter."

Ireland never quite forgave England for its comparative callousness during the terrible time. Religious differences were, of course, a factor in the two areas' bitter estrangement; but the Irish refusal to fight in the Second World War and the rise of the Irish Republican Army stemmed in no small measure from smoldering resentment over the famine. When Victoria and Albert paid a sympathy call in 1849, they were, to be sure, politely enough received (the 1847 potato crop had been satisfactory, though 1848 was another ghastly season), but the British were held blameworthy on a number of counts; for one, they never made any serious effort to teach the bulk of the Irish how to grow anything other than potatoes.

It is now known beyond any reasonable doubt what caused the horror of 1845. The villain was *Phytophthora infestans,* a rapacious fungus that causes late blight. It begins its deadly work on the leaves of the plant, and works its way down to the roots.

(Only a few days after the bad news first came out of Ireland, a Belgian botanist rightly analyzed the situation and suggested that if each stricken potato plant had its stalk amputated just above ground level, the tubers nesting underneath might survive; that might inhibit their growth, but runty potatoes would be better than none. There is no evidence that anybody paid him any heed.) Late blight was, and still is, a universal scourge. It was responsible for a potato-crop loss in Chile, in the 1950s, almost as devastating as that in Ireland a century earlier. It has ruined crops in Kenya, in India, in Sikkim; wherever the potato has gone, late blight has followed, an unflagging pathogenic nemesis. CIP devoted an entire scientific conference to *Phytophthora infestans* in 1973. In 1981, the Peruvian center screened seventy thousand potato seedlings, hoping to find one with the capacity for withstanding it. In 1983, a CIP researcher engaged in the never-say-die struggle to breed resistance to late blight said of it, with grudging respect, "It's one of the most versatile enemies we have got." But to the Irish peasants of the 1840s it was unknown by any name. What it did they attributed variously to the steam released by locomotives, to the use of guano for manure, to insects, to drought, to dampness, to frost, to electricity, to unidentified fungi, and, inevitably, to God. One Englishman, Alfred Smee, who deemed the potato "a plant of indolence," in 1846 delivered himself of a 174-page book entitled *The Potatoe Plant, Its Uses and Properties: Together with the Cause of the Present Malady.* Smee, who was surgeon to the Bank of England, to the Central London Ophthalmic Institution, and to the Royal General Dispensary (he dedicated the volume to Prince Albert), confidently laid the onus on *Aphis vastator,* an insect with which he claimed close acquaintance. He had tried to kill just one he spotted on a potato at Finsbury Circus, but "these little rascals crawl into chinks and crannies, from which they come forth at their convenience, and rapidly multiply," he wrote. Smee thought that for those Irish who were still alive the future might be more promising. "Let the husbandman be of good cheer," he wrote, "and remember, that if nature deviates for a time from its wonted relations, it always returns to its normal condition, and ultimately maintains the proper balance of animated beings. Let all people remember the promise in Malachi, 'that God will rebuke the devourer for your sakes, and he shall not destroy the fruits of your ground.'" Smee had delved into earlier famines. He reported that Rome had had one in 1708 B.C. that lasted seven years; that during an English one in 440 B.C. people ate tree bark, and during an Italian one in A.D. 446 parents ate their children; that in another English one, in A.D. 1251, people ate horses, dogs, cats, and vermin; and in yet two more British famines, those of 1389 and 1438, bread was made of fern roots. The Irish, he suggested, should similarly get by with makeshifts: "It is absurd to suppose that it is the duty of Government to supply food, except under extraordinary circumstances." In any event, "a nation of potatoe-eaters does not feel those relations and dependencies which bind other societies together.... This effect of depending too exclusively on the culture of the potatoe is fearfully exhibited in the Irish people, where the potatoe has begotten millions of paupers, who live, but who are not clothed; who marry but do not work, caring for nothing but their dish of potatoes." Left on their own, he concluded, the Irish would be helpless. "Fortunately for the Irish people," he added, slightly changing his tack, or perhaps judging that the circumstances were after all extraordinary, "they have a rich and powerful country to sympathize with and relieve them in their distress, and also desirous of alleviating their suffering." There is no reason to believe that if Smee had been more knowledgeable in his diagnosis of the plague he'd have come up with any less severe a remedy than what, in effect, he prescribed: tree bark.

By 1856, Elizabeth Barrett Browning, in *Aurora Leigh,* was wondering whether the potato would become extinct like the moly. (The moly was the plant Hermes gave to Odysseus to prevent Circe from turning him into a pig.) Three years later, however, Ireland had nearly the same acreage planted to potatoes as it had had in 1846, with only three-quarters as many people to sustain on the produce. At present, the 3.5 million inhabitants of Ireland still consume substantial quantities of potatoes; of their recommended per-capita daily intake of about 2,500 calories, potatoes provide 240, as opposed to a mere 21 from alcohol.

The great hunger brought a million Irish to the United States, among them Patrick Kennedy, the thirty-fifth president's great-grandfather. The immigrants were so closely identified with the plant that had upheld them and then undone them that for a while Boston policemen were called Boston Potatoes. All those who came were glad to learn that their new homeland had plenty of potatoes. To some of them, any other kind of food required getting used to. (It may be illustrative of the degree of assimilation of the Irish into the American mainstream that the per-capita consumption of potatoes in the United States in 1982 was only two-fifths of what it had been in 1912.) The potato, of course, had arrived on the Atlantic coast of North America long before the Irish. Englishmen introduced it to the Bermuda Islands in 1613. Eight years after that, the governor of the Bermudas fraternally sent the governor of Virginia two cedar chests filled with fruits and vegetables; there were some cassava and potatoes in the lot. (Thomas Jefferson, who is believed to be the first president of the United States to have served french fries in the White House, thought that the British had found potatoes growing in Virginia when they first set foot there; he had been misinformed by John Gerard's not entirely accurate *Herball* of 1597.) The cassava never caught on; the potatoes were so warmly received that the following year the Virginia colonists sent a bark to the Bermudas to bring back a shipload of them.

Potatoes were still largely unknown in the more northerly American colonies for nearly another century, however. Then, in 1719, some new settlers, Ulstermen from Londonderry, came to New Hampshire, established a town they named after their point of departure — it is now called plain Derry — and began to cultivate the crop they knew best. Potatoes got to Cambridge, Massachusetts, even before that, but how is something of a mystery. All that is known is that an eight-penny batch of them was purchased by Harvard College in January 1708 for a banquet celebrating the inaugural of President John Leverett. (The cost of the entire meal, for several dozen dignitaries, came to just over ten pounds, more than one-third of which was expended for beer, Madeira, port, and "green wine.") However much the fellows and overseers of Harvard and their guests may have relished the novel fare, potatoes were not appreciated on all levels of early-eighteenth-century society. It was the custom in New England then for apprentices to sign contracts specifying the housing and food their masters were to furnish them. Some young men would not commit themselves unless it was agreed in writing that they were not to be fed potatoes.

In due course, potatoes made their way westward. They reached Mantua, Ohio, which had a loamy soil admirably suited to them, in 1850, and they became pivotal to that community's economy. Not long afterward, a storage depot with a capacity of fifty thousand bushels loomed over the Mantua railroad station. An annual Mantua Potato Festival, where a potato queen was solemnly crowned, featured a fifteen-kilometer footrace called a Potato Stomp, and, among other competitions, a baked-potato-cooking contest, a potato-chip-eating contest (potato-peeling-speed races seem to have been exclusive to Australia), and wrestling bouts held on a mat of potatoes that had been mashed in a cement mixer. Mantua was generally conceded to have devised the world's best-known mess of mashed potatoes until Steven Spielberg had a plate-sized scale-model mountain built of them for his *Close Encounters*. (Earlier moviemakers had sometimes used dehydrated potato flakes to simulate snow in wintry scenes.) At the beginning of the twentieth century, just as in other sections of the country special trains lumbered across the Midwest to urge farmers to grow more and better corn, so in potato-growing regions were there exhortatory potato trains. The Denver & Rio Grande Railroad sent one around Colorado; the Oregon Short Line covered the Northwest out of Salt Lake City. As there were Corn Clubs for teenage farmers in the Corn Belt, so were there Potato Clubs elsewhere. A 1913 bulletin published by the Department of Agriculture, *Potato Growing as Club Work in the North and West,* offered guidelines for judging potato contests at state and county fairs: out of a possible 100 points, 40 were to be awarded for the greatest yield, 30 for the largest profit; 15 for the handsomest exhibit (one peck of seed potatoes), and 15 for the best essay on "How I Made My Crop of Potatoes."

Another Midwestern city on which potatoes had a resounding impact was Battle Creek, Michigan, where starting in 1876 John Harvey Kellogg, a Seventh-Day Adventist vegetarian physician and the older brother of the breakfast-food man, managed a sanitarium, which was at first called the Western Health Reform Institute. Dr. Kellogg frowned on a number of consumables without which many an American would hardly find life worth living — among them, caffeine, meat, and alcohol. He had been a health-food addict from way back; at medical school, his regular breakfast was graham crackers and apples. He believed that "man was intended to eat the plants and fruits and not the animals," and he sometimes proudly described himself as "a grass-eater." At Battle Creek, he served his patients meat and butter substitutes made from nuts and grains. In 1894, he and his brother Will Keith accidentally discovered how to flake wheat and other cereals. Ten years later, Battle Creek, though its turn-of-the-century population was under thirty thousand, harbored thirty wheat-flake companies. Most of them foundered, but meanwhile Will Kellogg was starting to make a fortune from cornflakes. Dr. Kellogg's Battle Creek Sanitarium could accommodate, when it was in full swing, fifteen hundred patients; one of them was Charles W. Post, who arrived in a wheelchair in 1891 and soon walked out, feeling much better, to launch Postum ("Makes red blood") and Grape-Nuts. Dr. Kellogg was pleased to be able to disclose that his patients consumed an average of seven bushels of potatoes apiece a year, despite his resigned awareness that, as he put it, "various malicious libels against the good name of this most innocent and wholesome of foodstuffs [its alleged affinity, for instance, with leprosy and lust] are still afloat."

Eventually, potatoes were grown, with few reservations, in every state of the Union, including even Alaska, where the natives of the southeastern portion of the territory were taught by white men how to distill a potato drink beguilingly called hoochinoo. Russian fur traders had brought potatoes from Siberia to Kodiak Island in 1783. For a while, the Aleuts there, like so many other people in other areas, were wary of the strange new tuber. But in time potatoes became the most important agricultural product of that frigid realm; they could be grown within seventy miles of the Arctic Circle. During the Alaskan gold rush, some of the more popular regional varieties were Gold Coin, Extra Early Pioneer, Extra Early Triumph, and Extra Early Eureka. Another northerly region where potatoes flourished was Aroostook County, in Maine. It had the kind of climate potatoes thrive in — short, cool summers and plenty of rain. Its dark brown, loose, and silty soil, sometimes called caribou loam, was ideal for potatoes. In 1923, for example, when the average United States yield for potatoes was 108 bushels an acre, Aroostook averaged 266. (That splendid seedbed is not quite what it used to be: a third of an inch of its topsoil vanishes every year because of erosion.) The Maine potato industry got under way in 1890 when the Bangor & Aroostook Railroad, constructed to expedite the transport of timber, was completed. It was to feed the laborers in lumber camps that potatoes first were planted there. Eventually, they took over a strip of Maine 110 miles long and from 20 to 40 miles wide. Some individual potato farmers had storage barns that would hold twelve thousand bushels. Between October and May, a railroad car crammed with potatoes would pull out of the county every ten minutes around the clock. At the peak of the fall harvest season, schools would shut down so the students could pick potatoes. Around Presque Isle, the hub of the potato traffic, it was not uncommon for a man with a hearty appetite to eat seven large potatoes as part of his Sunday dinner. There was an annual Potato Blossom Festival, a high point of which was the enthronement of a young woman who for twelve proud months could call herself the Maine Potato Blossom Queen.

Of all the states, Maine — though now eclipsed in production by both Idaho and Washington — ranks second in potato acreage only to Idaho, which leads in all statistics, and where the potato has been emblazoned on license plates and the covers of high-school yearbooks. In Idaho, to nobody's surprise, a founder of the Denver-based Potato Board — which annually confers on one potato-booster or another a Spuddy Award — was himself honored by the governor in 1972 with one of the state's most coveted awards: a Certificate of Highest Merit for distinguished service to the potato industry. (Idaho also raises rainbow trout — enough of them so that, it was revealed not long ago by the Agricultural Research Service of the Department of Agriculture, if the seven million pounds of feces they excrete every year could be collected for manure, the stuff would nicely fertilize a thousand acres of cropland.) In 1976, when Cecil D. Andrus, later Jimmy Carter's secretary of the interior, was the governor of Idaho — he considered it a routine part of that job to appear in television commercials touting Idaho potatoes — he told *The New Yorker,* off camera:

What makes Idaho potatoes unique is our elevation, along with our volcanic soil, our warm days and cold nights, and the purity of our water, which we use for irrigation in almost metered quantities. The result of all this is a fluffy, mealy-quality potato, instead of the soggy, watery kind you might get from other, nameless places, and in a premium fresh-baked potato this difference is crucial. . . . I know what you're going to ask: Aren't potatoes fattening? Well, I'm long and lean, so perhaps I'm not exactly your average person, but I do know that the average Idaho baker is an eight-to-ten-ounce, one-hundred-and-twenty-calorie, practically-full-meal-in-itself item, and not fattening at all. The problem arises from slopping on butter and sour cream. The medical society is somewhat at fault for creating the wrong image of potatoes. Instead of maligning them by saying "Stay away from them," it should be saying, "Stay away from all that stuff you pile on them." If you're on a diet, potatoes can actually be helpful. They're filling, and they're a source of protein. Why, some of the dehydrated potatoes that have been shipped to underdeveloped countries have sustained life for months when people have been able to get very little else. Spuds are amazing. We like to call potatoes "spuds" in Idaho. We even have an Idaho Spud candy bar, which has nothing to do with potatoes beyond its name and its shape. . . . The key to baked potatoes, as I wish more restaurants would realize, is to serve them immediately after they're cooked. No self-respecting restaurant would serve a steak that's an hour and a half old, but nobody has the proper respect for potatoes. There's absolutely no reason not to treat them as decently as you treat your meat.

Missionaries have often been responsible for the introduction of food plants to places where they were previously unfamiliar — they brought wheat in 1769 to what is now California, and potatoes in 1833 to what is now Lesotho — and it was a Presbyterian, the Reverend Henry H. Spalding, who is credited with having brought the potato, in 1836, to what is now the state of Idaho. Today, nearly 20 percent of all Idahoans are involved in one way or another with the potato business — a one- to two-billion-dollar one. Idaho is the home base of the J. R. Simplot Company, the biggest private potato enterprise on earth. Just one of its potato-processing plants can mangle a hundred thousand pounds of spuds an hour. One of the automobiles registered in Idaho to John R. Simplot, whose wealth from potatoes has put him, according to *Forbes,* in the $500-million category, bears the vanity plate "MR SPUD." The variety principally grown by Simplot is the Russet Burbank, a descendant of a potato developed in Massachusetts in 1873 by Luther Burbank from a seedball he found, as a young man, in his mother's garden. The Russet Burbank lends itself admirably to french fries, and Simplot is the major domestic supplier to the McDonald's chain, which, although it does not go in much for fancy language, has called french fries "the *pièce de résistance* of our menu." At least one sociologist has speculated, perhaps partly in jest, that were it not for these particular *pommes de terre* the hamburger might long since have become extinct. Russet Burbanks do not thrive especially well in Europe. To accommodate its outlets there, McDonald's has tried to send harvested ones across from America, but the European Economic Community, to protect its own potato farmers, hasn't let them in. McDonald's has had easier going in Asia. Its self-promotional arches are a familiar sight in Hong Kong. In Singapore, the younger set has considered it socially uplifting to be seen sauntering along Orchard Road conspicuously consuming a pack of McDonald's french fries. Potato people are sensitive. They often wish it could have been some other edible out of which John Dillinger carved a fake pistol that, after he'd coated it with iodine, facilitated his escape from a prison. Potato people speak ruefully of "a cereal mentality" — a tendency to regard roots and tubers as inherently inferior to grains — and it heartens them to hear that in some parts of the world, at least, it is a status symbol to be a potato eater. In parts of Indonesia, for instance, potatoes are reserved for such special occasions as weddings and birthdays. In the Philippines — where Simplot used to have an experimental potato-growing agreement with the government — when women go to market they sometimes buy potatoes last and spread them across the top of their shopping baskets, to demonstrate how high-class they are. At some Filipino markets, potatoes are handled like luxury items — they are individually wrapped in plastic. (A Ketchum, Idaho, mail-order entrepreneur once went even further. He peddled gift-wrapped "Awesome Potatoes" — four of them, in an imitation-mahogany box, for $12.95.) Even so, potatoes have not yet entirely shed the lingering suspicions that have plagued them throughout history. On the island of Luzon, there is a widespread belief that it is dangerous to eat them at more than three meals in a row.

In the United States today, more than half of all potatoes that are consumed each year have been processed (five billion pounds of them in the form of french fries) — a state of affairs that has prompted the nutrition polemicist Susan George, the author of *Feeding the Few: Corporate Control of Food* and *How the Other Half Dies: The Real Reasons for World Hunger*, to write, "Americans are perhaps the only people on earth privileged to buy unbreakable, perfectly calibrated, dehydrated, rehydrated, parabolic potato chips packed in vacuum-sealed tennis ball cans — at dozens of times the cost of the original, long-forgotten potato." Frito-Lay, the snack-food division of PepsiCo, Incorporated, earned its parent company over $300 million in 1982, which was more than Pepsi-Cola did. Potato chips, sales of which in the United States alone totaled nearly $3 billion in 1983, are popularly believed to have originated out of spleen, in the 1850s, at Moon's Lake House, a restaurant near Saratoga Springs, New York. Apparently a diner there complained that the fried potatoes he ordered were too thick. The chef, a temperamental fellow named George Crum, was miffed; he thereupon sliced a fresh batch of potatoes as thinly as he could, dumped them in hot oil, and slammed the end result down on the patron's table. It is thought by some potato historians that the finicky diner was none other than Cornelius Vanderbilt, alias the Commodore. Saratoga historians have disputed that; but Marylou Whitney, the fourth wife of the Commodore's great-great-grandson, Cornelius Vanderbilt Whitney, gave it such credence that she once assembled a *Potato Chip Cookbook* — she didn't need the proceeds to live on and assigned them to the Saratoga Performing Arts Center — and got practically the whole county government of Saratoga embroiled one sweltering August in a much-publicized controversy as to whether or not her great-great-grandfather-in-law, who was unarguably associated with the spread of the New York Central Railroad, played a similar role with respect to potato chips.

Saratoga Springs already has a horse-racing museum. Otherwise, it might have proved an admirable location for one of the world's most esoteric institutions — a Potato Museum that has been in existence, though for a good part of the time in cartons and crates, since 1975. That year, E. Thomas Hughes II, a monomaniacal young Philadelphian who was teaching fifth grade at the International School of Brussels, in Belgium, assigned his class, which was made up mainly of children of foreign businessmen, to bring in something interesting about potatoes, to which he had never previously given much sustained thought. What the students came up with — mostly, at first, recipes from their native lands — so fascinated him that he began to collect everything he could lay his hands on that pertained, however remotely, to the potato. He had soon accumulated enough objects to open a museum in the home he shared with his wife Meredith, a European representative of Wrangler bluejeans, at Maransart, fifteen miles outside Brussels. Hughes became incurably addicted to potatoes. "Others may find the potato inelegant — why, when Norwegians dislike their political leaders, they call them 'potatoheads,' " he says. "But to me potatoes are elegant." Every month, he gets out a little publication called *Peelings,* which contains such potato esoterica as "in Lithuania it was the custom for people dining together to pull each other's hair before digging into a dish of new potatoes." The paper at last count had only eighty subscribers, but Hughes is confident it could attain a much wider readership if he ever launched a concerted circulation drive. By 1982, his hoard consisted of more than two thousand items — specimens of potatoes of all sizes, shapes, and colors; jars full of Colorado beetles; jewelry and toys made out of or resembling potatoes; planting and cultivating tools and kitchen implements; van Gogh reproductions; postcards, sometimes humorous, showing soldiers on kitchen-police duty; an 1828 New Hampshire "Wanted" poster describing a scoundrel who had swiped a potato still — but since his return to the United States he had never found a suitable home for it until, in mid-1983, he moved to Washington, D.C., and into a commodious old house situated not far from another incomparable respository of rare memorabilia, the Library of Congress. When Hughes was offered a teaching job at the Potomac School, in McLean, Virginia, his joy was boundless. "It sounds almost like the 'Potato School,' " he wrote a friend. In 1976, an organization in London called the Potato Marketing Board, which wanted to encourage farmers to send only their best potatoes to market and to make sure they were properly dressed, distributed a poster showing a sexy young woman clad solely in a potato sack, with the name of the variety Désirée imprinted on it. For nearly a decade now, Hughes has been searching for an invaluable trophy he would love to add to his trove — the actual potato sack in which Marilyn Monroe, before she was in a position to shrug at such frivolities, herself posed near-naked for a publicity photograph. (Someone had apparently remarked that she was so attractive she'd look good even in a potato sack, and a hovering press agent had been inspired to act.) If Hughes never gets the sack of his desire, there is always the possibility that some patron of his museum will confer on him the original manuscript of Booker T. Washington's *Up from Slavery,* which contains a line that other potato buffs, when they are feeling put-upon, cite to comfort one another: "There is as much dignity in tilling a field as in writing a poem."

III

WHEAT
Fiat Panis

Let husky wheat the haughs adorn,
An' aits set up their awnie horn,
An' pease an' beans at een or morn,
Perfume the plain.
Leeze me on thee, John Barleycorn,
Thou king o' grain!

On thee aft Scotland chows her cood,
In souple scones, the wale o' food,
Or tumblin' in the boilin' flood
Wi' kail an' beef.
But when thou pours thy strong heart's blood,
There thou shines chief.

— ROBERT BURNS

I T is a sobering fact of life — or, perhaps, of minimal existence — that although hundreds of millions of inhabitants of the earth have far too little to eat, billions of
bushels of the staple plant foods on which mankind has always
been dependent are used annually for the concoction of alcoholic beverages. All over the world, throughout history, people
have gone hungry because they allocated too much of their
just-ripened crops to the brewing of potions with which to cel-
ebrate those very harvests. The authors of *Wheat in Human
Nutrition,* a publication put out by the FAO, said, "We can as-
sign to wheat the credit, or discredit, of having contributed to
the evolution of the intoxicating alcoholic drinks which en-
liven human existence." It was at least implicit in that statement that at harvesttime or any other time the great grain
drinks can make life a little more bearable for the otherwise
disadvantaged. Indeed, it has been argued that Bantu beer,
more than 100 million gallons of which are imbibed by South
African blacks every year, is highly nutritious. Bantu beer,

which, in keeping with the incongruities so characteristic of South Africa, is made from a kind of sorghum called "white Kafircorn," was given its due in a 1937 book published at Cape Town: "In times of plenty it is not only freely consumed, but often is the principal or sole food of many men for days on end. But it also plays a very important part in their social life. The whole social system of the people is inextricably linked with this popular beverage, which is the first essential in all festivities, the one incentive to labour, the first thought in dispensing hospitality. . . ."

Robert Burns, being Scottish, naturally had a fond spot for barley, which has been a base of beer and malt whiskey (malt is sprouted barley) since the start of recorded history. The Egyptians have a barley beer they called "*booza*"; gypsies carried that word as far north as England, where it evolved, the nature of its original ingredients having been forgotten along the way, into "booze." Burns would probably not have been surprised by some twentieth-century American statistics. In 1918, the United States produced 225,067,000 bushels of barley on 9,198,000 acres of land. That crop clearly did not all go into barley soup, for when Prohibition came along the following year barley acreage plummeted to 2,619,000 and production to 93,981,000 bushels. Of the half a billion bushels of barley that are annually grown in the United States nowadays, a good deal is used for livestock feed — and some, on the eve of Jewish holidays, to fatten carp — but a quarter is earmarked for malting and brewing. By 1935, the first year American farmers had a chance fully to react to Repeal, both barley totals were back to and well above their 1918 levels — 12,436,000 acres and 288,667,000 bushels. Such robust figures would surely have heartened an anonymous contributor to the *Memoirs of the New York State Board of Agriculture* in 1821, who wrote of barley:

This grain, at present, is only cultivated in the vicinity of breweries, which being unfortunately few in number, the market is circumscribed, and the price of consequence altogether at the mercy of a few consumers. Nothing is more to be desired than that barley should be extensively grown; for next to wheat and corn, it is the most valuable of grains. A more general cultivation of barley, would be proof of the increase of breweries, and of the substitution of malt liquor for ardent spirits. These from their cheapness, are the bane of our labouring population, and furnish a delusive poison to our harvest fields, in the place of a refreshing beverage. Children, as soon as they are able to lift a rake, are accustomed to coarse rum and whiskey, and the habit growing up with them to manhood, too often destroys their usefulness and happiness. I know of nothing which promises so efficaciously to root out this pernicious habit, as the multiplication of breweries: the establishment of every new brewery, it is to be considered as an additional safeguard to the morals and welfare of the most numerous part of the community.

Burns's Scotland was not only a barley worshiper's mecca, but, with its damp, cool climate, was singularly hospitable to oats, or, as the poet put it, aits. In the eighteenth century, the standard ration there for unmarried plowmen consisted almost entirely of seventeen and a half pounds of oatmeal apiece a week, with enough milk to moisten it. "The beggars of London, and within ten miles of it," Daniel Defoe wrote in *The Complete English Tradesman,* "eat more white bread than the whole kingdom of Scotland." The man generally credited with being the first serious breeder to try to improve oats was a Scotsman, Patrick Shirreff, of Haddingtonshire, who in the 1860s released three varieties called, with commendable directness, Early Fellow, Long Fellow, and Fine Fellow. (Other Scot-

tish breeders came up with other names that were descriptive of
their environment: Angus, Drummond, Highlander, Sandy,
Black Tartarian, Royal Scot.)

Long before that, oats, which may have been in the British
Isles as far back as 400 B.C., had acquired a reputation there for
more than mere sustenance. John Gerard, in his 1597 *Herball,*
wrote that colic, or a stitch in the side, could be much relieved
by the application of some heated oats secured in a linen bag;
that chapped hands or feet, or other abrasions, could be treated
by holding the afflicted parts over the steam from a pot of boiling oats; and that an application of oats could make a ruddy
maiden's complexion fairer — give it the paler hue, indeed, of
tallow. (In the fourth century A.D., a popular remedy for a col-
icky horse was to stir up some oats in wine and pour the mixture into the ailing animal's left nostril.) Oats are still an
ingredient of some specialty skin soaps; they also help heal
wounds in trees.

Wild oats are a weed, and a mean one. They caused nearly
$200-million worth of damage in North Dakota in 1973, a year
in which they so infested the wheat fields of that state that
those looked like oat fields. Fortunately, the United States
harbors only 16 species of wild oats; Great Britain had at last
count 228. Wild oats are sown by the wind. The phrase "sowing one's wild oats," may, as H. L. Mencken has asserted, be of
sixteenth-century English origin. It also may stem from an old
Jutland legend, in which the earth mother Hulda, or Bertha,
put werewolves at each corner of her grain fields to scare off
predators, and then the larksome fire god Loki stole past the
sentinels at night and scattered wild oat seeds; thus the connec-
tion between oats and naughtiness. Still another tale has it that
God once gave Satan oats, and then changed his mind and
wanted them back. But how to get them? Saint Paul said he'd

take care of it. When he saw the Devil heading his way, skipping along and jubilantly crying "Oats! Oats!" Paul hid under a bridge. He leapt forth and scared the devil out of Satan, who complained that Paul had made him forget the name of his precious burden. Was it rye, Saint Paul asked, or perhaps wheat? No, neither. How about sow thistle? The poor addled Devil said that sounded right, and that was what he ended up with.

Cultivated oats have not always been treated with the deference their fanciers believe they deserve, although Caligula is said to have fed them to his horses out of a golden receptacle. Franklin L. Coffman, for decades an oats specialist of the United States Department of Agriculture, grumbled in 1961, after forty-four years' unswerving devotion to his favorite cereal, that wheat, corn, rice, and cotton had all "received more attention from publishers than oats." Coffman, in his book *Oats and Oat Improvement,* did his best to rectify that. Still, there was no gainsaying that much more widely remembered writings about oats were Pliny's observation that, wild or tame, they were only a noxious weed; and Dr. Samuel Johnson's definition of them as "a grain which in England is generally given to horses, but in Scotland supports the people." (Johnson later confessed to Boswell, "I own that by my definition of oats I meant to vex them.") To which Lord Elibank, a Scottish military officer, gallantly retorted, "Very true, and where will you find such horses, and such men?" Coffman did not live long enough to know that the unappreciated oat, as part of a scientific experiment, would in 1982 soar skyward on a spacecraft.

The family of grasses to which most staple food plants belong — the *Gramineae* — can be proud of its place in literature. Take the Bible. What love-smitten poet has improved on Solomon's song lyric "Thy belly is like a heap of wheat set about with lilies"? While it is true that Abel, the good guy, was a shepherd and that Cain, the bad guy, was a farmer, and while the authors of the Book of Judges did elect to recount an unflattering Israelite dream in which some Midianites are stunned by a cake of barley bread that falls into their camp, did not God, very early in Genesis, create food plants before he created fish, before birds, before animals, before man? In prebiblical times, Egyptians, not unlike the crocodiles with which they warily shared the Nile, are alleged to have been cannibals. The crocodiles never much adapted to civilized eating, but the Egyptians were weaned from their crude ways, their high priests informed them, by the goddess Isis, who returned from a journey to Lebanon with some wheat and barley. Osiris, who was both husband and brother to Isis, taught his flock how to cultivate the wheat and, inevitably, how to make beer from barley. This, to be sure, was only when his sister-wife had put him together again after he had been dismembered in a spat with yet another sibling, the fratricidal god Seth, who had scattered parts of Osiris's body every which way. Isis patiently retrieved the pieces, reassembled them, and breathed new life into Osiris. There is a statue of him in the main lobby of the FAO, in Rome. The inscription hails him as "Food Promoter and Protector of Agriculture in Ancient Egypt." Another effigy of Osiris, found in the tomb of Tutankhamen, is a hollow figure with some grains of barley embedded inside it in the expectation that they would germinate and be a symbol of resurrection. Other regal mummies were bedecked, also to accelerate resurrection, with barley necklaces. (A European count once contended, in Prague, that he had planted some thousand-year-old wheat seeds found in an Egyptian sarcophagus and that they had germinated — a metamorphosis that most botanists consider not only unlikely but impossible. The count could have been duped; somebody could have slipped some fresh seeds into the coffin. In any event, guides at the Pyramids still occasionally tell tourists about the mummified wheat that came back to life, and the story had a brief flurry in the American press. One Chicago newspaper — apparently unaware that in the rest of the world, as in the Bible, "corn" is used to describe all grains — had it that a retired minister from Pennsylvania planted some *three*-thousand-year-old kernels of corn and was eventually rewarded with fourteen-foot-high stalks bearing two-foot-long bright red ears; and on the stalks perched voracious devil-horned worms that, when transferred to latter-day corn plants, refused even to nibble at them.) Not long after receiving Osiris's agronomic instructions, Egyptians were dividing their years into three seasons — Flood, Sprouting of the Seed, and Harvest of the Grain. For a while, they believed that barley grew out of man and wheat out of woman, and that the sex of an unborn child could accordingly be ascertained by putting the urine of a pregnant woman on both cereals; whichever sprouted first determined the outcome. (Twentieth-century spoilsports discovered that nonpregnant urine stopped all sprouting and that pregnant urine fostered sprouting 40 percent of the time no matter which grain it was applied to.) The old Egyptians were also persuaded that barley had medicinal properties — though, to be sure, only when used in combination with salt, papyrus, burnt leather, ox grease, wax, cow's milk, honey, dates, red ocher, and leg marrow; they were no less convinced that asps could be kept from biting if one set out a dish of barley and wine and then summoned snakes to the deterrent by clapping one's hands.

The Egyptians began to make bread around 4000 B.C., probably by accident, when some gruel went sour and yeast was formed. (Herodotus maintained that the Egyptians were contemptuous of both wheat and barley, and cited as his evidence that they kneaded clay with their hands and dough with their feet; but he may have been misinformed, as he was about other things.) The workers who built the pyramid of Cheops were fortified by beer and bread — three loaves a day apiece. When the city of Alexandria was being laid out in 332 B.C., its designers ran short of chalk. They used barley grains to mark the perimeter. Birds flew over and began to eat the barley, and Alexander's soothsayers regarded that as an exceptionally propitious omen for the municipality's future. Earlier, Rameses III (1198–1166 B.C.) set aside ten thousand measures of grain daily for divine offerings; and Thutmose III (1504–1450 B.C.) always gave barley to the gods at the new moon. For festivals, Egyptians baked loaves in the shape of pigs, asses, and hippopotamuses; when they didn't have a handy animal around to sacrifice, they would sacrifice its floury image. Various rulers fed grains to their sacred cats, their sacred ichneumons, and their sacred crocodiles, though the crocodiles, at least, might have preferred something meatier.

The domestication of wild grasses, and, simultaneously the domestication of man, because he no longer had to live nomadically, forever on the prowl for food, probably began about ten thousand years ago somewhere in that broad expanse of Asia stretching from the western slopes of the Himalayas to the Mediterranean — most likely in the valley between the Tigris and Euphrates rivers that was called the Fertile Crescent. (It is no longer fertile.) Cereal grains found at Jarmo, in what is now northern Iraq, have been dated by radiocarbon testing at 6700 B.C. (Archeologists have unearthed implements older than that by fifty thousand years or more which apparently were used for grinding or crushing *something* — conceivably edible seeds.) Schliemann thought he discovered some ancient bits of wheat at Troy, though they were more likely barley, which Pliny credited — as, later, did Sir James Frazer — with being the most venerable of all cultivated cereals and thus called it *Antiquissimum frumentum.* Pliny also ascribed to barley magical powers. Ancient seers, he recounted, would scrawl the letters of their alphabet in dust, put a grain of barley on each letter, and then watch a cock that had already been subjected to suitable incantations peck away at the barley. The letters the bird uncovered would spell a secret word. In *The Odyssey,* Homer asserted that wheat once grew wild, eons ago, in Sicily; but in his nineteenth-century work *Origin of Cultivated Plants,* Alphonse de Candolle rejoined cuttingly that "it is impossible to attach great importance to the words of a poet, and of a poet whose very existence is questioned."

The old-time Greeks, who were redoubtable grain-traders, did import wheat seeds from Sicily. One of their holiest of shrines was the temple at Eleusis dedicated to their goddess of agriculture, Demeter. (Her name may have come from an old Cretan word for barley: *deai.*) Demeter's sway over food plants was omnipotent, and was not lightly to be interfered with, as even her brother-consort Zeus was made to realize. Their mischief-making brother Pluto — the parallels to the Isis-Osiris legend are obvious — kidnapped Persephone, the daughter of Demeter and Zeus, and dragged her down from Olympus to Hades. The aggrieved mother at once curtailed the growth of plants on earth and, before leaving Olympus herself in a huff, told Zeus that she would permit no further agriculture until she got Persephone back. Zeus was in a dilemma; he didn't want to have his mortal constituency perish, but he couldn't get the girl permanently out of the underworld; it seemed that she had taken some nourishment there, which represented a binding commitment to the depths. But Zeus did manage to work out a compromise with Pluto, whereby Persephone could spend eight months a year with her mother, and the other four — the cold, unproductive winter months — with her captor. Demeter was appeased, and agreed to return to Olympus, and before doing so gave to Triptolemus, the son of King Celeus of Eleusis, a magic chariot and a supply of seeds, so that he could travel around the world and resow its barren fields. The grateful Greeks would thereafter always scatter seeds at their sacrifices. Around 1000 B.C., or even earlier, barley was the staff of life for the Greek peasantry, and that grain was considered so emblematic of physical well-being that quantities of it were awarded to the winners of the Eleusinian games. Later, Roman gladiators were served barley — *Hordeum soanteum* was its formal designation — at their training tables; they were called *hordearii:* barley-men. Barley's high repute was, however, not universally recognized; contemporary Bedouins still follow their ancestors' example of referring to their enemies as "cakes of barley bread," to show in what low esteem they are held.

The Greeks were master bakers. They made sixty-two different kinds of bread. Their proficiency so impressed the Romans that they used Greeks for bakers. In both Greece and Rome, white bread conferred social prestige; Romans called the coarse brown bread that they fed their slaves *panis sordidus.* Around A.D. 100, millers and bakers enjoyed such prestige in Rome that they had their own delegates in the senate, and eschewed fraternization with raffish folk like gladiators and comedians. Their activities were deemed worth immortalizing in bas-reliefs on the tomb of Marcus Vergilius Eurysaces, near the Porta Maggiore. At the height of the Roman Empire, bread was not considered supplementary to a meal: it was the meal. When Pompeii had a population of twenty thousand, it had twenty bakeries. Statues honoring one Roman deity, the goddess of the hearth, Vesta, sometimes depicted her holding a pan of *panis*. The Romans had another god, a rather special one, Robigus, to whom they would pray to deliver them from rust, then as now one of wheat's most merciless oppressors. Pliny, who had it on good authority that in sowing wheat seeds one should be careful to walk with one's right foot forward, said that "the rust of wheat is the greatest pest of crops." Ovid, for his part, described how on the twenty-fifth of every April, the date on which rust could be counted on to attack wheat plants, the rust god's acolytes would seek to placate him with a feast called the Robigalia, in the course of which there would be burned on his altar the entrails of a dog. The dog's coat had to be reddish — the color of rust. The Romans, of course, following the Greek precedent, also worshiped the goddess Demeter. They called her Ceres. Thus: "cereals."

The Wolofs of western Sudan have a proverb that succinctly illustrates how reliant so much of the world's population is on plants and how, in fact, to many human beings food and food plants are one and the same: "There are three things that sustain man — sowing, harvesting, eating." In 1970, when Addeke H. Boerma was director general of the FAO, he wrote, "Since cereals dominate the cropping pattern of most developing countries and are the main staple for both calories and protein, they have an overwhelming psychological, nutritional, and economic importance for farmers and governments." As cereals dominate crops, so does wheat — the rice-eating areas of the earth perhaps excepted — dominate cereals. Wheat is "a prime necessity of civilized life," according to *The Book of Wheat,* written in 1908 by Peter Tracy Dondlinger. "Herein lies the present and increasingly great importance of wheat, for it seems to be the tendency of the civilized world to raise its standard of living. As the standard of living rises, wheat becomes a relatively more important part of human food. . . . As an essential part of the food of civilized man it becomes of an importance so vital as to be dominating." Largely because of wheat, bygone human beings began to live in communities, to domesticate animals, and to build carts, wagons, roads, boats, and canals. As John H. Klippart impassionedly stated in *The Wheat Plant,* back in 1859:

With a map of the world before you, point, if you can, to the country or nation enjoying civilization and enlightenment, that does not cultivate the cereals, or point to a country or a nation in a state of savagism or barbarism that does cultivate the wheat plant; then reflect for a moment on the number of persons in our country whose occupations would be gone; how many millions of capital would have been uselessly invested, how many machines and implements would be left to decay in inglorious idleness, and how much calamity, moral, political and social would ensue, were the wheat plant to be suddenly and universally annihilated.

More of the globe's arable surface is given over to wheat — about 600 million acres in all — than to any other crop. There are parts of the world where you could fly a small plane over wheat fields and run out of fuel before wheat ran out of sight. If all the grain grown on earth in 1982 could have been assembled to form a highway at the equator, that road would have been about seventeen feet wide, seven and a half feet deep, and twenty-five thousand miles long. Unlike corn, unlike soybeans, unlike barley and oats, huge quantities of all of which are channeled into human food through animals, wheat — like rice — is produced almost exclusively for direct consumption by people, for whom, in developing and developed countries together, it now furnishes 20 percent of their calories and 45 percent of their protein — as much protein as is derived from all the meat and milk and eggs mankind eats. Wheat is the quintessential foodstuff for a billion people, in forty-five countries, from Albania to Yugoslavia — though not in some places (China, India, the United States, for instance) where it is grown on a massive scale. (We know little about present-day Albania, but we do know that bygone Albanians had a trenchant, if somewhat confusing, adage: "Bread is older than man.") Winter wheat is planted in the fall and harvested in the summer. Spring wheat's cycle goes from spring to autumn. Every single month of the year, some wheat is harvested somewhere on earth. Of the 1982 worldwide wheat production of more than 450 million tons — roughly, 16.5 billion bushels — the United States, on nearly eighty million acres, was responsible for almost one-sixth. About 2 billion bushels of that harvest ended up abroad — a more than $7-billion export crop. (It is uncertain whether the total production attributed to the United States took into account the modest harvest of the conceptual artist Agnes Denes, who, spurred on by a ten-thousand-dollar foundation grant, obtained six bushels of hard red spring-wheat seed from the North Dakota Wheat Commission in May 1982 and planted them, in the peculiar line of her work — she had earlier done a rice field in upstate New York — on a 1⅓-acre vacant lot on Manhattan Island.) Enough of the United States wheat crop remained at home for Americans to spend $8 billion that year on wheat and wheat-flour products, their per-capita consumption of which came to 115 pounds. A ton of wheat, with a few supplemental condiments and greens, will nicely sustain a family of five anywhere for a year.

Wheat — one should perhaps say "the wheats," for this exemplary seed-swollen grass (as many as fifty spikes to a plant, as many as a hundred grains to a spike) of the genus *Triticum* (from *tritus,* the past participle of the Latin *terere,* "to grind") comes, like most of the indispensable food plants, in many guises. There are at least a dozen known major species of wheat, among them einkorn, emmer — this the chief one, apparently, known to ancient Egypt — Persian, Polish, and spelt. The three principal commercial wheats of modern times are the common, or bread, wheat (*Triticum aestivum*); club wheat, used mainly for biscuits and pastries; and durum, the raw material of pasta. Wheat is the most traded of all edible commodities, in part because it is also the easiest to store. Its relative imperishability has made it the grain most fancied for shipments of food aid to the world's have-not nations from the haves. That has brought about radical changes in many of the seventy so-categorized developing nations where before the Second World War wheat figured minimally, if at all, in day-to-day eating habits, or desires. Tastes have been created that can be satisfied only by massive imports. The American and British and Australian soldiers who ranged the globe during that war had a lot to do with it. Wherever they went, they had bread; and the indigenes they encountered were impressed with a type of food that didn't rot and didn't have to be cooked and that came presliced. (The soldiers also often toted peanut butter; the world's leading importer of peanut butter today is Saudi Arabia — which shows what people who have a lot of money to throw around will spend it on.) In 1955, the developing countries imported one-fourth of all the wheat that was involved in international trade. By 1982, though few of them could afford it, their share of that commerce had risen to two-thirds, at a cost to them of more than 3 billion hard-to-come-by dollars.

The pattern was global. At the beginning of 1983, for instance, the Philippines, historically a rice-eating country, was spending $120 million a year to import some 750,000 tons of wheat. It had only fifty-one acres of its own in wheat. That year, President Marcos — responding, as any good politician must or should, to the actual or perceived demands of his fifty million constituents — decided to launch a major wheat-production program. Under reasonably good agronomic conditions, fifty-one acres will yield about twenty tons — enough wheat for five hundred people a year. The Philippines had a very long way to go. But once their rice crop was harvested they also had six million acres of land available for winter wheat. If merely half of that were to be sequestered, that could mean more than a million tons of wheat.

Today, Burma, where for centuries people have obtained most of their calories from rice and still get 70 percent from it, wants wheat. So does Thailand, where rice has been the staple for eight or nine thousand years and where for much of that time it was commonly believed that the human body was made of rice and thus needed to keep ingesting that cereal to keep itself functioning. So does Sri Lanka, a country in which one of its farmers — 46 percent of the population is engaged in agriculture — not long ago told a tourist, who wondered why he was smiling, "Happiness is seventy bushels an acre." Sri Lanka is tropical, and wheat, by and large, is not. Almost anything except wheat will grow splendidly there — exotic fruits and flowers, tea, coffee, rice, and the output of sixty million graceful coconut trees. Sri Lanka has one of the world's most elegant botanical gardens, where bamboo will grow taller before your eyes, if you have the patience to watch it long enough; today, in deference to the shifting demands of its consumers, it also has one of the world's largest flour mills. South Korea, where bread was virtually unknown before that nation's Westernization began during the war of the early 1950s, at last count had seven thousand bakeries.

Although Chiang Kai-shek was sufficiently influenced by the American way of life to tell the Taiwanese, when he moved over among them, that "wheat-eating is patriotic," it has been suggested by his enemies that he did not wax so enthusiastic when he was still influential in mainland China. An article in the January 1981 issue of the propaganda magazine *China Reconstructs,* published in the People's Republic, reconstructed an episode in the career of Professor Jin Shanbao, the then eighty-five-year-old president of the Chinese Academy of Agricultural Sciences. It seemed that while in Chungking during the Second World War Professor Jin, who had studied both at Cornell and the University of Minnesota, bred two promising new strains of wheat. "When they were ignored by the Kuomintang government," the story went, "he took the seeds to the office of the Communist Party's *Xinhua Daily.*" Zhou Enlai was the ranking dignitary in Chungking, and he not only didn't ignore the seeds but sent them to Mao Zedong's headquarters at Yan'an. "Learning that his new wheat seeds had been received in Yan'an and were being used," the article went on, "gave Prof. Jin food for thought about the different attitudes of the Communist Party and the Kuomintang toward science. He decided that China would do better to follow Yan'an." Mao apparently became so sold on the virtues of wheat himself that in the 1970s he decreed that his subject peoples in Tibet, who had always had highland barley as their staple grain — they used it in *tsampa:* fried barley powder mixed with tea, salt, and yak butter — had to start growing wheat instead. The Tibetans were unhappy; wheat didn't seem to fare especially well in their mountains and what crops they harvested were mostly allocated to the Chinese occupying forces. In 1983, to the Tibetans' delight, the Chinese relented and let them put nearly forty thousand acres of unwelcome wheat land back into barley. In contemporary Chinese high schools, where there are few elective courses, students get lectures on how to grow wheat along with how-to-grow-rice ones. By 1979, when China's production of rice came to 144 million tons, it was also producing 63 million tons of wheat — almost as much as the output of the United States. By the year 2000, China may reach the 100-million-ton mark. Despite all that, to satisfy its burgeoning wheat needs the People's Republic had to import a billion dollars' worth of wheat from America in 1982 — this to the great pleasure of a promotional organization called the U.S. Wheat Associates, which opened an office in Peking and had arranged for the shipment there of machinery for a bakery that could spew forth fifteen hundred loaves of bread an hour.

An American organization called the Western Wheat Associates had long before that established a beachhead in Japan, which, like China, had for so many centuries been a stronghold of rice. Not that all Japanese had always thought that rice was the sine qua non of comestibles. In 1927, for instance, an iconoclastic Tokyo journalist, delivering himself of an opinion that cannot have made him very popular at home, asserted that Asians — Chinese and Indians as well as Japanese — were retrogressive, and that their heavy dependence on rice was the reason. "The people of the Orient and of the South Seas feeding on rice," he wrote, "cannot keep step in the march of civilization with Europeans and Americans. This has been noted by the Occidentals. Therefore they fear Orientals no longer." He went on to say, astonishingly, that if Europeans stayed in Japan long enough and ate enough rice their skins would turn yellow. "There is no doubt," he concluded unqualifiedly, "that diet has a great deal to do with the color of human bodies." Per-capita rice consumption in Japan is still high (in 1981, the average Japanese household spent $1,100 per annum on food, of which $200 went for rice), but wheat has been making inroads, although comparatively little of it was used there until the United States occupying forces introduced it in 1946. Before the Second World War, the per-capita consumption of wheat flour was thirty pounds a year; by 1955, it was ninety pounds. By 1956, the Oregon Wheat Growers League — soft wheat from the American West Coast is admirably suited to the manufacture of *udon,* the hot boiled noodles sold by bicycle-pedaling street venders — was on the scene, distributing posters in rural areas that read, "Tasty wheat foods will bring you good health tomorrow"; and the Japanese themselves had a Food Life Improvement Association that sent demonstration-kitchen buses around the countryside and gave instructional courses to small-town bakers. The industrialists who ran Japan were not displeased; they had already determined — as had their counterparts in Taiwan and South Korea — that they could expect greater productivity from wheat-eating factory workers than from the rice eaters of yesteryear.

Much the same situation has evolved in other traditionally non-wheat-growing-and-eating regions. In Brazil, between 1961 and 1980, the average per-capita per-annum consumption of wheat rose from 75 pounds to 120; in Bolivia, from 98 to 128; in Central America, from 18 to 51; in the Caribbean, from practically nothing to 160. (Columbus, who took corn from the West Indies to Europe in 1492, had reciprocated by bringing wheat over the following year, but nobody had then paid it much heed.) Even more striking have been the changes in Africa. In most of Zaire, where cassava had been the staple food while the region was a Belgian colony, there was no wheat to speak of at independence time in 1960. Then Zairians became acquainted with bread through United States food-aid benefactions, and grew fond of it. But they couldn't grow wheat in their torrid climate. In 1980, they imported two hundred thousand tons of American wheat. By 1981, fifteen million tons of wheat and wheat flour were imported into all of Africa at a cost of $3 billion. That $200-a-ton outlay was more than the average annual earned individual income for the entire continent.

What, compared to pre-Colonial levels, was an avalanche of wheat was still, compared to the overall African scene, more of a trickle. Two hundred million or so sub-Saharan Africans remained utterly dependent on sorghum and millet — drought- and heat-resistant cereals (sorghum has a slightly larger grain) that thrive on sere soils, and that are believed to have originated in what is now Ethiopia. The African continent as a whole receives more nourishment from sorghum and millet than from any other source. Some countries there carry their stalks in their festival parades. Burundi — better known outside Africa for its coffee — has a bundle of sorghum on its national flag. Sorghum, the more widespread of the related cereals, is not easy to prepare. Its hull is hard and indigestible. To crush its inner kernels into a form suitable for cooking takes a person — usually a woman — an hour for every couple of pounds; if there is a family to feed, that may entail five hours of labor every day. And sorghum flour doesn't keep well; it turns rancid in twelve hours. All things considered, it is an unprepossessing food (West Africans sometimes call it "the poor man's rice"), inferior in protein and calories not only to wheat but also to corn, rice, and potatoes. Even so, the home-economics department of the University of Nairobi, on behalf of the East African Industrial Research Organization, has hailed sorghum as "a vastly underrated cereal." To the hundreds of millions of Africans — and not a few Asians, too — who are beholden to it its ratings are of little consequence: they have no alternative to it, and they would die without it.

Across the globe, the sorghum family bestrides 110 million

acres of cropland, a tract exceeded in size only by the fields given over to wheat, corn, barley, and rice. Worldwide sorghum and millet production in 1980 amounted to 100 million tons. In the United States they are often called "milo" or "milo maize." Broomcorn, a variety of sorghum that has especially long panicles and is used, not surprisingly, to make brooms, has been on the American scene ever since Benjamin Franklin, a tidy man, brought it over from Europe in 1725. Fifty-six years after that, Thomas Jefferson, who was as knowledgeable about agriculture as about statecraft, would proclaim sorghum one of the most important agricultural crops of Virginia. In the United States, sorghum is now to be found predominantly in Texas. In sorghum's honor, the town fathers of two nineteenth-century Texas farm communities gave them the names of Sudan and — perhaps being unaware of the Southern African connotations of the word — Kafir. (There is also a Milo, Oklahoma.) Americans use sorghum mainly for syrup and for animal feed — only very rarely for human consumption. In Africa, by contrast, 90 percent of it goes into pastes, porridges, soups, and beverages like Bantu beer; and most of it is consumed, in one form or another, right where it is grown. Ugandans are partial to a home brew of boiled sorghum and cattle blood. The International Crops Research Institute for the Semi-Arid Tropics (ICRISAT), near Hyderabad, India, harbors a collection of twenty-one thousand cultivars of sorghum and fourteen thousand of millet. A symposium on "Sorghum in the Eighties" was held there in 1981, with 245 scientists from thirty-seven countries in attendance. A major topic on the agenda was how to improve sorghum as a human food. "Failure to do so will be a disaster for the world" was the consensus. An increase in yields, through better seeds or better cultivation, would be one obvious way of averting that disaster.

The United States and Nigeria, for example, have just about the same number of acres — some twelve million — planted to sorghum. At the start of the eighties, however, largely because of the superiority of American soil and American cultural practices, the average sorghum yield for the United States was 3,200 pounds an acre, and for Nigeria, 550. Over an eight-year stretch, American yields had gone up by 10 percent; Nigerian, down by 4. Americans can get along without sorghum; Nigerians can't. In a 1981 report on its activities, ICRISAT did not sound particularly optimistic about the closing of that sort of gap. "Living standards are not going to be miraculously upgraded by the advent of one or two new discoveries for [semiarid tropical] farmers," it said. "Instead, the spectrum of improved agriculture and life styles is made up of many vital inputs — improved seeds, essential fertilizers, effective soil management, better utilization of rainfall, appropriate cropping systems, supplementary irrigation, motivation for adoption of technologies, and the elimination of socioeconomic constraints."

Sorghum grows taller than most grains — its name stems from the Latin *surgere,* "to rise" — and Africans use its stalks as building materials for homes and fences. Like all food plants, it has its special deadly enemies. More than a hundred and fifty kinds of insect — prominent among them the shoot fly, earhead bugs, and the armyworm — prey upon it. So does the parasitic witchweed, *Striga.* So does an extraordinary creature, the small red-billed weaverbird, or *Quelea quelea aethiopica,* whose ravages were much discussed, with head shaking and hand wringing, at the 1981 ICRISAT convocation. Forty thousand of these birds can live on one acre of thorn scrub, waiting patiently to pounce on an emerging nearby stand of grain. A flock of a million of them has been credited with ruining twenty tons of sorghum in a single day. People have tried, with not much success, to dynamite their nesting sites. In 1959, when Kenya and Tanzania had better relations than they did later, those neighbors embarked on a joint *Quelea*-extermination program. In one year, they dispatched, by somebody's awesome count, ninety-one million of the pesky birds. The survivors seemed unruffled. It was in 1959, too, that locusts destroyed a quantity of grain in Ethiopia that would have been sufficient to feed a million people for twelve months. Soon afterward, the FAO gloomily estimated that "fifty-five million Africans could be fed for a year from the . . . grain finding its way to the wrong consumers — rats, locusts, quelea birds, beetles, moths, and weevils and countless microorganisms." Sorghum breeders at ICRISAT and elsewhere have tried to come up with strains of the plant that the quelea might find unappetizing, but they suspect that if they do, whatever they contrive will also prove to be deficient in nutrition and digestibility for human beings.

Outsiders who now and then attempt to chide Africans for craving staples other than those they can readily grow themselves are apt to be rebuked for expressing colonialist views. Wheat is not the only grain involved. The FAO once urged Kenyans to plant sorghum and millet on some of their arid soil, to which these plants were admirably suited. But no — in Kenyan eyes, corn was much more prestigious, and that was what they wanted even if they couldn't grow enough of it and had to purchase it abroad. Not that there was not legitimate resentment among newly emerging countries toward the policies of their erstwhile colonial rulers. Had not the British raj encouraged the culture of soybeans in India in 1937 — not out of any particular penchant for that plant, but because Indians were beginning to eat wheat that had been earmarked for profitable export? Had not the European powers that for so long presided over Africa often dictated that its most fertile fields be set aside not for sustenance for natives but, rather, for cocoa or coffee or other export crops that could fatten distant exchequers? And what about the French regime in what was then Upper Volta? During a famine there in 1932, a French civil servant at Ouagadougou wrote home:

One can only wonder how it happens that populations who always had on hand three harvests in reserve, and to whom it was unacceptable to eat grain that had spent less than three years in the granary, have suddenly become improvident. They managed to get through the terrible drought years 1912–1914 without hardship. . . . Now these people, once accustomed to food abundance, are living from hand to mouth. I feel morally bound to point out that the policy of giving priority to industrial cash crops has coincided with an increase in the frequency of food scarcity.

It may say something about past attitudes of developed nations toward developing ones that when a new, cheap macaroni substitute was fabricated in the United States some years ago out of wheat, corn, and soybeans, it was designed with two sets of consumers in mind — the Third World and the inmates of American prisons. The colonial nations didn't have to be unduly concerned if their policies led to malnutrition; their subjects couldn't exert any real pressure on them. But after independence food became a national and immediate, not international and remote, concern. Indigenous governments had to be more sensitive than satraps to the aspirations of their people, people who were more stridently than ever before articulating their needs. Starvation was no longer to be tolerated —

although there was little any government, no matter how sympathetic or solicitous, could do on its own to alleviate a severe famine. And what increasingly large numbers of those people were asking for — ironically, it was the colonial powers that, by example and precept, had stimulated their demands — was wheat and the baked products it generated.

North Africa had grown wheat since the days of the pharaohs. The only East African countries that grew much of it at all in modern times were — since Australian merchantmen had introduced it there in 1910 — Kenya, Tanzania, Sudan, and Ethiopia. (Ethiopia has a cereal of its own, teff, a small-grained, weak-strawed, low-yielding plant that is the basis of the national dish *injera,* a flat pancake with the consistency of a towel. Teff is cultivated on twelve million mountainous Ethiopian acres and, for reasons no botanists have yet fully fathomed, nowhere else.) Notwithstanding, consumption of wheat has increased throughout Africa by 5 percent every year for the last two decades. In Nigeria, which grew 25,000 tons of it in 1981 and imported 1.5 million, the rate of escalation has been more than twice as steep. The number of calories furnished by wheat to all Nigerians increased more than fourfold over those twenty years, while those from sorghum and millet were concurrently decreasing by 25 percent. One reason for the shift in consumption is that Africa, like much of the rest of the world, is becoming more and more urbanized. Self-sufficiency is on the wane. The FAO has estimated that by the end of this century half the human race will be living where it has no direct access to farm produce. The agricultural economist and author Lester Brown, who presides over the Worldwatch Institute in Washington, D.C., calculated, in his 1978 pamphlet *The Worldwide Loss of Cropland,* that if by the year 2000 there were 1.58 billion more urban people on earth, and that if each of them required one-tenth of an acre for living space, the cities they inhabited would have to expand by usurping some sixty million acres of cropland — acreage from which enough food could have been produced to sustain eighty-four million human beings.

The population of Lagos has already swelled enormously — from 1.4 million in 1960 to 3.5 million in 1983. Nigerians who move from rural communities to their congested capital can't easily grind sorghum and millet, or pulverize cassava, even if they bring their implements along: their neighbors are apt to complain about all the noise their incessant pounding creates. So they turn to preprocessed city foods, and for the majority of them that means bread. (Late in the nineteenth century, Nigerians called bread "shackleford." That was the surname of a Caribbean entrepreneur who came to West Africa from Jamaica, moved eastward, and along the way established some bakeries.) Nigeria has its own flour mills, but until recently its grain elevators couldn't handle large bulk shipments. Consequently, most of its imports of wheat had to arrive in bags, and bagged grain usually costs a dollar a bushel or so more than bulk grain. Nonetheless, because of government subsidies residents of Lagos can frequently buy sliced wrapped bread more cheaply than its equivalent, in food value, in homegrown sorghum. (Sliced bread was not common on New York City grocery shelves until 1930, and up to the beginning of the Second World War 50 percent of all floury goods consumed in the United States were baked at home. Now 95 percent, including fifty million loaves of bread a day, are store-bought.) Subsidies like those prevalent in Nigeria are perhaps unavoidable if the country's authorities — or the authorities of any country with large urban-population masses to cope with — are to maintain tranquility. As a publication of the United States Agency for International Development (AID) put it in the spring of 1983,

"After all, city people can riot and farmers are spread all over the country."

The FAO flaunts an ear of wheat on its official seal. The title of a bimonthly magazine it gets out is *Ceres*. Its motto is *Fiat panis* — "Let there be bread." Man cannot live by bread alone (it lacks essential vitamins), but nothing has happened in the ten thousand years or so of civilization to refute Matthew Henry's commentary on Psalm 104: "Here is bread, which strengthens man's heart, and is therefore called the staff of life." The word "bread" — sometimes used in the broader context of "food" — appears in the Bible 322 times, far more than the mentions altogether of wheat, corn, barley, and loaves. Bread has been almost universally recognized as the world's chief item of food — the one seeming dissenter being Ignazio Silone. His anti-Fascist novel *Bread and Wine* was published in the United States before it could come out in his native Italy. After Mussolini was toppled, Silone chose for the title of its Italian printing *Wine and Bread*. He explained that "in a democracy, wine is more important in our lives than bread." When bread was democratized in France after the French Revolution, it certainly seemed more important than wine even in that stronghold of oenophiles. In 1793, for instance, there was a shortage of bread. Ration cards were issued to the citizenry. Everybody was entitled to a pound a day. But there still wasn't enough to go around, and when one baker was discovered to have a few loaves unethically stashed away, he was dragged off his premises by a mob and hanged. Wheat is the peerless grain for bread making, because it contains gluten, which permits flour to absorb water and then, when yeast is added to it, to rise and form leavened bread. Hard wheats have more gluten than soft ones; french bread is made from soft wheats, and its relative lack of gluten is what makes it go stale so quickly. Bio-engineering specialists hope within the next few years to be able to transfer gluten's DNA genetic codes into sorghum and millet and even corn; if they succeed, that could revolution-ize bread making. A synthetic substitute for gluten, which can make dough rise, already exists: glyceryl monostereate (GMS), which is the offshoot of a catalyzed reaction of glycerol with lard or with a hardened vegetable oil. GMS-made bread consist-ing of eighty parts cassava starch to twenty parts soy flour — plus a pinch of salt, a tad of sugar, and some compressed wheat — has been assayed as more nutritious to rats (who will go to any lengths to help out human experimentation) than white bread. Not that unleavened bread does not have its fit place in graminivorous history. That was, after all, what Jesus ate at the Last Supper. The corn bread of North America, the tor-tillas of Latin America, the matzoth of Judaism, the chapatties of Asia are various types of unleavened bread. During the Sepoy Mutiny of 1857, chapatties were used in India to spread the word about scheduled uprisings against the raj. If some-thing was supposed to happen on, say, the tenth day of May, messengers would go from town to town and cut one chapatti into five parts, for the month, and another into ten, for the day. It was correctly anticipated that any British officials who hap-pened to be watching would take this to be just another quaint native way of parceling out sustenance. At least one English co-lonial official in India, however, was far from obtuse. That was a colonel who, suspecting merchants of bilking pilgrims by selling them chapatties made from adulterated flour, got them to quit by the simple method of directing them to eat their own tainted fare. The British themselves, over the centuries, had had their own peculiar habits when it came to bread. Take, for instance, the sin eaters of the seventeenth century — practitioners who could be engaged to devour a loaf of bread at a funeral, and thus transfer unto and into themselves the transgressions of the deceased. Earlier, it was believed in England that the best way to keep witches from molesting a sleeping child was to put some bread under his pillow. (Across the Channel, a fairy tale with which the Dutch sometimes put their children to bed involved a rich, ship-owning woman who wouldn't give a wizard any bread. He said she would suffer for it, and she did. When she dispatched one of her ship captains to fetch her the most precious cargo on earth and he returned with a boatload of wheat, she was furious and ordered it jettisoned, even though the captain suggested she give it to the poor if she had no use for it herself. Where the grain was dumped, a wheat field soon materialized, clogging her harbor and putting her out of business.) Quite a few of the humans who have been accused and convicted of witchcraft over the years were undoubtedly not in the clutches of evil spirits but had merely had the bad luck to eat rye bread contaminated with ergot, a fungus that grows on rye in excessively damp and cool weather. People who contracted ergotism would foam at the mouth and have tingling and burning sensations — the symptom called Saint Anthony's fire. There were dreadful outbreaks in the Middle Ages; at Limoges, in A.D. 943, forty thousand deaths were attributed to ergotism. As recently as 1951 there was an epidemic in the Rhône Valley. The afflicted thought they were being chased by lions or smothered by snakes, went berserk, jumped into the river, and drowned. Notwithstanding, rye bread was for many years the bread most regularly consumed by the poorer classes of northern Europe. In the Middle Ages, thick, hard slabs of it were used by the upper classes in lieu of plates. They were called trenchers. One would put one's meat on one's trencher, and it would soak up the juices and prevent one's meal from becoming a mess. Once a trencherman was sated, the trenchers would be fed to dogs, or to servants. The custom in the Middle Ages of carving a cross on loaves had Christian connotations; it also made the loaves easier to break apart. As late as the eighteenth century, some of the bread that English laborers got as their pitiful share of the available bounty of grain was so hard it literally knocked out their teeth. And in France, at about the same time, the bread most peasants ate could often not be carved with a knife; it had to be chopped with an ax.

In the Bible, "breaking the bread" had nothing to do with the food's texture but stood, rather, for hospitality and fellowship. The word "companion," from its Latin and Old French antecedents, literally means "one who shares bread with another." The word "wheat" stems from the Middle English "whete" and, further back, from the old English "hwaete," which is in turn almost the same as "hwit" — "white." (The German for "wheat" is *"Weizen"* and for "white," *"weiss"*; the French for "wheat," *"blé,"* is, similarly, akin to *"blêmir"* — "to pale.") The white bread in which so much wheat ends up is not necessarily, as nutritionists have long been pointing out, the most wholesome. To make it, the wheat's tonic husk of bran has first to be removed. In the 1820s, a French physiologist put a dog on an exclusive diet of all the white bread it cared to eat, and to the grim satisfaction of such white-bread detractors as his American contemporary Sylvester Graham, the dog died in fifty days. Graham, whose surname is best remembered nowadays as a modifier of a cracker, was an outspoken Protestant clergyman who thought that white bread, among its other failings, was a major cause of constipation, and that people who insisted on stripping wheat of its bran were guilty, like adulterers, of putting "asunder what God has joined together."

Graham was also a vegetarian (Emerson dubbed him the "poet of bran bread and pumpkins"), the general agent of the Pennsylvania Temperance Society, the organizer of the Popular Health Movement, and a heated proponent of cold showers. In his tract *Health from Diet and Exercise,* published in the 1830s, he passed along a letter he'd received from the sort of person he could unstintingly admire: a seventy-one-year-old man who, at sixty, had given up smoking, drinking, and flesh-eating (it had earlier been his pernicious practice to have a beefsteak for breakfast and smoked tongue with his tea), and who as a consequence could walk ten or fifteen miles a day and saunter with impunity into cholera wards — all this from subsisting solely on corn porridge, plain boiled rice, potatoes, and a bread fashioned largely of unbolted wheat. In his *Treatise on Bread and Bread-making,* Graham came out so vehemently in favor of homemade bread as against bakery bread that he was physically assaulted by a gang of irate bakers, who were vigorously abetted, because of his no less stern dicta against the consumption of flesh, by some vengeful butchers.

Across the Atlantic, a couple of generations later, one of wheat's most rabid, and most racist, spokesmen was the chemist Sir William Crookes, the discoverer of the element thallium and the president of the British Association for the Advancement of Science. In 1898, Sir William delivered himself of the following:

Wheat is the most sustaining food grain of the great Caucasian race, which includes the people of Europe, United States, British America, the white inhabitants of South Africa, Australia, parts of South America, and the white population of the European colonies. . . . If bread fails — not only us, but all the bread-eaters of the world — what are we to do? We are born wheat-eaters. Other races, vastly superior to us in numbers, but differing widely in material and intellectual progress, are eaters of Indian corn, rice, millet and other grains; but none of these grains have the food value, the concentrated health-sustaining power of wheat, and it is on this account that the accumulated experience of civilized mankind has set wheat apart as the fit and proper food for the development of muscle and brains.

In 1773, another Englishman, who signed himself "J.H.," had said in a treatise called *Advocate for Public Welfare* that "the prejudices of the people are strong; but they relate chiefly to the magic of the two syllables, *white* and *brown*." At the start of the twentieth century, in Australia, the *Queensland Agricultural Journal* would be stating, reiteratively, "It is very hard to remove a prejudice, especially when it has to do with the food one eats." There have been strange parallels between the alleged superiority of white bread to other breads and of white people to other people. A pro-white-bread editorial in the British magazine *The Lancet,* in 1940, was entitled "The Colour Question." (Another editorial it ran that same year said that if the British armed forces didn't get enough white bread they "would be the first to revolt.") In the American South, before the Civil War, it was customary for plantation owners to eat white corn and to give yellow corn to their slaves; the practice diminished when it became known that the slaves were, in that respect at least, better off than their masters, because what gave the yellow corn its nonwhite tinge was carotene, an estimable source of vitamin A. It has been argued by parlor sociologists that what has made the white man's white bread so popular among nonwhite Africans is, to a degree, its whiteness. President Kenneth Kaunda of Zambia expressed his displeasure not long ago when his citizens let it be known, after a drought had curtailed their own corn crop, that they would rather have white corn imported from the Republic of South Africa than yellow corn from the

United States. (It is perhaps inevitable that South Africa should be the world's principal exporter of white corn.) Seneca once wrote, "Nature does not care whether the bread is black or white: She does not want the stomach entertained but filled." People seem to care, though. Petronius reported that in ancient Rome — where white bread was the status food for the rich and the poor had their *panis sordidus* — young blades would box the ears of servitors who proffered them bread that wasn't quite bleached enough for their finicky tastes. Caesar, on the other hand, exhibited admirably democratic traits when he clapped one of his bakers in chains because the fellow had made the mistake of serving him better-quality bread than that tendered to his guests. In London, during the Middle Ages, the dividing line between different colors of bread was so sharp that there were separate companies for the bakers of each kind. (In Holland, until recently, some farmers would partake of white bread only on Sundays; for the rest of the week, dark rye bread would suffice.) There have been deviations from all this fuss about whiteness. By the end of the eighteenth century, milling techniques had become so advanced in England that white bread could be bought more cheaply than dark. When the poor accordingly began gobbling up the white bread they'd so long envied the rich for, the rich, who were not prepared to tolerate any such egalitarianism, promptly switched to dark.

> *O beautiful for spacious skies,*
> *For amber waves of grain,*
> *For purple mountain majesties*
> *Above the fruited plain! . . .*

The grain that the anthem writer Katharine Lee Bates thought made America beautiful did not exist in the New

World — aside from what little Columbus carried over on his second voyage — until the Spanish introduced it in the sixteenth century. Wheat was then traveling across the Atlantic in one direction and corn — to the vast and lasting benefit of the inhabitants of both landfalls — in the opposite. The founders of the Jamestown and Plymouth colonies brought wheat with them; Bartholomew Gosnold had planted some of it near Martha's Vineyard as early as 1602. Missionaries, circumnavigating the great central plains which wheat now bestrides, took it to California in 1769. When wheat moved around, as precious to man as was his family that it succored, so inevitably did the grain's pursuing foes. The rusts, for deliverance from which the ancient Romans had prayed to their god Robigus, were conspicuous among them. Wheat-rust spores proliferate at so dazzling a rate that even with a slow start they can multiply by a trillion a month. The barberry bush, which to some horticulturists has an ornamental appeal but to all agriculturists is a pariah, is notoriously hospitable to stem rust. As many as twenty-five strains of that nuisance (there are probably several hundred altogether) have been known to nestle on a single barberry bush. In the early eighteenth century, while some New Englanders were preoccupied with ridding their communities of witches, others were spiritedly debating the pros and cons of whether the pretty barberry bush should be held culpable because of what rust could do to wheat. Connecticut outlawed the barberry bush in 1726. Neighboring colonies fell into line, though slowly. The Massachusetts General Court called for the extirpation of barberries in 1754. Rhode Island didn't join what some colonial chroniclers called "the war against the barberry bush" until 1772.

Then came a real war, and with it a new and deadly weapon against which America's wheat growers were all but defenseless — *Phytophaga destructor,* or, as it quickly became known, the Hessian fly. Its larvae suck the juices from young wheat plants' stems; the weakened stalks collapse before harvesttime. That fly — an insect half the size of a mosquito — got its popular name because it was believed to have traversed the Atlantic hiding in shipments of straw for mercenaries' horses. The Hessian fly, which became, and still is, one of wheat's unrelenting adversaries (in 1900, for instance, it was credited with destroying 10 percent of the entire United States crop, a $100-million loss), came ashore on Long Island in 1776 and, proceeding at its own leisurely pace, got to California in 1884. (Accelerating, or perhaps helped by favorable tail winds, it took only four more years to reach New Zealand.) Such notable farmers of their era as George Washington and Thomas Jefferson were much concerned about the pesky bug — Washington in part because some Tory propagandists in England spread the nasty rumor that it was *he* who was somehow responsible for the infiltration of the Hessian fly into the Colonies, although he no doubt would have been just as happy if the Hessians themselves had stayed home. (In a letter dispatched soon after the end of the War of Independence, Washington said, "No wheat that has ever yet fallen under my observation exceeds the wheat which some years ago I cultivated extensively, but which from inattention during my absence of almost nine years from home has got so mixed or degenerated as scarcely to retain any of its original characteristics properly." Things improved. By 1795, Washington's Mount Vernon brand of flour was selling nicely — it was especially popular in the West Indies — and in the last letter he is known to have written he said that "wheat and flour are my principal concerns." He once had a variety of wheat named after him: large head, brown chaff, long beard.) As for Jefferson, he wrote to Thomas Mann Randolph in May 1791 that "a committee of the Philosophical Society is charged with collecting material for the natural history of the Hessian fly." Twelve years after that, Jefferson was the grateful recipient of a few grains of a French wheat with a stem so comparatively tough that he hoped it could withstand the enemy. He would be disappointed. Another decade after *that,* in June 1813, he would be writing to James Madison that "the fly" — by then he knew that the recipient would understand the unembellished reference — had undermined one-third of his wheat crop. Jefferson added, philosophically, that "in the lotteries of human life you see that even farming is but gambling."

Today the United States, which is sometimes called the breadbasket of the world, has about twenty million acres planted to wheat. Canada has half as many more. Wheat did not get *there* until 1811, when Thomas Douglas, the fifth earl of Selkirk, decided to establish a colony in what is now Manitoba. Wheat's debut was inauspicious. Selkirk's first settlers had no plows or harrows; their only agricultural implements were hoes. Their first two crops failed, even though Selkirk had offered a prize of fifty pounds for the best wheat anyone could produce. They survived, at the start, on potatoes and turnips. When they began, following an inspection visit by their patron himself in 1817, to do a little better with their wheat, they were plagued by locusts. (They were also plagued, in the 1820s, by a governor, Alexander Macdonell, who was so universally disliked that they began to call him the Grasshopper Governor. They claimed he drove them to drink. The only orderly aspect of his otherwise untidy incumbency was that his subjects kept track of their consumption of liquor by removing a grain of wheat from a bottle every time they drew a flagon of rum from a cask.) Wheat production in Canada did not get under way on any appreciable scale until 1842, in what was then Canada West and is now Ontario. That year, David Fife, a Scotsman who had emigrated twenty years earlier from his birthplace at Kincardine, resolved to plant some hardy wheat at his new homestead in the township of Otenabee, in Peterborough County. Fife wrote to a friend in Glasgow and asked him to send over some seeds. The Glaswegian took a dockside stroll one evening and espied a few grains of wheat that had been spilled during the unloading of a ship. He had a hole in the lining of his tam-o'-shanter. He picked up the wheat, carried it off in his cap, and sent it to Fife, who duly planted it. Only five spikes ripened. A wandering cow had eaten two of them and was about to devour the other three when Fife's wife came running out of her kitchen, flapping her apron, and routed the invader. Thus was Red Fife wheat, destined in the years ahead to become the progenitor of many celebrated varieties, saved from death at birth.

One drawback to Red Fife was that it was susceptible to early frosts. Canadians wanted a wheat that embodied its laudable traits — it possessed exceptionally laudable milling and baking qualities — but would more rapidly mature in their often chilly climate. They began crossbreeding Red Fife with varieties from the Himalayas. One of the wheats they obtained from India was called Hard Red Calcutta. In 1892, that was crossed with Red Fife by Arthur and Charles Saunders, brother cerealists affiliated with the government's Central Experimental Farm, at Ottawa. (Their father, William Saunders, was a well-known breeder of currants, raspberries, and gooseberries.) An offshoot of that mating was a wheat called Marquis, whose yields proved to be agreeably higher than those achieved by Red Fife. Marquis was quickly embraced by the farmers of Manitoba and Saskatchewan, where wheat was already a major crop. Wheat made Winnipeg — wheat and the Canadian Pacific Railway that took it to market. The railroad had got there in 1886, and the

Winnipeg Grain Exchange had been established five years later. By 1915, a thousand freight cars were passing through Winnipeg every day, most of them stopping just long enough to be loaded with wheat. Earlier, James J. Hill, the swashbuckling proprietor, south of the border, of the Great Northern Railway, had offered a gold cup worth a thousand dollars for the best bushel of hard spring wheat produced in the United States. (Hill, the prosperity of whose rail line was inseparable from wheat, once predicted that because of the availability of United States grain China would eventually become a nation of bread eaters; he expected that his trains and the ships he also owned would handsomely benefit from that.) Canadians were miffed because Hill declared them ineligible for his competition, so in 1911 the Canadian Pacific announced that it would give a thousand dollars in gold for the best bushel of wheat produced anywhere in all of North America. A Saskatchewan man won that year with a bushel of Marquis; and for the next four years Marquis continued to reign triumphant. By then — in 1913 — the variety had moved south, and had caught on in the United States. "Farmers and also millers, bankers, and real-estate dealers have had their attention attracted to it," a United States Department of Agriculture bulletin reported. After just one year in residence in the United States, Marquis occupied five hundred thousand acres of cropland that had previously been given over to other wheats. It got to Minnesota in 1913, and four years later the annual value of the wheat grown in that one state alone increased by seven million dollars. Charles Saunders had produced just twenty-three pounds of Marquis seed in 1907. A decade later, the total crop of Marquis wheat in North America amounted to nearly 300 million bushels — a monumental resource without which it might have been far more difficult than it was for the Allies to wage the First World War.

Perhaps someone should have awarded a posthumous medal for heroism to Mrs. Fife.

Wheat and its hounding nemeses began to drift westward from the Atlantic Coast in 1783. In the 1830s, 60 percent of all United States wheat came from New York, Virginia, Pennsylvania, and Ohio. By the 1850s, Illinois, Indiana, and Wisconsin were in the van. By the 1870s, wheat was firmly entrenched in Kansas and Nebraska. The proliferating railroads of the country were instrumental. The Santa Fe, for example, had been granted three million acres of trackside land in Kansas. That rail line naturally wanted people to settle there and keep its train crews busy. It learned about some Mennonites who were living unhappily in the Ukraine. Because their religion forbade them to bear arms, they had left Prussia for Russia in 1786, on being promised an exemption from military service by Catherine the Great. But in 1870 Czar Alexander II had reneged. The resentful Mennonites were looking for a new haven. The Santa Fe sent an agent named Carl Schmidt — he would later become known as the Moses of the Mennonites — to Russia to accommodate them. He offered free transportation to Kansas for themselves and their belongings; he had a guarantee from the state of Kansas that it would never let them be conscripted. On August 16, 1874, thirty-four Mennonite families, 163 people in all, arrived at Marion County, Kansas, and on an eight-thousand-acre tract founded the town of Gnadenau. Their most precious possessions were some gold into which they had converted their savings and some earthen jars filled with seeds of a hard, red, drought-resistant winter wheat called Turkey Red.

Today, nearly three-quarters of all United States wheat is winter wheat, and Kansas derives more revenue from the production of wheat than any other state of the Union. Turkey

Red had much to do with that. It roosted high on the family tree of a later, much-prized, and widely-sown variety testimonially called Kanred. Another strain of wheat that was fancied in its day was called Kansas Mortgage Lifter. England had a wheat dubbed, in the same vein, Rentpayer. Breeders outdid themselves paying nomenclatural tribute to the wheats that prospered and that made them prosperous. Australia had a Triumph, Canada a Superlative, Italy a Miracle. (Germany, to be sure, had a Frankenstein.) Miracle was a name so alluring that early in the twentieth century, when patent medicines were in vogue, seed salesmen often appended it to wheats of questionable merit. One Miracle, purportedly discovered in Alaska, in 1904, by a farmer from Idaho, was glowingly advertised in seed catalogues as having the capacity to grow anywhere, under any conditions of soil or climate, and to increase its yields tenfold or more year after lucrative year. The Wheat Investigation office of the Department of Agriculture looked into that one, felt impelled to put out a warning against it, and got the postal authorities to issue a fraud order against its sale by mail; one public-spirited agronomist urged all farmers to "shun it as you would the smallpox."

Soon after the Department of Agriculture attained cabinet level, in 1862, it began sending emissaries abroad to seek out varieties of many of the food plants that came under its jurisdiction. In 1864, for instance, it dispatched an expedition to China to hunt for promising strains of sorghum. An important functionary of the department was its cerealist. One of them prominent at the end of the century was Mark Alfred Carleton, who was born in 1866 at Jerusalem, Ohio. Not long after joining the department in 1894, Carleton, one of whose self-determined missions was to find a rust-resistant winter wheat, betook himself to Kansas — where earlier he had studied and then taught agriculture at Kansas State Agricultural College — to visit the Mennonite community. His association with the Mennonites made him resolve to go to Russia and hunt varieties that might emulate their Turkey Red. Carleton prepared himself by learning Russian. In 1898, he persuaded his superiors in the department to send him to Russia. He came back with two fine wheat trophies — Kubanka and Kharkov — that eminently justified his time and trouble. For when a black-stem-rust blight savaged many American wheats in 1904, Kubanka, by that time rooted in four million acres of the Dakotas, and Kharkov, sprawled across twenty million acres of the Midwest, held their ground. Carleton's sturdy wheats may have prevented a lot of people from going hungry, but in the long run they did him precious little good. He got into a jam because of nonpayment of debts, lost his job, and, with no other apparent recourse, emigrated to Peru, where he died, in 1925, of malaria.

There can have been few Americans who had less in common — unless one counts their unfulfilled presidential aspirations — than Henry Agard Wallace and Douglas MacArthur. Yet they both had a hand in sparking "the Green Revolution," or that part of it, at any rate, involving the radical turnabout in the role of wheat in human affairs. Wallace was most celebrated, occupationally, as a pioneer in the development of hybrid corn. MacArthur was much celebrated, nonoccupationally, as an addict of corncob pipes. (When President Truman relieved the general of his command in Korea in the spring of 1951, a corncob-pipe company in Washington, Missouri, where the manufacture of that device began in 1872 and where a brisk-selling item was the "Mac," received a slew of orders from ruffled adherents of the general who wanted to send him the pipes as evidence of their unwavering loyalty. People who had seen MacArthur off-camera, though, had the strong impression that he preferred to smoke cigars.) MacArthur established bread in Japan at the start of the occupation over which he imperiously presided. Among the American specialists the supreme commander invited over there in 1946 was S. C. Salmon, an agronomist who hoped to help the Japanese bake more and better bread. The Japanese had long been renowned, of course, for their dwarf trees, or bonsai. They had also long been experimenting with the dwarfing of food plants. The shorter a stalk, the less likely it is to have its grains damaged from falling over — lodging — when buffeted by severe winds or hailstorms. Furthermore, dwarf wheats tend to be higher-tillering — that is, to have more stems. Back in 1873, Horace Capron, a former U.S. commissioner of agriculture (at a time when Agriculture was a subdivision of the Patent Office), had been invited to Tokyo as a consultant during the Meiji era, and had marveled that his hosts had bred wheat stalks down to a height of only twenty or twenty-five inches. "The Japanese farmers have brought the art of dwarfing to perfection," Capron had written home. In 1917, Japanese breeders had crossed a famous dwarf wheat called Daruma with a first-rate American variety, Glassy Fultz; and in 1925, they had crossed the offspring of that mating with the Mennonites' Turkey Red. Now, in 1946, Salmon, prowling around MacArthur's empire with an eye out for promising wheats, encountered a still more recent product of that lineage: a mid-thirties wheat called Norin 10. Salmon was impressed by it — its glittering ancestry alone made it a wheat to be reckoned with — and he brought some of it back to the United States. Soon Orville A. Vogel, a breeder at the Washington Agricultural Experiment Station, had some of it. Vogel crossed Norin 10 with a domestic winter wheat called Brevor and eventually came up with some new varieties that were appreciably shorter than most standard wheats — which pleased just about everybody in the wheat world except, perhaps, those traditionalists who were fond of long stalks because they used them to fashion wheat-straw images called corn dollies. (In bygone Russia, the last sheaf of a harvest was believed to embody the Corn Spirit. A woman in the vicinity would volunteer to feign giving birth to it, and it would be dressed in swaddling clothes and pampered until the next harvest. In very olde England, similarly, corn dollies, dressed in white and beribboned, would be taken to church on Sunday.)

So much for General MacArthur. Henry Wallace came into the picture in December 1940, when he was vice-president-elect. He went to Mexico, representing Franklin Roosevelt, for the inauguration of a new president. At the suggestion of the incoming minister of agriculture, Wallace traveled around the country, talking to farmers and inquiring about their cultural practices. He told his hosts that he hoped the United States would help Mexico establish a network of stations to do agricultural research. Back in Washington, he concluded that there was little chance of arousing congressional interest in such an undertaking: Congress had a war in Europe on its mind. So Wallace got in touch with Raymond Fosdick, the president of the Rockefeller Foundation, which had been active abroad, mostly in the area of public health, for a quarter of a century. In the fall of 1941, the foundation sent three American scientists to Mexico on a fact-finding trip: Richard Bradfield, an expert on soils; Elvin C. Stakman, who specialized in rusts and other fungi; and the corn breeder Paul C. Mangelsdorf. They agreed with Wallace that there was a great deal that should be done, and perhaps could be done, to ameliorate the lot of Mexican farmers and their crops. Not much happened for another couple of years, by which time J. George Harrar, a botanist and plant pathologist, had set up a program of agricultural research in Mexico for the Rockefeller Foundation. (From 1961 to 1971, he was its president.) What ultimately happened would have a profound impact on the production of wheat around the globe.

Enter Norman Borlaug. When Borlaug received word in the fall of 1970 that he had been awarded the Nobel Prize for his prowess in wheat breeding, he was up to his knees in a stand of Mexican wheat, as he had been for a good part of twenty-six previous sunbaked years. He was born on an Iowa farm, the son of Norwegian immigrants, on March 25, 1914. He was raised on johnnycake and wheat cake. He went to a one-room grade school and then to high school at Cresco, ten miles from the Minnesota border. The principal, David Bartelma, had been an alternate on the American wrestling team at the 1924 Olympics. Bartelma got Borlaug, who had already demonstrated a flair for baseball, into wrestling as well. The boy hoped to become a high-school science teacher and athletic coach, and planned to prepare for that at Iowa State Teachers' College, in Cedar Falls. He was persuaded by a Cresco alumnus to apply instead to the University of Minnesota. Baseball practice there conflicted with his forestry classes, so he concentrated extra-curricularly on wrestling. At the end of Borlaug's junior year, Bartelma became the Minnesota wrestling coach. He sent Borlaug and another protégé all over the state to put on wrestling exhibitions for PTAs and similarly influential groups; years later, after he won his Nobel, Borlaug was invited back to Minnesota and was gratified to learn that there were more high-school boys participating in wrestling in that state than in any other sport save basketball. He is probably the only Nobel laureate who while performing the feats that won him his accolade sometimes wore an Amateur Wrestling Hall of Fame cap. Normally a mild-mannered man, Borlaug once lost his temper and almost punched a classmate. He was testy because he had been on a rigorous diet, trying to lose ten pounds to make a weight limit. "I was starving," he said years afterward, "and I found out that a hungry man is worse than a hungry beast."

In graduate school, Borlaug specialized in plant pathology, and wrote his doctoral thesis on wilt resistance in flax. During several summer vacations, he had jobs with the U.S. Forest Service. (In later years, he taught part-time at Minnesota and Cornell. In 1983, he was appointed Distinguished Professor of International Agriculture at Texas A&M.) Just before Pearl Harbor, he went to work for the agricultural-chemicals division of du Pont, in Wilmington, Delaware. He was assigned to a microbiological laboratory, and was soon working on projects that got him a War Manpower Commission deferment from the draft — the purification of drinking water, the refinement of camouflage paints, the improvement of packaging for military field rations, and the development of DDT, which evolved from a louse powder that Russians had taken from captured German soldiers and had shared with their British and American allies. Borlaug has been a defender ever since of DDT and similar chemicals, with the proviso that they should be employed like medicine, in proper, supervised dosages. He likes to point out that while he had no strong objection to the banning of DDT in the United States, where malaria is rare, when it was banned in India, following worldwide protests against its use anywhere, the annual incidence of malaria rose from 250,000 to 7.5 million. In mid-1943, Borlaug met George Harrar at a scientific conclave in Philadelphia. Harrar invited him to join the agricultural program that the Rockefeller Foundation was launching in Mexico. Borlaug was interested, although there were drawbacks. He didn't know a word of Spanish, for one thing. In any event, the War Manpower Commission wouldn't release him from du Pont until mid-1944. By then, Borlaug was ready to move on. He wasn't being paid much, and he had concluded that a microbiologist who had never studied chemistry didn't have much of a future there. In October 1944, he went to Mexico, and for the next thirty-nine years that would be his home.

For his first six months in Mexico, Borlaug worked mostly on the prevention of diseases. Then he took charge of wheat. There hadn't been much change in the varieties of wheat grown in Mexico — for the most part, tall, weak-stemmed ones — since the Spanish introduced the plant in the sixteenth century. Mexico had two wheat research stations of a sort — a high-altitude one at Chapingo, just outside Mexico City, and a lower-altitude one, a thousand miles to the northwest, at Ciudad Obregón, in the state of Sonora. For three straight years before Borlaug arrived, there had been bad epidemics of stem rust. He wanted to breed some rust-resistant wheats, and to breed them fast. He figured that if he didn't succeed, he'd be deported. (Today, there is a street named after him in Obregón.) It usually takes ten years or more to produce and test a new variety of wheat before it can be offered with any assurance to farmers. To speed up his breeding program and produce two generations of plants a year instead of the conventional one, Borlaug grew wheat at Obregón from November to April, and at Chapingo from May to October. It was not easy at first. Both research stations were ill equipped. Worse yet, the farmers he tried to work with were leery of aliens preaching a foreign gospel. "For a while, hardly any of them would even talk to me," Borlaug recalled years later. For a while, too, lacking the kinds of machinery that United States farmers took for granted, Borlaug would till the fields he cultivated literally hitched to a plow. By 1948, he had developed five promising varieties, but the first time he held a field day to demonstrate them to local farmers, only twenty-five people showed up. (The following year, there were seventy-five; after that, hundreds.) He might have been even more discouraged than he was had it not been for the heartening presence on the Mexican scene of John S. Niederhauser, who was running a potato program for the Rockefeller Foundation. Niederhauser eventually became known throughout Mexico as Mr. Potato. Borlaug was Mr. Wheat. He was also Mr. Kid Baseball. In what spare time he had, with Niederhauser as an enthusiastic collaborator, he had introduced Little League baseball to the country. A team that Borlaug coached for about ten years, Las Aguilas, or "the Eagles," won his first important prize — a national championship. When he was not wearing his Wrestling Hall of Fame cap at work, he sported an Aguilas one, with a big *A* on it.

The wheats that Borlaug bred in those first four years were agreeably rust-resistant, but they were aggravatingly tall, and tended to lodge. He concluded that he would have to get some dwarfing genes into his plants. In 1953, he heard about the short-stemmed wheat that Orville Vogel — using the Norin 10 genes he'd received from MacArthur's Japan — had bred in Washington. Vogel sent Borlaug some seed. It was a winter wheat, however, and Borlaug wanted to implant its dwarfing gene into spring wheats, which do better in warm-weather climates. He embarked on another patient round of breeding. It was always a time-consuming, backaching process. Wheat flowers are bisexual. One would sit out in the blazing sun day after day and with tweezers carefully remove the male anthers from each floret (a single spike of wheat may have fifty florets), so they couldn't produce pollen. Then one would slip a paper jacket over the emasculated spikes, so their pistils, the female organs, couldn't be accidentally pollinated by any drifting pollen before one was ready to dust them with pollen of one's own choice. "If you're a plant breeder, you pay your dues," the geneticist Garrison Wilkes, who has paid his several times over with corn, once told an acquaintance. "There's a saying that any plant breeder has to be dumb, because it doesn't take much in the way of brains to sit on a stool in the sun for hours on end and pollinate a few hundred, or a few thousand, plants. But it sure does take a cool hand." Borlaug, who while walking through an experimental wheat field has much the air of a dog-show judge appraising a lineup of nearly identical purebreds, has been accused now and then of talking to his plants. He would tell his assistants — they were known as Borlaug's Apostles — that that was a false charge, that actually the plants were talking to *him*. "But you have to listen to them with your eyes," he would add. While he may not actually converse *with* his plants, when talking about them he often endows them with human characteristics. He refers to their traits, for instance, as "personalities," and he has described the sound of wind-stirred beards of wheat rubbing against each other as "a sweet whispering music."

Different wheats fare differently in different areas. A variety that may do well in one part of South Dakota may be ill suited to another in that very same state. Borlaug was never especially concerned about improving varieties for any part of the United States, or for Canada (though some of his resistant varieties helped alleviate an outbreak of stem rust in those countries in the mid-1950s), or Australia, or any other developed nation. They usually had plenty of wheat, far more than they could use themselves, and their inhabitants were, by and large, adequately nourished. Mexico was his immediate concern, and beyond that, the rest of the developing world, where to so many hundreds of millions of people food meant food plants and little else. (A United States ambassador to Bangladesh said not long ago that for the nearly 100 million inhabitants of that hard-pressed country "the availability of cereals becomes a life and death matter.") By 1957, even before dwarfing genes had come into play, Mexico had achieved self-sufficiency in wheat. By the early 1970s, however, it was importing one-fifth of the wheat it needed; its farmers had diverted some land to the production of export crops — onions, cucumbers, asparagus, strawberries, watermelons — that they could profitably sell abroad. But since 1974, wheat acreage has been increasing. It peaked in 1982 at 2.2 million acres, while over the past two decades wheat consumption has about tripled.

In 1962, after still more full-throttle crossbreeding, Borlaug had the first of what were to be many spring wheats incorporating the dwarfing genes. Word spread to countries that were desperate for more wheat — notable among them India. Borlaug had already been there. After a 1960 visit, he had persuaded the Rockefeller Foundation to underwrite the travel to Mexico of several dozen young foreign wheat scientists. Borlaug had been distressed, on meeting them abroad, to perceive how few of them, unlike him, came from farm families. Their farms were laboratories. "To this day," he would reflect two decades later, "the curse of the developing nations is that if you have a chance for a higher education you don't want to have anything to do with agriculture." He went back to India, at the invitation of its government, in 1963. A few, a very few, of his new wheats had by then been planted in a New Delhi nursery by M. S. Swaminathan, who was then the head botanist of the Indian Agricultural Research Institute. Not until 1965, however, when India purchased 250 tons of Mexican semidwarf wheat seed, and Pakistan 350 tons, did the dwarfs have much impact on that region. (A number of influential Pakistani civil servants maintained that no chapatties were worth eating unless they were baked from flour milled from home-bred white wheat. A higher government official stifled their complaints by making them take a taste test, blindfolded; they couldn't tell a white domestic chapatti from the imported red vintage.) In 1966, the Indian government decided to import 18,000 tons of the seed from Mexico. Two varieties of wheat that evolved from that hefty shipment, called Sonalika and Kalyan Sona, became great favorites in India and also in Pakistan, Nepal, and Bangladesh. They thrived, unprecedentedly long for any single lines, from 1967 to 1979; and then a new race of leaf rust caught up with them and began to render them obsolete. Borlaug had gone back to India once again in 1967, and Swaminathan had invited him to a lunch at a tractor factory. "If you get this new wheat established," Borlaug told the assemblage, "you'll get so many tractor orders you'll never catch up." Over the next fifteen years, wheat production in India tripled. And Borlaug personally was invested with saving graces. In a 1969 citation accompanying the conferring on him of an honorary degree by the University of Punjab, his name was said to be a household word worldwide, and he was likened to a prophet sent to earth by heaven to uplift mankind.

By 1968, the progress that had been made in wheat breeding in Mexico and, more or less concurrently, in rice breeding in the Philippines, had led to the phrase "the Green Revolution."

The actual words were first uttered that March by William S. Gaud, the director of the U.S. Agency for International Development. Today, 44 percent of all wheatland on earth is given over to short-stemmed, high-yielding, disease-resistant varieties that were undreamed of before the Second World War. In Bangladesh, where the percentage was 96 in 1981, the production of wheat skyrocketed from 89,000 tons to 1.1 million tons in eight years. "The state of Sonora," Borlaug said in 1983, "has had a greater influence on food production than any other agricultural research station on the surface of the earth."

The much trumpeted Green Revolution had its critics, and deservedly so. The new varieties could not merely be shoved into the ground and expected to take off from there unaided. They often required irrigation, fertilizers, herbicides, and pesticides that were beyond the reach and the purse of many small farmers. "There are no miracle cereals," one plant physiologist declared, "except in the headlines." The director general of the FAO in 1971, Addeke H. Boerma, said soberingly that year that the Green Revolution "does not yet have enough of the general economic and social thrust behind it which we have all along said would be necessary and without which it will fail in its broader objectives for bettering standards of life in the developing countries." By 1974, only six years after the Green Revolution had been defined and acclaimed, its verdancy had begun to pale. Borlaug, who in India had seen small country farmers stand in line for two days vainly hoping to obtain enough petrol to slake their irrigation pumps, was not surprised. "There was no green revolution," he said. "There was only a peaceful struggle to gain the respect of farmers. The seed alone cannot revolutionize things, without technological and cultural change."

When Borlaug's wife came out to the wheat field near

Obregón, on October 21, 1970, to tell him she'd just had a phone call to the effect that he'd been awarded the Nobel — he was the first agricultural scientist ever to receive it — he wouldn't believe her, and he remained where he was, skeptical, until a television crew descended upon him. (When a cameraman trampled a wheat plant Borlaug had been meticulously harvesting, the fledgling laureate flared up in anger he hadn't exhibited since he near-starved himself as a college wrestler.) His Nobel citation hailed him as a man who, "through his work in the laboratory and in the wheat fields, has helped to create a new food situation in the world, and who has turned pessimism into optimism in our dramatic race between the population explosion and the production of food." Borlaug, who was then fifty-six, did not entirely share that optimism. He believed that what he and his cohorts might have brought about by increasing wheat production was simply to delay a nutrition crisis by perhaps thirty years. He was afraid of what he likes to call "the population monster," and had no confidence that food was keeping pace with fecundity. He once declined an invitation to the Vatican because he disagreed with the papal views on birth control. "Food is the moral right of all who are born into this world," Borlaug has declared, and he has frequently expressed his regrets that so many people are born into it who have preciously little chance of even aspiring to that human right. He likes to point out that when he got to Mexico, in 1944, its population was twenty-one million, and that in forty years the figure had come close to seventy-eight million. "No government can do a decent job of providing the basic necessities with that kind of growth," he said in 1983. The year before, in a speech at the World Bank entitled "Feeding Mankind in the 1980's," Borlaug had said: "I believe that there can be no lasting solution to the world food-hunger-poverty problem until a more reasonable balance is struck between food production and human population growth. The efforts of those on the food production front are, at best, a holding operation which can permit others on the demographic, educational, medical, family-planning, and political fronts to launch an effective and humane attack to tame the population monster. . . . I am deeply concerned that we are taking mankind to the brink of disaster in hopes that a scientific miracle will save the day. . . . If this unrelentless growth in human numbers goes on unabated, *Homo sapiens* will no doubt end up as an endangered species itself."

Borlaug has been no less outspoken on the subject of agricultural chemicals, for which he has had an unabashed affinity ever since his stint at du Pont. "As a Nobel laureate," one high-placed agriculturist at the World Bank remarked not long ago, "Norman's allowed to say things that some of us can't." Not only has Borlaug criticized "irresponsible environmentalists" for having banned the DDT he helped perfect, but he has ruffled other feathers:

There are some organic gardening enthusiasts who insist that the wide use of organic fertilizers could satisfy all our fertilizer needs. It is true that organic manures are very effective for growing six beautiful high-yielding tomato plants, six lovely rose bushes, or a small vegetable garden in one's back yard. But it certainly doesn't follow that the same procedure can be effective for producing the food needed to feed 4.3 billion people in a land-hungry world. The amount of composted organic animal manure . . . that would be needed to produce the 47 million metric nutrient tons of chemical nitrogen used in 1978 would be about 3.2 billion tons — quite a dung heap and quite an aroma — were it available. This volume of organic material is equal to twice the weight of current world cereal grain production and would require a 2.9-fold increase in the world animal population. . . .

The environmental movement, undoubtedly well-intentioned but badly informed, is fostered, controlled, and popularized by relatively small, well-organized groups of elitist environmentalists and neo-ecologists. They play on the public's fear by employing propaganda campaigns to convey the idea that civilization is on the verge of being poisoned out of existence by the reckless and unnecessary use of agricultural chemicals. The leaders of this campaign seem to imply that the world can, and should, go back to producing its food with pre-World War II technology. . . . It is my belief that much of the confusion, misunderstanding, and litigation that has evolved in the past over the use of chemicals in agricultural production could have been avoided if suitable educational programs had been developed to explain to the non-rural public the complexities and difficulties of protecting our crops, together with an explanation of the precautions that are taken to protect human health and safeguard non-target wildlife species.

. . .We should not be misled that high yields, the key to feeding mankind in the years ahead, are possible without adequate plant nutrition. When I am asked, which happens quite often, whether good plant breeders will soon succeed in developing varieties which do not require fertilizer to produce high grain yields, my reply is that this will occur about six months after we have succeeded in producing a race of man that needs no food to grow strong bodies, maintain health, work effectively, and enjoy life.

When I see the world's continuing profligate misuse of gas, one of the basic raw materials for the production of nitrogenous fertilizers that are so essential for restoring fertility to nutrient-deficient, low-yielding soils, I lose my patience with those who ask plant breeders to perform miracles.

I am optimistic that, from a scientific point of view, we have the knowledge to double the current level of the world food production in the next forty to sixty years. To achieve these production increases and to distribute the food equitably will require the sustained and focussed support of governments and international development assistance agencies. The task will not, and cannot, be achieved without massive new investments in the agricultural sectors of the developing countries, particularly in the areas of water resource development and fertilizer production.

Borlaug — who by 1983 was getting slightly deaf and said that pleased him; it meant he couldn't hear some of the aspersions of environmentalists who buzzed around him like Hessian flies — concluded that declamation with a quotation from the nutritional savant Jean Mayer (the president of Tufts) and his historian son André:

Few scientists think of agriculture as the chief, or the model, science. Many, indeed, do not consider it a science at all. Yet, it was the first science — the mother of science; it remains the science which makes human life possible; and it may well be that before the century is over, the success or failure of science as a whole will be judged by the success or failure of agriculture.

In 1966, the Rockefeller Foundation's agricultural operations in Mexico evolved into the International Center for the Improvement of Maize and Wheat — known acronymically, from its name in Spanish, as CIMMYT. Borlaug became director of CIMMYT's wheat program. He had no further need to hitch himself to plows. CIMMYT, supported by both foundations and governments, soon had at its beck just about all the machinery and laboratory equipment that any breeder could ask for. (It still engages field hands, though, whose main duty is to patrol growing areas and scare off intruding birds by snapping whips through the air.) Among CIMMYT's nearly seven hundred employees nowadays is a core staff of eighty scientists, most of them of the Ph.D. stripe: pathologists, taxonomists, cytogeneticists, biochemists, agronomists, economists, entomologists, et al. (One of its entomologists developed a gadget to infest corn plants with the larvae of the fall armyworm. The device resembled a bazooka and was dubbed "bazooka." A visiting Turkish insect man admired it and asked to have some replicas sent to him at home. A crate stenciled "BAZOOKAS" was soon dispatched, and when it arrived there was a flurry of excitement at Customs.) CIMMYT has experimental growing fields at five widely scattered Mexican locations, its own flour mill, and its own test kitchens, where spaghetti makers and tortilla bakers engage in their own arcane research. It has a working relationship with twenty-five hundred agricultural scientists in other countries, as ideologically disparate as West Germany and Vietnam; on its own, it conducts regional programs in Chile, Ecuador, Kenya, Portugal, Syria, Pakistan, and Thailand. CIMMYT has furnished wheat germ plasm to just about every place except Albania and Mongolia. About 50 percent of all the wheat currently grown in the developing nations of the world is descended from CIMMYT stock. CIMMYT wheats got to Communist China via Pakistan and via capitalistic intermediaries in 1967, long before Henry Kissinger was admitted. One of the middlemen was Haldore Hanson, who as a journalist had had a long acquaintance with Mao Zedong and who in 1972 became CIMMYT's first director general. Another was Robert D. Havener, a dwarf-plant specialist then working in Pakistan for the Ford Foundation; he succeeded Hanson at CIMMYT in 1978 and has presided over it ever since.

The increase in value of the wheat crop of India alone accruing from CIMMYT inputs has been calculated at five billion dollars a year. Alluding to CIMMYT's own annual budget of twenty million dollars, an editorial in the April 16, 1982, issue of *Science* said, "Seldom has so modest a sum produced such significant results." As a safeguard against the loss of varieties of wheat that, once extinct, could never be resurrected, CIMMYT maintains and carefully nurtures a germ-plasm bank of some forty-five thousand cultivars. From that bulging repository, in 1983, it doled out to grateful supplicants almost nine tons of wheat in ten-gram packets. The center also hoards thirteen thousand varieties of corn, and sends off twenty-kernel packets at the rate of about fifty thousand a week; that entails the examination, by hand and eye, of more than two hundred thousand separate kernels every day.

Borlaug stepped aside as head of the CIMMYT wheat program in 1979, although he remained very prominently on the Mexican scene in an elder-statesman role, and spent just about as much time communing with plants as he ever had. "I used to be able to fly into New Delhi at three in the morning and be out in the fields at six," he said when he was sixty-nine, "but I'm afraid I've slowed down a little." His wheat job was eventually filled by a fugitive from private industry, Byrd C. Curtis, a onetime paratrooper who'd been in charge of wheat breeding for Cargill, Incorporated, the Minneapolis-based grain-trading multinational. One of Borlaug's contemporary preoccupations is high-protein corn; another is the first cereal ever made not by nature but by man: triticale. It is a cross of wheat *(Triticum)* and rye *(Secale)*. Triticale was invented in Scotland in 1875, and some research on the crossbreed was conducted before the end of the nineteenth century in Russia and Germany. Few people gave it more than sporadic attention until some Canadians began working on it in 1954. Borlaug first encountered it at

Winnipeg in 1958, and he began growing it in Mexico in 1962. Triticale, which combines wheat's prodigious yields with the drought- and disease-resistant traits inherent in rye, can be more auspiciously grown than wheat on acid, impoverished soils. But it cannot reproduce itself any more than a mule can. Rye can fertilize wheat; triticale itself, so far at least, is sterile. Also, while triticale has a slightly higher protein content than wheat, it is weak in gluten — good for chapatties and tortillas, accordingly, poor for leavened bread. Nonetheless, when Canada's International Development Research Centre embarked on intensive research into triticale in 1971, it acclaimed the plant as a "a new food crop, the agronomic characteristics and nutritional value of which will be superior not only to those of either of its parents, but to all other cereal grains, particularly those grown in food-deficient areas of the world where climatic conditions are often unfavorable for cereal grain production." The encomium went on: "It is anticipated that triticale will provide a valuable new source of protein and essential nutrients for many people of the developing world." Triticale is now grown on a million acres in a dozen countries, but it has not yet fulfilled that glowing promise. Its very name may be a hindrance; "triticale" sounds like something the doctor declined to order. Plant geneticists, however, are patient if nothing else. "There's plenty of time for triticale to make its mark," Byrd Curtis said in 1983. "After all, we've only been looking at it seriously for about a quarter of a century, and it took wheat bread eight to ten thousand years to get to where it is today."

After Anthony Trollope visited the United States in 1861, he wrote in *North America* that "in the corn lands of Michigan, and amid the bluffs of Wisconsin, and on the high table plains of Minnesota, and the prairies of Illinois, God prepared the food for the increasing millions of the Eastern world as also for the coming millions of the Western." In Chicago, Trollope said he saw wheat "running in the rivers." That was thirteen years after the establishment of the Chicago Board of Trade, often called The Pit, where commodities — wheat a swollen stream among them — have been spiritedly bargained over ever since. Ships laden with wheat used to ply the seas toward Europe in what were called grain races — from Adelaide, South Australia, around Cape Horn; from Odessa, on the Black Sea, through the Mediterranean — to the nourishment of millions and to the enrichment, by millions of dollars, of their transporters. Watery metaphors bobbed in their wake. The novelist Frank Norris was inspired almost to the point of breathlessness by Chicago's Board of Trade. He wrote in *The Pit* that wheat, "like a tidal wave, was rising, rising. Almighty, blood-brother to the earthquake, coeval with the volcano and the whirlwind, that gigantic world force, that colossal billow, Nourisher of the Nations. . . ." In *The Octopus,* Norris disposed of a villainous character by having him buried alive — drowned, as it were — in an avalanche of wheat.

The eleventh chapter of Proverbs has it that "he that withholdeth corn [meaning wheat or barley], the people shall curse him: but blessing shall be upon the head of him that selleth it." Though to people dealing in commodity futures it is simply another way of earning — rather, making — a living, trading in grains has for centuries figured importantly in commerce. Men and women can get by, however, without most of the other goods that are bartered or sold. They cannot survive without their staple foods. In Greece, twenty-four hundred or so years ago, there were special laws governing the grain trade, and special magistrates to enforce them. Of all the magistrates in office, only those responsible for grains were liable to execution for dereliction of duty. A similarly grim lot awaited merchants who exceeded the quotas on wheat imports that the state decreed. In more modern times, numerous attempts have been made to bring order to the grain business, which the vagaries of nature — a drought here, a flood there — can render highly speculative, and lucrative. (Such giant trading octopuses as Cargill, Continental, and Louis Dreyfus are almost in a class with the big oil companies.) In 1930, the League of Nations appointed a committee to look into "Agriculture as a World Problem." Partly as a result of that inquiry, twenty-two countries convened in London in 1933 and signed an International Wheat Agreement, which among other things established export quotas for the then leading sellers: 200 million bushels a year for Canada, 110 million for Argentina, 105 million for Australia, 47 million for the United States. (The United States hung back in fourth place until after the Second World War. Since then, it has forged into first; it now exports 45 percent of all the wheat and wheat flour in international trade — a $7-billion slice of the business.) But in 1934 Argentina had a record harvest, and not enough facilities to store it all, and it exported 30 million bushels more than its stipulated share; by 1935, the short-lived agreement was null and void. A subsequent one was ratified in Washington, in 1948, by thirty-six countries. "It provides for maintaining a high level in world wheat trade and consumption," the U.S. undersecretary of agriculture declared. "Importing countries are assured of ample supplies at fair prices. And the farmers of exporting countries are assured of markets at fair prices. No more practical and concrete action could be taken towards early and lasting improvement of the basic world food problem." (The Soviet Union was not a signatory. It shies away from participation in such group enterprises; it has never, for instance, joined the FAO.) The food problem continued, notwithstanding, to vex the world.

When grain yields in South Africa fell off drastically in 1982, the chairman of its Wheat Board said he wasn't sure that that republic could afford to import what it needed to meet demand, and he added, "The last time it had to be done, there was only one country with wheat to export. If they decided not to export to us, we could find ourselves in a serious situation." (There are many parts of the globe, of course, in which it is believed that the situation in South Africa is always serious.) Nowadays, about 100 million tons of wheat figures in foreign trade each year; 90 percent of that is exported by a few developed nations; and it is all imported — at great strain to purchasers' exchequers — by the developing world. Wheat can be and is used by one country to punish, or seek to punish, another: viz., the curtailment in recent years of American sales to Russia after it invaded Afghanistan, and to Iran after the hostage crisis. (When the United States tried to put the Soviet Union in its place in 1980, Argentina blithely sold the Russians some 75 to 80 percent of its grain crop.) Embargoes may not always have their intended effect, but, as the World Food Institute at Iowa State University observed in 1982, "they continue to be used for diplomatic communication." At just about the same time that an American diplomat was revealing, in the spring of 1981, that the United States had demonstrated its distaste for the government of Nicaragua by refusing to extend it any more credit to buy American wheat, the Soviet Union was announcing an agreement to ship 20,000 tons of wheat to Nicaragua.

The practice of selling American wheat and other agricultural products to the Soviet Union — many midwestern farmers who are otherwise hard-line anti-Communists are among its heartiest advocates — is relatively recent. (In the spring of 1983, the National Corn Growers Association let President Reagan know that unless he endorsed a then pending grain agreement with Russia he would risk losing the farm vote. That bloc had dwindled between 1920 and 1980 from just over 30 percent of the population to just over 2.5 percent, but it was still to be reckoned with: Had it not, four years earlier, been garnishing its pickups with blunt bumper-stickers that read "Cheaper crude or no more food"?) Until the First World War, Russia itself was a substantial wheat exporter. In 1847, sixteen million bushels left Odessa docks. The peasant farmers of imperial Russia could not have been enthusiastic about that sort of commerce, but they had no say in the matter. During a famine there that began in 1891, some twenty million of them had to subsist on "hunger bread" — an unappetizing blend of rye, bark, chopped straw, sand, and weeds; it gave them, not surprisingly, terrible stomachaches. The United States compassionately rushed over a shipload of unadulterated flour. Throughout it all, the czarist regime, apparently untroubled by portents of revolution, continued to export wheat. It was available for purchase at home, to be sure, but the masses couldn't afford it, and nobody was giving any of it away. After the Revolution, peasants long deprived of grain began eating it so voraciously that the residents of Russian cities suffered themselves from a sharp reduction in their customary allotments.

On the eve of the ratification of the 1948 wheat agreement, another Department of Agriculture functionary warned, "Non-agreement points toward the possibility of an eventual world war in wheat, the consequences of which may have a far-reaching effect on the national and political economy of nations." The United States and the Soviet Union have been warily, and praiseworthily, engaged in grain-trade negotiations ever since. It has not been only in its relations with Russia that American foreign policy has been geared to grains. In 1981, when the administration deemed it highly desirable to maintain amity with Egypt, of $800 million earmarked by the United States for long-term, low-interest loans to countries the world over for agricultural purposes, $275 million was allocated to Egypt alone. The following year, the American ambassador to Bangladesh said, quite accurately, that "food is absolutely fundamental to stability in Bangladesh"; and the envoy added that "therefore it is directly tied in to our foreign policy objectives." Wheat has always been one of the most fundamental of foods, and no political leader, of whatever ideological bent, can afford to slight it. Lenin, who had little use for the monetary benchmarks of capitalism, once grandly dismissed them all by stating, "Grain is the currency of currencies." And Socrates, when the world was far smaller and far less complicated, but every bit as dependent on a few frail staple food plants as it is today, had presciently delivered himself of the maxim that "no man qualifies as a statesman who is entirely ignorant of the problems of wheat."

IV

RICE
Everybody's Business

Planting rice is never fun;
Bent from morn till set of sun;
Cannot stand and cannot sit;
Cannot rest for a little bit.

— from an old Filipino song

AT A GATHERING of plant scientists in Washington in the fall of 1982, Dr. Amir Muhammed, the chairman of the Agricultural Research Council of Pakistan, recounted an incident that had occurred during a meeting of his country's cabinet in 1978. Pakistan's production of wheat was then running at a rate of 10 million tons — $2-billion worth — annually. But that year rust, a fungus that has been ravaging wheat just about ever since human beings started keeping records, had wiped out 2.5 million tons of that vital Pakistani crop in three weeks. Food plants, which are infrequently discussed at high-level government conclaves, made the agenda. Dr. Muhammed said that urgent steps were needed to stop rust before it overran the nation. A military man proffered a solution: Ban the use of metal fencing near wheat fields. It took Dr. Muhammed half an hour, he told his Washington confreres, to make everyone understand what kind of rust he was talking about. Then the finance minister, who the previous year had turned down a recommendation to spend $100,000 on rust-resistant wheat seed, said he guessed he could come up with $5 million to save the next year's crop. "It's only when a disaster hits that people think of money for agriculture," Dr. Muhammed said.

Not all national leaders are indifferent, or obtuse. The late prime minister Indira Gandhi of India, where about 80 percent of the population devotes most of its waking hours to the sowing, cultivating, harvesting, and processing of food plants, observed at a November 1981 conference of the FAO that for the price of a single intercontinental ballistic missile it would be possible to "plant two hundred million trees, irrigate one million hectares, feed fifty million malnourished children in developing countries, buy a million tons of fertilizer, erect a million small biogas plants, build sixty-five thousand health-care centers or three hundred and forty thousand primary schools." Her concept was not entirely new. Back in 1898, Sir William Crookes, the outspoken president of the British Association for the Advancement of Science, had said, "We eagerly spend millions to protect our coasts and commerce; and millions more on ships, explosives, guns, and men; but we omit to take necessary precautions to supply ourselves with the very first and supremely important munition of war — food." He added, concerned about fertilizers, that "the nitrogen which with a light heart we liberate in a battleship broadside has taken millions of minute organisms patiently working for centuries to win from the atmosphere." Five months after Mrs. Gandhi's own broadside, the director general of the FAO, Edouard Saouma, remarked that the total gross national product of fifty-three developing countries of the world amounted to less than the cost of one nuclear aircraft carrier. The FAO's bimonthly magazine, *Ceres,* had its own variation on that theme.

It put the price of a nuclear submarine at $1.7 billion. Then it translated various statistics into Submarine Units — SMUs. The sum of all the rice imported by all of Asia in 1977 — $1.991 billion — came to 1.17 SMUs. The sum of all the wheat imported by all of Africa the same year — $1.676 billion — came, it said, to .98 SMUs. The FAO's accumulated budget for thirty-four years — $1.011 billion — equaled .59 SMUs. All the money spent on international agricultural research from 1960 to 1980 — $.629 billion — came to .37 SMUs — slightly more than one-third the cost of one submarine.

Sir William had also told his association, "It is through the laboratory that starvation may ultimately be turned into plenty." Not all agricultural scientists believe they can turn the trick alone. Nature and the farmers who must cope with its capriciousness will probably always be leading protagonists in the struggle. ("The real experts are those millions of human beings who have inherited green fingers down the centuries," an article in the *Economist* stated in 1954.) Few scientists would disagree, though, that far too little has been and is being spent on agricultural research. Worldwide, only $5 billion is presently allocated to that specific end — a mere 3 percent of all the funds devoted to research in general. A message from President Reagan to a National Wheat Research Conference at the Department of Agriculture's Beltsville, Maryland, station in October 1982 said that "we are dedicated to basic agricultural research"; but the $460 million committed to that research by the department — that is, about one-third of 1 percent of the proceeds generated by American agriculture — comes to a mere 7 percent of the funds set aside for military research, of the president's dedication to which he probably knew the conferees were already aware. (Part of that agricultural-research expenditure had a quasi-military purpose: to study the decontamination of food, water, land, and air after a nuclear war and the possibility of breeding plants resistant to radioactivity. Whether or not radioactivity-resistant humans could themselves be bred was not one of the stated goals.) Still, however comparatively trifling may be the American outlay for agricultural research — it was enhanced, late in 1984, by the creation of a new and largely Rockefeller-funded group called the Winrock International Institute for Agricultural Development — the situation is a lot better than it was not so long ago. Although land grant colleges came into being in 1862, the year of the establishment of the Department of Agriculture, it was not until 1887 that they began to engage in any research; and not for another twenty-five years after that did the federal government do much about conveying the results of that research to the farmers who could best profit from it. Up to the twentieth century, hardly any consequential agricultural research was conducted in Asia, Africa, or Latin America. Today, the developing countries of those continents budget about $1 billion a year among them for that purpose; but much of the money is spent, as research money generally was in the colonial era, for the furtherance not of subsistence crops but of export crops.

"CGIAR" is an awkward, unpronounceable acronym, but that may be of little importance, because it is rarely used in headlines. If it were, it would probably be taken for a typographical error, or perhaps the initials of an anti-tobacco lobby. To the relatively few people, however, who worry, day in and day out, about how most of the other people on earth are ever going to have enough to eat, CGIAR is an institution of no mean significance, and so are its scarcely more identifiable affiliates: IRRI, CIMMYT, CIAT, IITA, CIP, ICRISAT, ILRAD, ILCA, ICARDA, IFPRI, WARDA, IBPGR, and ISNAR.

"CGIAR" stands for "Consultative Group on International Agricultural Research." The group was formed in 1971, largely at the instigation of the Rockefeller Foundation, the Ford Foundation, the World Bank, and the United Nations Development Program. From its headquarters in Washington, its modest secretariat of nine coordinates and supports the activities — most of these aimed squarely at enhancing the production and quality of food in the Third World — of the International Rice Research Institute (in the Philippines), the International Center for the Improvement of Maize and Wheat (in Mexico), International Center for Tropical Agriculture (in Colombia), the International Institute of Tropical Agriculture (in Nigeria), the International Potato Center (in Peru), the International Crops Research Institute for the Semi-Arid Tropics (in India), the International Laboratory for Research on Animal Diseases (in Kenya), the International Center for Agricultural Research in the Dry Areas (in Syria), the International Food Policy Research Institute (in the United States), the West Africa Rice Development Association (in Liberia), the International Board for Plant Genetic Resources (in Italy), and the International Service for National Agricultural Research (in the Netherlands). This widely extended family spends about $180 million a year — or .11 SMUs. CGIAR's funds — one-quarter of them from the United States — are almost entirely contributed by a few industrial nations and even fewer foundations. The Soviet Union and its allies, though they have sent trainees to CGIAR's centers and have availed themselves of their considerable outflow of technical literature and assiduously bred germ plasm, have never yet chipped in. "We've sent the Russians a couple of solicitation letters," one high CGIAR official said in 1982, "but they haven't answered." Although China did come into the fold in the fall of 1983, some Communists appear to regard the scattered organizations under CGIAR's umbrella as part of a capitalistic conspiracy to take over the Third World, when in fact it is exactly to the woes of that world that the centers have chiefly been addressing themselves since their inception. Norman Borlaug said not long ago, "A big difference between the international centers and research laboratories in the United States is that — with the usual exceptions — the latter operate essentially for the profit of a few and the former for the survival of the many." It is hard to calculate such matters precisely, but knowledgeable folk in the food world have maintained that the efforts of the centers have increased global production of food by enough to sustain 300 million people. Much of this increment can be attributed to the high-yielding wheats and rices developed in the mid-1960s at two centers that subsequently were embraced by CGIAR — CIMMYT, in Mexico, and IRRI, in the Philippines. Together their breakthroughs in plant breeding constituted the Green Revolution. According to M. S. Swaminathan, the director general of IRRI since 1981, CGIAR is "the most meaningful affirming flame shining in our spaceship world today."

You earn your bread — wheat breads, mainly — and if you're lucky you become a breadwinner. You never become a sorghum- or millet- or potato- or cassava-winner, let alone a rice-winner. Asians familiar with the English language must find this terminology amusing. For there are far more people utterly dependent on rice — of all the plants, the only one consumed almost exclusively by humans — than on any other food plant; and unless unforeseeable changes occur in the breeding patterns of both plants and human beings, that is unlikely to change. In a booklet put out by the FAO under the title *Rice: Grain of Life,* the grain was acclaimed as "the most important single food-stuff today." Rice — *Oryza sativa* — is the staff of life for, according to another FAO publication, "approximately half the human race"; there are over a billion men and women who do very little throughout their lives except to try to grow enough of it to keep on living. Among cereals, rice is doubly unique: it is the only one that is cooked and eaten as a whole grain, and it is the only one that grows under water. The oxygen its submerged roots need to thrive is drawn from the air by its upthrust leaves and passed along downward. Rice can grow just about anywhere — in Malaysian swamps, in Kashmir hills, in melting snow. There are only seven countries on earth with more than 100 million inhabitants, and in five of these — China, India, Indonesia, Japan, and Bangladesh — rice is indispensable. Their residents get 70 to 80 percent of all their calories from rice. One-quarter of the entire caloric intake of the human race is furnished by rice — 505 calories a day, the average works out, for everyone on earth. (Wheat, although it occupies more land than does rice, is still, at 465 calories, only the runner-up.) In Asia, where 92 percent of all rice is grown across a swath that stretches from Japan to West Pakistan, 320 million acres are given over to this one lush green crop. The cultivation of rice — the planting, the transplanting, the weeding, the reaping, the threshing — is still largely done by hand, perhaps assisted by a carabao with a small boy on its back. It takes a thousand man- or woman-hours in Asia to bring a single acre to fruition. (In the United States, where most farmers have machinery and some rice is sown by airplane, it takes seven hours.) The per-capita average works out to eighty hours a year for every person on earth, including those who never get any closer to rice than Rice Krispies.

In many ancient languages, "rice" is synonymous with

"food." *Dhanya,* the Indian word for rice, means "sustainer of the human race." (The name of the sixth-century-B.C. king of Nepal, Suddhodana, who was the father of the Gautama Buddha, means "Pure Rice.") A thousand years before Christ, Japan was called "Mizumono Kuni" — "The Land of Luxuriant Rice Crops." All the names for *Oryza sativa* today (*sativa* is the Latin for "sown") — the Italian *riso,* the German *reis,* the Spanish *arroz,* and, of course, "rice" — stem from the Greek *oriza,* which itself means "of Oriental origin." Rice is not exceptionally nutritious — few grasses are — made up as it is of 80 percent starch, 12 percent water, and only 7 or 8 percent protein, along with traces of fiber, fat, mineral ash, thiamine, riboflavin, and niacin. These last three, however, vitamins of the B stripe, diminish when rice is milled — that is, when the bran enveloping its grain is removed. Unmilled, brown rice is healthier than milled white, but is harder to preserve; the oil in the bran makes the rice spoil if it is kept around too long. (Since 1950, millers in the United States have been required to add some vitamins to the rice they have just finished devitaminizing.) In the Philippines, rice growers can often get their produce milled free of charge, because animal-feed distributors are happy to pay the millers for the discarded bran. However cogent the arguments may be for leaving rice alone and nourishingly brown — the Japanese temporarily outlawed debranning during the Second World War, as one way of obviating a crucial shortage of all food — they have had minimal impact, for the simple reason that the majority of rice eaters prefer their rice to be white, and if it must be dusted with talcum powder to embellish its chasteness, so be it.

One malign result of the low protein content of white rice is that people who have access to no other food at all are susceptible to beriberi. (Their chances of succumbing to it are somewhat reduced if rice is "undermilled" — that is, parboiled before it gets to the milling stage.) On the other hand, rice is admirably nonallergenic. Sufferers from sprue, an affliction induced by wheat, turn up at dinner parties carrying packets of rice cakes as a substitute for bread. Japanese physicians have prescribed rice vinegar for arteriosclerosis, fatigue, and hot tempers, and, especially, for limbering up the muscles of performers in circus troupes. Bygone Chinese, for their part, treated wounds with rice-stalk ash and hemorrhoids with rice cakes fried in camel fat. Therapeutic as some practitioners have contended rice and its by-products to be, it would be foolish to think that anything so popular has not also had its detractors. The ooze through which rice growers so often must slog has inspired a fair amount of criticism. "It is this system especially," a doctor in Mexico informed the American Public Health Association in 1891, "that is meant when competent authorities denounce the cultivation of rice as homicidal, declare its history to be one of blood, and contend that every sixteen hectoliters of rice are bought at the price of one man's life." An American physician added, for his part, "It has even been suggested that the origin of leprosy might be in the malarious mud through which the rice laborers are continually wading." "Malaria" means "bad air." Because it was believed in mid-nineteenth-century Spain that there was some affinity between rice and that disease, a royal edict was promulgated in 1860 to the effect that the plant could be grown solely in treeless swamps where air could freely circulate, and in any event not within fifteen hundred meters of any residential area, and even then not without a permit. In the light of all that, medical researchers began to study the relationship of rice-growing to all fevers. The doctors were mildly surprised — Edwin Bingham Copeland was exultant — to discern that in areas where rice was rife, death rates were markedly lower. Between 1905 and 1909, for instance, fatalities from malaria throughout Italy came to 14 per every 100,000 of population; but in the Italian rice-growing provinces of Novara and Pavia, the rate was only 2.4 per 100,000. The inference was that mosquitoes dislike breeding in rice water; in a later experiment, when mosquito larvae were scattered across some rice fields in California, most of them died without maturing. Nonetheless, rizoculture has been and continues to be blamed every now and then, usually by nonscientists, for neuralgia and pneumonia (getting one's feet wet is rarely conducive to good health), for diseases of the spleen and liver, and for purple blemishes on the skin. A rice grower in Georgia, when the United States South was still the Old South, once asserted that "Negroes . . . are constitutionally less liable to fevers than whites." An American physician thereupon urged the Japanese to import some field hands from Georgia and the Carolinas to work in their paddies. The Japanese, perhaps because their skin was neither black nor white, were unimpressed. Some of their forebears, though, had believed that rice — rice wine, anyway — was an effective, perhaps the only, palliative for droughts. It was the practice in the Aomori prefecture at arid times to send a forceful message to the errant gods of rain by plying the chief priest with sake and throwing him into a pond. Each time he came up, he would be given another dose and tossed back in. When he failed to surface, that was evidence that the gods were listening. Eventually he would be fished out — sometimes, if he was lucky, still breathing.

Rice itself comes in several colors. There are black rices — actually, like black tulips, they are purple — which are much fancied in Burma for the concoction of both beer and spirits. There are red rices, which are comparatively high in protein and are quite popular in Madagascar, in Iran, and in northern Ghana, though elsewhere their robust hue has made people shy away from them. (A Southeast Asian legend about the origin of *Oryza sativa* has it that there always was a rice plant, but its ears were bare of grain. Along came the goddess Kuan Yin, who squeezed her breasts over the worthless plants, and her milk spilled into the ears, and that created white rice. But she squeezed too hard, and some blood came out, too, and that accounted for red rice.) Tastes in rice vary widely. Part of its starch content is amylose. When cooked, high-amylose rice is drier and less fluffy than sticky, low-amylose rice. High-amylose is favored in India, Pakistan, Bangladesh, Malaysia, southern China, most of Latin America, and Sri Lanka, where astrology is taken very seriously and some women would not dream of planting rice until their neighborhood seer has told them what clothes they should wear. Indonesia and the Philippines are partial to medium-amylose. The chopstick-wielding countries — Japan, Korea, Taiwan, northern China — fancy low-amylose. (For much Korean rice, the starch has a 22- to 24-percent amylose content, as opposed to only 20 percent for much Japanese rice. Habitual rice eaters can detect such nuances. Japanese, accordingly, sometimes dismiss Korean rice as being far too dry.) For all the rice that is grown in Japan, its emperors of yore were usually served imports from Taiwan, which were held to be peerless in causing imperial taste buds to flower. Chinese emperors often had rice shipped in from the environs of Hong Kong, even though by the time it reached Peking the delicacy was apt to be a trifle moldy; accordingly, Pekinese considered it prudent to express unstinted admiration for moldy rice. (Confucius was not fussy. "With coarse rice to eat, with water to drink, and my bended arm for a pillow," he wrote, "I have still joy in the midst of these things.") Wealthy Vietnamese, not to mention East Pakistanis, are partial to rices that are, or are perceived to be, perfumed. In parts of India where there is enough rice to be able to set some aside, aroma is so highly esteemed that selected grains are sealed in jars for five years before they're consumed, by which time their redolence is awesome. Most Filipinos, like most Arabs, prefer longer-grained rice. Filipino farm families usually cook all the rice they intend to eat on any given day in the morning; it is imperative for them to have rice that, when it cools, won't turn unacceptably sticky. Some Asians are so finicky about rice that the Filipino troops who served in Korea during the war there insisted they couldn't function properly on Korean or Japanese rice; once familiar rice was shipped to them from home, they were content. One primitive Filipino tribe, the Ibaloi, traditionally grew a kind of rice they *didn't* like the taste of. Their rationale was that they never seemed to have enough rice, and the more disagreeable the taste of what they could produce, the less of it they would want to eat. They could probably have produced more if they'd been willing to use insecticides, but they were loath to do that because their children, who had few other enjoyable diversions, liked to pluck leafhoppers from their rice plants and munch on them as snacks. The Ibaloi children — and their elders — also ate tadpoles, bats, snakes, and snails when they were excessively short of rice, but they would not, unaccountably, eat rats, even though rodents sometimes did away with half their crop. Instead, the Ibaloi prayed for the rats to go away and leave them alone — religious ceremonies in the ebullient course of which a good deal of rice wine was consumed, thereby further depleting the already scarce stocks. To the Ibaloi, according to an American anthropologist who spent some time with them in the 1960s, "Rice is the cultural focus, . . . the nub of a man's life. It is what he does the most, thinks about the most, and talks about the most." When that visitor gave one Ibaloi six-year-old a pencil and a piece of paper and asked the child to make a drawing of something of special concern to him, what emerged was a crude and angry portrait of a stem borer, rice's main entomological adversary. In 1953, another anthropologist made an exhaustive study of the relationship of rice to tribal Filipinos. "Rice is the crop of greatest concern to all," he wrote. "It is the most highly valued real food. In most ritual offerings, curing rites, and for major feasts it is an essential for which there is no substitute. The success or failure of one's agricultural activities is gauged almost entirely in terms of harvested rice."

For many years, one of the most popular undergraduate courses at Harvard — taught jointly by the Japanological diplomat Edwin O. Reischauer and the Sinological prosopographer John K. Fairbank — was called, formally, "The History of East Asian Civilization." Its informal designation was "Rice Paddies." In a 1962 article, an eminent analyst of paddy soils, Felix N. Ponnamperuma, pondered the relationship of rice to Asians and flatly concluded, "Rice rules their lives." Rice, which has long loomed large in the spiritual as well as the temporal lives of most Asians, has often dictated not merely their diet but also their social and economic status. In Japan, where *Oryza sativa* is sometimes called "the fundament of life," the belief prevailed, in the time before pizza and McDonald's french fries stormed ashore, that anyone who didn't eat rice at least once a day was beyond the pale, and even beyond the assurance of waking up the following morning. A generation ago, Japanese housewives did not think in terms of breakfast, lunch, and supper; the three meals they served were *asa gohan* (morning rice), *hiru gohan* (afternoon rice), and *yoru gohan* (evening rice). The table manners they sought to inculcate in their children had to do primarily with the rights and wrongs of handling chopsticks. And no wonder: the sacredness of rice was secondary only to that of the emperor, who was himself, the youngsters were reminded, the direct descendant of the Rice Prince, who was the grandson of Amaterasu, the Goddess of Day.

In Indonesia, some rice paddies were themselves considered sacred, and were not to be defiled with fertilizer, organic or inorganic. (No Javanese girl was deemed fit for marriage until she knew how to cook a perfect bowl of rice.) Sumatrans working on rubber plantations insisted on being paid for their efforts in rice rather than cash; their employers, accordingly, had to allocate part of their acreage to the cultivation of wages. Women who transplanted rice on the nearby Malay Peninsula were expected to use their left hand only, meanwhile making sure that their tongue clung to the roof of their mouth. At harvesttime, they stripped to the waist: the less bulk they exhibited, it was reasoned, the thinner, and thus easier to thresh, the ripe rice plants would be. Men had their standardized rituals, too. At planting time, they would engage in mock battles, flailing away at one another with three-foot rods, and thus putting to rout any evil spirits that might be hanging around. In ancient Siam, where rice was well known to be the gift of the perennially fruitful womb of the goddess Mae Phosop, the paddies reverberated with a prayer to her: "O, Rice Goddess, come up into the rice bin. Do not go astray in the meadows and fields, for mice to bite you and birds to take you in their beaks. Go to the happy place to rear your children and grandchildren in prosperity. Come!" The incantations were usually uttered by Thai women. They did not want their men to get too close to Mae Phosop. They were afraid they would become infatuated and try to run away with her.

In Hong Kong, social workers often used to determine whether or not a family that had applied for welfare was eligible not by checking their garage for automobiles or their living rooms for TV sets but by evaluating the quality of the contents of their rice bins. On mainland China, to have a secure job is to have an "iron rice bowl"; conversely, to be unemployed is to have "broken the rice bowl." Chinese who elected to be baptized by foreign missionaries, hoping thereby to obtain a better education and a better job, were called "Rice Christians." To knock over someone's rice bowl with malice aforethought was an affront tantamount to slapping his face. A polite way of saying hello was "Have you eaten your rice today?" As Japanese emperors ceremonially tilled their rice plots behind the walls of their palaces — Hirohito continued to do so past eighty — so did the emperors of China when they still reigned. They would inaugurate the planting season by pulling the first plow. The dirt they turned over was carefully doled out and scattered by the lucky recipients on their own paddies, which would then assuredly be fertile. And, of course, rice, the perpetual symbol of fecundity (Was it not conceived, after all, according to Balinese legend, when Mother Earth was ravished by the God of the Underworld?), has been a feature of imperial and commoner weddings worldwide, although not in every instance thrown at the bride. Greeks sometimes put it in her shoe.

Latter-day Asians and others respectful of rice take a more prosaic, less deistic view of it and its powers. But they do not take chances, either. The library of the International Rice Research Institute in the Philippines contains several thousand highly technical books and papers about rizoculture. It also contains a statue of a rice god worshiped by the Ifugao, a primitive Luzon tribe whose terraced rice plots, at an altitude of five thousand feet, have been tended in pretty much the same fashion for more than three thousand years. To ensure the success of Expo '70, the Japan World Exposition in Osaka, three years before the gates were opened priests flew over the site in helicopters and sprinkled it with holy rice. Lebanese Christians greeted Israeli tanks lumbering into Beirut in June 1982 with showers of flowers — and also of rice. And when, the year before, dedication ceremonies had been held in New York City for a new home of the Asia Society, a feature of the program was the pelting of the audience with colored rice by a Balinese dancer — part of a ritual that was supposed to thwart any evil spirits who might have infiltrated the premises.

One old-time Japanese myth had it that the first human being to lay eyes on rice was a priest — theretofore an ill-fed eater of roots — who tied a string to the leg of an obliging mouse and was led to it. Botanists are not certain quite how rice originated — probably from some wild grass — but they generally agree that it was first involved in human nourishment about 5000 B.C., in India and China. Migrants took it thence to Burma and Thailand. It reached China by about 3000 B.C., and the Philippines not long afterward. Malays took it to Madagascar, and also to India, where by 1000 B.C. there was enough of it around for different varieties to be rated according to their nutritiousness. The Japanese were introduced to rice much later, perhaps not before 200 B.C. The Greeks got it from Persians, the Egyptians and the Spanish from Arabs — who thought that they and the rest of the world had got it initially from the sweat off Muhammad's brow. Just how rice got to Guam is uncertain, but Magellan was glad to find it there when he stopped by in 1521. There is an old saying that goes, "The history of the introduction of Asian food crops into Africa is written on the wind, but the wind cannot read." Latter-day historians know that the Portuguese took *Oryza sativa* to West Africa (where rice has been a staple ever since and is so vital to the Kissi tribesmen of Guinea, Liberia, and Sierra Leone that they are sometimes called "The People of Rice") early in the sixteenth century, but for more than a thousand years before that the continent had had its own indigenous rice, *O. glaberima,* which apparently sprang up along the banks of the Niger River at just about the same time that *O. sativa* emerged in Asia.

In the scholarly view of the plant historian Edward Lewis Sturtevant, rice was introduced to the United States, in 1647, when Sir William Berkeley brought some to Virginia. It did not make much of a splash. Nearly half a century later, a Dutch ship out of Madagascar ran into trouble in a storm and anchored off Charleston, South Carolina. The South Carolina governor, Landgrave Thomas Smith, had been in Madagascar sometime earlier, had fond remembrances of the rice he'd eaten there, and asked the ship's captain if he happened to have any on board. The governor was given a sackful and planted it in his garden. Rice burgeoned so splendidly in the American Southeast that by 1852 the East India Company sent an emissary to Savannah to pick up some tips on growing the crop. That quest prompted the author of a report to a South Carolina farmers' society to burble, "Here, then, was an embassage from the banks of the Ganges, a spot where rice has been cultivated probably for twenty centuries, to inquire into the method of cultivation and preparation, of a people amongst whom the grain had no existence one hundred and sixty years ago." Sturtevant thought that inquiry was eminently sensible. "The finest rice in the world," he wrote in 1919, "is that raised in North and South Carolina."

Up to 1861, the Carolinas produced three-quarters of all the rice grown in the United States. After the Civil War, they faltered, and Louisiana rice, sown on abandoned sugar plantations along the Mississippi River, became dominant. Farmers from the Midwest, attracted by the warm climate and plentiful irrigation of the South, drifted down and turned from wheat or corn to rice. Crowley, Louisiana, in the heart of the rice district, became known as "the new Iowa." A man who had much to do with the proliferation of rice that ensued was Seaman A. Knapp (1833–1911), who was born in New York but moved to the old Iowa at thirty-two and went into farming — corn and hogs. Then he turned to academe. He became a professor of agriculture at Iowa State College, and in time its president. He was also an explorer for the Division of Botany of the U.S. Department of Agriculture. Secretary of Agriculture James Wilson, a native Iowan, twice sent Knapp to Asia, in 1899 and 1901, to gather plants, and he brought back new rice varieties from Japan and the Philippines. With almost evangelistic fervor, he gave demonstrations throughout southwest Louisiana and east Texas of how best to grow it. (Knapp must have been an uncommonly modest man: In *Rice Culture,* a bulletin that he wrote for the department in 1910, the year before he died, he alluded to the blossoming of Louisiana rice because of the Japanese strains that had come there; nowhere did he mention that it was he who was responsible.) Crowley began to call itself "the Rice Capital of America"; its principal hotel was the Rice. Next, early in the twentieth century, rice production surged in Texas and Arkansas. Texas had had just 175 acres in rice in 1892; by 1909, it had 238,000 acres. By the spring of 1983, Stuttgart, Arkansas, was the seat of a Rice Research and Extension Center of the University of Arkansas, and it was proclaiming itself "the rice capital of the *world*" — which, considering that there were only 14,000 rice farmers in the United States and that altogether their three-million-odd acres produced only 1.5 percent of the global crop, might have been a slight exaggeration. (At the same time, because the Environmental Protection Agency had authorized the use of the herbicide 2,4,5-T to combat aquatic weeds in Stuttgart rice fields, the cancer mortality rate there was revealed to be half again as high as that for the nation as a whole.) Rice had moved along to California in 1909, and seventy years later occupied more than half a million acres of that hospitable state and reciprocated by adding more than $300 million to California's agricultural income. (In the South and the Southeast, most of the rice grown was long-grained — suitable for canned rice, soups, and baby foods. California rice was short-grained — stickier, more adapted to Japanese tastes and to breakfast cereals.) Farther yet to the west, out in Hawaii, rice had been on the scene since 1857, when the Royal Hawaiian Agricultural Society imported some seeds from China, and kernels were offered free, along with land to grow them on, to any residents who were interested. Just about the only people who seemed to care were some Chinese laborers who'd been imported in 1852, on five-year contracts, to work on sugarcane plantations. When they had fulfilled their obligations, they gladly took up rice farming. Ever since, every spring, the descendants of those Hawaiian rice pioneers have solemnly decorated their graves with bowls of rice, which, not wishing to be wasteful, they have then proceeded to eat. To most Chinese, wherever they are, the gourmet food that Americans call wild rice is virtually unknown, and for good reason: it is not a true rice at all, but an unrelated grass, *Zizania aquatica*. Most of the wild rice grown nowadays — three million pounds or so a year — comes from Wisconsin, Minnesota, and Manitoba, and much of it over the years has been raised by American Indians. For the old Dakotas, wild rice was featured on the menu of a rather exclusive feast: you had to have killed an enemy to be invited.

Most of the people for whom rice is *the* food inhabit subtropical or tropical regions, but that is not necessarily where rice grows best. It needs sunlight as well as rain to thrive, and the yields of rices in temperate zones like the American South have regularly been far higher than those in places where typhoons abound. Laos grows four times the amount of rice that Australia does, but requires thirty times as much acreage to do so. While the rice plant is primarily esteemed for its edible grains, as with other cereals quite a few non-nutritional uses have been found, over the years, for its inedible parts. (Also for the edible: Steve Carlton, the Philadelphia Phillies' star pitcher, coddled his precious left arm by rotating it inside a tub of white rice.) Rice husks have served as aggregate in cement, and as an ingredient of anhydrous alcohol. Koreans thatch their roofs with rice straw, and India has lately been looking into the substitution of rice straw for jute in the manufacture of potato sacks. In Louisiana, the straw is converted into corrugated fiber boxes. Among the artifacts made by the Peking Handicraft and Art Factory for sale to tourists and for export are miniature dolls (Santa Clauses among them) fashioned out of rice-flour paste. In Thailand, rice husks end up as logs — twelve hundred tons of these a year compressed from a mountain of 3.5 million tons of residue. The Japanese and Taiwanese sometimes use a little broken rice for animal feed.

Such utilization of the components of *Oryza sativa,* however, amounts to nothing compared to the versatility of another tropical marvel, the coconut, which in Asia often grows on the fringes of rice paddies and which on some palm-shaded Pacific atolls is called "the tree of life." Coconut trees figure importantly in the lives of at least 300 million humans. An official of Puerto Rico's Department of Agriculture and Labor once declared that "no other tropical crop comes so close to being indispensable to the human race in limited areas, in islands particularly." *Cocos nucifera* was once apostrophized in verse by George Herbert as "clothing, meat and trencher, drink and can, boat, cable, sail, mast, needle, all in one." Herbert could have added "shelter," for the coconut tree is singular in that it can provide for all the basic needs of man except sex — and to some Westerners who visualize romance as a full moon hovering over a graceful coconut palm, *Cocos nucifera* may at least induce passion. "*Coco*" is Portuguese for "cat"; the nut's triangular shape and two eyelike spots put early seafarers in mind of a mewing feline. (How the "eyes" got on the shell in the first place was, according to an ancient Chinese legend, perfectly simple to explain: Prince Lin-yi had the Prince of Yüe's head chopped off and tossed into a palm tree, where it lodged and was transformed into a nut.) Coconuts also vaguely resemble monkeys' faces, and monkeys have been prominent in coconut lore. The *Arabian Nights* had men throwing stones at monkeys in palm trees, and monkeys retaliating by throwing back coconuts; the story may have been inspired by the fact that in some places — the Malay Peninsula, for one — men have trained monkeys, who are less likely to fall out of trees than they are, to harvest their coconuts. A somewhat more fanciful yarn out of India involved a crocodile who invited a monkey to climb on its back and be ferried across a river. Halfway over, the crocodile stopped and told the passenger he was going to eat him. The monkey thought fast. "Wait!" he cried. "The most delicious portion of me is my heart, hanging on that tree there on the far shore."

Because coconuts are both dependable and profitable, they

have been called "the Consols of the East." In a preface to a 1914 book thus titled, Sir William H. Lever, the British soap man whose far-flung plantations kept him tidily supplied with coconut oil (it makes soap foam), wrote, "I know of no field of tropical agriculture that is so promising at the present moment as coconut planting, and I do not think in the whole world there is a promise of so lucrative an investment of time and money as in this industry." Nowhere is the indispensability of the coconut more apparent than on the two thousand tiny Pacific islands known as Micronesia. They cover an expanse of the ocean as vast as the continental United States, but altogether they have only 450,000 acres of land. Of that, 75,000 acres are given over to coconuts.

Every bit of the coconut tree is precious to Micronesians and to others — Indonesians, Filipinos, Sri Lankans — who bask in its shade. From the towering trunk (sometimes seventy-five or eighty feet tall) they make boats and houses. From the spreading fronds (sometimes seventeen feet long) come clothes and mats. From the coir — the hairy fiber on the outside of the shell — come fishnets and ropes. From the shell itself, fuel and utensils. From the copra — the dried meat — food and oil. The juice, before it hardens into meat, is a delicious thirst quencher, as thousands of American servicemen thitherto unacquainted with coconuts in their own milieu were happy to discover during the Second World War. (Forty years later, a new generation had the same refreshing initiation on Grenada.) From the sap of the trunk — the servicemen liked this, too — came the mildly alcoholic toddy, a fermented drink; and the much-higher-proof arrack, a distillation. (The residents of the American island territory of Guam did not consider themselves unduly inconvenienced by Prohibition; their consumption of toddy and arrack went on unabated — though, to be sure, as there were risks in drinking bathtub gin, so were there in clam-bering up trees to tap them. "Frightful accidents often occur," one toddy chronicler has observed, "usually resulting in death or disfigurement for life.") Somebody once took the trouble to calculate that various parts of the coconut palm had one use for nearly every day of the year — among the 360 of them being confectionery, cattle feed, arrowheads, dagger handles, cosmetics, diesel fuel, fencing, pickles, dentifrices, shaving cream, bridges, furniture, curtains, margarine, plastics, explosives, rope, hats, mats, canes, carpet felt, fishhooks, fishnets, brooms, baskets, buttons, ladles, ice cream, fertilizer, and an alternate to mother's milk. The roster did not include the heavy reliance on coconut-palm-tree photographs of Army and Navy recruiters, resort hotels, travel agents, and the Florida Chamber of Commerce.

How the coconut palm got from one part of the world to another has been spiritedly debated by *Cocos nucifera* scholars. Most of them agree that it originated in Southeast Asia, or perhaps western New Guinea, or perhaps Sri Lanka. Coconuts float, and they have been said to germinate after bobbing around in salt water for more than a hundred days — a span of time in which, given favorable conditions of wind and wave, they could travel for three thousand miles. (After the Bikini atom-bomb test of 1946, which destroyed all the trees there, one nut floated over to a nearby island and took root; the coconut crabs that loitered around it ended up laced with strontium 90.) In the pre-Christian era, outriggers could and did make the thirty-five-hundred-mile voyage from Java to Madagascar in a month or so, and they might have had coconuts aboard for propagation as well as for eating. The explosion of Krakatoa in 1883 covered three Indonesian islands with volcanic ash to a depth of one hundred feet. In 1906, without the known intercession of any human hand, coconut trees popped up.

Today, nearly 300 million coconut trees decoratively cover

15 million acres of the earth's surface. Each of them, when mature, bears thirty or thirty-five nuts a year. That's 10 billion coconuts. Three billion nuts alone are harvested on Sri Lanka, where people sometimes measure their worth in terms of the number of coconut trees they own, where 20 percent of all the calories consumed derive from coconuts, and where coconut juice — to cite still another of its noteworthy uses — was once esteemed as a cure for ringworm, eye inflammations, hemorrhoids, diarrhea, and gonorrhea. CGIAR does not have an international research center devoted to coconuts, but Sri Lanka has a national one; the coconut has been a much more lasting part of its civilization than the Portuguese and Dutch and British occupations under which it was (as Ceylon) successively a colony until its independence in 1948. A roadside statue at Weligama commemorates an ancient Ceylonese king, Kustaraja, who, whatever his other claims to fame, is best remembered now for having been cured of a terrible itch by subsisting for three months on nothing but coconut juice and a little salt water. Coconuts have an affinity for salinity. Some Sri Lankans maintain that the palms lean out toward the water, as they often do at bizarre, seemingly precarious angles, because they want to get as far away as possible from inferior vegetation; others argue that the trees have to be near to and to smell the sea to prosper. People there whose groves are out of earshot of the Indian Ocean sometimes try to make it up to their deprived and frustrated trees by sprinkling salt on their roots.

In the spring of 1952, Sri Lanka had rubber to export and needed to import rice. The People's Republic of China had some rice to spare and it needed rubber. The two countries made a deal; over the next five years, they would swap 50,000 tons of rubber for 270,000 tons of rice — a bargain for both sides. (The agreement marked China's reentry into commerce with the non-Communist world.) In subsequent years, Iranian oil has been bartered for Thai rice. Compared to wheat, corn, and soybeans, however, rice has never been much of a factor in international trade. The United States exports half of the 6 million tons it raises annually. (Iran used to be a good customer.) Thailand exports about the same amount. The two nations together account for half of all the rice that is exported; the 12 million tons that change hands each year are a mere drop in the worldwide-rice-production bucket of 400 million tons. That averages out to 200 pounds for everyone on earth. Americans eat 6 pounds of rice apiece a year. Vietnamese, if they could get that much, would gladly eat 600. Ninety-five percent of all rice is consumed within the borders of the country where it is harvested — more often than not, indeed, within two miles of its production site. In much of the Far East, transportation facilities are so minimal that rice growers can't get their grain to regional mills and have to mill it themselves. There are stone slabs emplaced along some rural Indonesian roads for the express purpose of pounding rice. Communist China, similarly, maintains communal granaries in isolated areas — some of these being round stone watchtowers that in ideologically different days landlords had erected so they could keep an eye on their toiling peasants.

Robert F. Chandler, Jr., the first director of the International Rice Research Institute, wrote in his 1979 work *Rice in the Tropics: A Guide to the Development of National Programs,* "So dependent upon rice are the Asian countries that throughout history a failure of that crop has caused widespread famine and death." Comparatively modest the international rice trade may be, but rice is of such immense importance to Asians who are not self-sufficient in it that any alteration of their access to it can have disastrous consequences. India — thanks in large measure to research at IRRI — now grows just about all the rice it requires. Before the Second World War, though, its eastern provinces were heavily reliant for their rice on Burma, a country that then grew three-quarters of all the rice exported. When the Japanese cut off the flow of rice in 1943 from Burma to Bengal, two million Bengalis starved to death. Today, India and China have between them less than half the population of the globe. They produce more than half the rice. Their dependence on it is such that they consume more than 99 percent of what they grow.

In 1949, the government of Japan established a Commission for Rice Competition, because, as the newspaper *Asahi Shimbun* put it, "the most vital problem for the reconstruction of postwar Japan is that of food. And that is, in short, none other than that of increasing her rice crop." That year, thirty-five hundred Japanese farmers vied to see who could coax the most rice from their paddies; by 1953, thirty thousand of them had entered eight regional contests. The winners got to meet the emperor, became instant celebrities, and were thus hard-pressed to find enough time to grow any more rice. Some of their accomplishments were also illusory. For throughout Japan, as throughout the rest of Asia, rice yields had not appreciably increased for five hundred years. And as the 1960s approached, the population of Asia was increasing by nearly a million a week. There was not much more arable land available to take care of their looming needs. The alternative was to find ways of making existing rice fields more productive and more nourishing.

Among the global thinkers who addressed themselves to this problem was J. George Harrar, who had got the Rockefeller Foundation interested in agricultural research. It was he who had launched the wheat-breeding program in Mexico in the

1940s that, twenty years later, would bequeath to the bread eaters of the world a dazzling array of high-yielding varieties of *their* staple grain. Now, in 1958, Harrar (who died, at seventy-five, in 1982) was brooding about rice. "We had learned enough in Mexico to be able to mount a full-scale attack on a basic human problem," he recalled a few years afterward. "Even so, I suspected that rice was a little large for us to swallow alone [the play on words was doubtless unintentional]." The Rockefeller Foundation had never before collaborated on any major venture with the Ford Foundation. Harrar thought it was time it did. On October 8, 1958, he composed a memorandum for Dean Rusk, then the president of the Rockefeller Foundation, to pass along to Forrest F. Hill, an agricultural economist and the Ford Foundation's vice-president for overseas development. Harrar wrote, in part:

Rice is the single most important food crop grown today. It dominates agricultural production in essentially every area of the world which is well adapted to its production and has been extended to and beyond its optimum ecological limits. Most of the world rice production occurs in those areas thought of as being underdeveloped with the result that methods are primitive and inefficient, production is low and prices relatively high. Although research in rice is in progress in a number of parts of the world the great advances lie ahead. There are immediate opportunities to make significant benefits in the quantity and quality of rice available each year to feed the ever increasing number of individuals who depend on this crop for sustenance. . . .

It has been estimated that the annual world yield of rice could readily be doubled if scientific and technical information now available could be universally applied. By extrapolation, the total yield might conceivably be doubled again as a result of fundamental research on those problems of rice production which are still only partially understood. While this situation is obviously utopian, it would seem clear that very great improvements in production could be expected as a result of intensification of research efforts and the extension and application of their results. . . .

Examination of world production figures on rice in comparison with numbers of so-called rice eaters in the world and their average caloric intake very clearly emphasize the fact that there is an enormous imbalance between demand and supply. This suggests that any well-conceived and effective effort to produce information and materials could readily be applied over wide areas with benefit to rice yields and would have important social significance. One approach to this objective might be the establishment of an International Rice Research Institute. . . .

The Ford Foundation was interested. "At best, the world food outlook for the decade ahead is grave," Forrest Hill told its trustees the following year. "At worst, it is frightening." By the end of 1959, the two foundations had formally committed themselves to a joint venture: Ford would provide $7.9 million in capital funds; Rockefeller would provide $.75 million a year in operating funds and would recruit a staff.

The Philippines, Harrar had concluded after an exploratory swing around Asia, would be a logical place for the research center. Rice furnished 50 percent of the calories and 40 percent of the protein for its population. Its rice yields were low — only 1,280 pounds, on the average, per acre. (Japan's contest winners had got close to 10,000 pounds.) It was importing rice. Moreover, at the suggestion of the Filipino government, the College of Agriculture of the University of the Philippines offered to turn over to the proposed institute, near its campus at Los Baños — thirty-four miles southeast of Manila — 220 acres of vacant land. It was a tract that seemed to warrant redemption; during the Second World War, the Japanese had interned three thousand prisoners there, who'd had very little to eat except rice and not much of that. (Thirty-seven years after V-J Day, a definition in an American crossword puzzle was "A U.S. general, WW II, who hated rice"; the answer was "Wainwright.") Los Baños had plenty of rain and a pleasing uniformity of temperature; there was only a five-degree-Fahrenheit difference between January, its coldest month, and April, its hottest. It had promising soil — young and fresh as soils go, only ten thousand or so years old — soil so potentially productive that some scientists feared at the outset it might skew their research. Construction of the institute — offices, laboratories, dormitories, swimming pool, tennis court, and, most important of all, 200 one-acre growing plots spread over a honeycombed network of concrete irrigation pipes fed by three big wells — began in 1960. (The Ford Foundation, at one point, sent the architect Ralph Walker over to inspect the plans and make recommendations. He had a typical American view of what a tropical paradise should look like. He suggested more coconut palms.) By the time the institute formally became operative, in February 1962, it had an official emblem (three peasant women in big, round rice-straw hats transplanting rice at the foot of Mount Mayon, the Fuji of the Philippines), a collection of three thousand varieties of rice from all over the world, an 881-page *International Bibliography of Rice Research,* and a board of trustees that, along with George Harrar and Forrest Hill (who long before he got involved with tropical agriculture had acquired the nickname Frosty), included members from Japan, India, Thailand, Taiwan, and, of course, the Philippines. At the start, IRRI was something of a tourist attraction — so much more splendid, with its modern buildings and gushing fountains, than most institutions in the area that busloads of sightseers, a thousand a week, took the hour-and-a-half drive down from Manila just to gawk at it. Eminences, too, came by to pay their respects — the king and queen of Thailand, the crown princess of the Netherlands, the prime minister of Japan, and Norman Cousins, the editor of the *Saturday Review*. "Any genuine improvement in the human condition on this planet," Cousins wrote on his return from Los Baños, "must be concerned with rice. If rice yields can be increased in the hot countries and if the protein content can be stepped up, the benefits would be among the most far-reaching in human history." The VIPs were often escorted by the man· then chiefly responsible for whatever history was about to be made — Robert Chandler. A resident of the potato country of Maine, Chandler had become a soil scientist and taught that subject at Cornell for twelve years. He had spent a 1946 sabbatical working for the Rockefeller Foundation in Mexico. The following year, he became dean of agriculture at the University of New Hampshire. From 1950 to 1954, he was its president. Then it was back to the Rockefeller Foundation's agricultural program for five years. Chandler was fifty-five in 1962. He had never seen a rice plant growing until he was forty-one. For much of his adult life, he had had a fairly low opinion of rice, which as a boy he had chiefly encountered, grudgingly, as an ingredient of rice pudding. He had believed that rice, considering its fairly low protein content, was a second-rate food. By the time he was put in charge of IRRI, he had changed his mind: If you can't lick 'em, join 'em. He told an early group of visitors to IRRI that "we sincerely believe that by our combined efforts Asia can continue to feed its teeming millions for some time to come. I cannot make this statement, however, without adding what every thinking person knows — viz., that we must curb population growth. It is the only ultimate solution to man's food problem. The land area of the world has a definite limit and eventually population must be brought into equilibrium with this area and its capacity for food production." One of the challenges Chandler faced when IRRI opened its doors was to establish its credibility — especially, to begin with, in the Philippines, where most of the rice growers were farmers with landholdings of five acres or less, were xenophobic, were set in their habits, and were like as not illiterate. Some IRRI men were distressed to find that in one Filipino area stem borers had grievously damaged the rice crop. But the scientists couldn't convince the farmers there of what had happened; *they* attributed their misfortune to lightning, or to the fact that their soil had been contaminated by tobacco grown on it previously, or to almost anything except the worms that were visible when a rice-plant stem was snapped in two. IRRI's staff became resignedly aware that to persuade some farmers that a novel seed was better than an accustomed one, the new variety would have to at least double its predecessor's yield. And even that was often not enough. IRRI had heard from a Japanese agriculturist how he had gone to Cambodia not long before and on a demonstration plot had easily doubled the rice output in that neighborhood. The natives had been impressed, but the following year they didn't seem to have any more rice than they'd had before. It turned out that, having learned to increase their yields of rice by 100 percent, they had saved themselves a lot of time and trouble by only planting half as much of it. An IRRI anthropologist probing the Philippine hinterlands concluded, for his part, that he could accelerate acceptance of a new variety by inventing a god for it and promising to put on a first-rate religious ceremony if the natives in that area would just plant some of its seed. He added, offhandedly, that the variety he was touting made a crackerjack rice wine.

In 1964, a committee set up by the FAO reported that "the fundamental need was for a technological revolution in rice production such as has already occurred in the developed wheat-producing areas so as to bring about a substantial rise in productivity." IRRI was in the process of responding to that challenge. Many of the rices popular in Asia had a tendency to fall over, or lodge. If their panicles were heavy with grain, it would rot before it could be reaped. IRRI wanted a shorter, stiffer stalk. (When it came up with one, some Filipinos complained they had to bend over too far at harvesttime, and there were jokes about that: "Did you bring your stool?" In rebuttal, Chandler liked to point out that people had to bend over even lower to handle plants that had lodged.) There were three basic kinds of rice in the Far East: *Indica,* a tropical strain, which grew best in South and Southeast Asia; *Japonica,* a temperate one, which flourished in Japan, Korea, and Taiwan; and *Javanica,* confined mainly to Indonesia. The idea was to produce a new rice that would combine the more desirable characteristics of all. It could not be the perfect rice for everyone everywhere, rice eaters being as idiosyncratic in their tastes as wine drinkers. The IRRI ambition was to develop a rice, from crossbreeding the by then more than ten thousand varieties in its custody, that would grow in most climates and soils, that would be a little richer in protein than other varieties, that would satisfy most palates, and that would have a consistently higher yield than the rices of yesteryear. It was not an easy task. As a rule, only about one in every ten thousand crosses made by rice breeders results in a strain that meets enough criteria to justify sending it out to farmers. The variables are infinite. A single one-acre IRRI test plot might have hundreds of them — different kinds of rice, planted at different times, with different applications of fertilizer and water. As three IRRI breeders put it in a 1979 collaboration called *Rice Improvement,* "Rice improvement requires years of constant, hard, dirty work, with many failures and rare successes. . . . There is no easy way to improve rice production; it demands patience, dedication, continuity, and total physical and mental commitment to field work. Successful rice scientists live with their plants. Unsuccessful ones delegate hard work to assistants and seek physical comfort while writing progress reports and attending conferences." IRRI rice scientists could not even pursue their drudgery in peace. They were in a no-holds-barred war with rats and birds. They built electrical barriers against the rats. They put up nets to foil the birds. They could not help admiring the countermeasures resorted to by some especially rice-hungry birds, who would fold their wings and dive like arrows through the interstices of the nets.

In 1962, one new strain looked especially promising. It was a cross between a tall Indonesian variety called Peta and a semidwarf from Taiwan called Dee-gee-woo-gen. It was tested and tested worldwide and further refined. By 1964, it had evolved into a rice that ended up with the prosaic name of IR-8. IR-8 was a rice for all seasons. It did not care much how long or short a day it had to grow in. It was short and stiff and stood up straight. It had abundant tillers. Its grain was sticky but not too sticky, although after it was cooked, it hardened when it cooled. Its upright leaves permitted greater penetration of sunlight. It did not resist all pests (there are at least a hundred species of insects that, like birds and rats, dote on rice) but it was moderately inhospitable to the dread stem borer, and also to blast, a rice disease so epidemic that in 1963 IRRI had held a symposium exclusively devoted to that affliction, with sixty concerned scientists from seventeen countries in attendance. (Twenty-nine scholarly papers had been presented, one of which was entitled "A Proposal for an International Program of Research on the Rice Blast Disease" — an implication, at least, that its author regarded the whole gathering as a mere kickoff.) And IR-8's yields were heartening. At IRRI — under, to be sure, carefully controlled conditions — they were computed at fifty-eight hundred pounds an acre, and that whopping productivity had been realized in just eighty-five days, less than half the time it took many rices to ripen. What *that* meant was that farmers who'd had to make do in the past with one or two crops a year could now reasonably look forward to two or three.

When George Harrar heard that IR-8 would soon be available for distribution, he said, somewhat optimistically, "There is no longer any excuse for human starvation." Robert Chandler, less sweepingly, said, "To those of us who are living our days close to the rice plant, it seems that the near future is rather bright." Politicians in the Philippines had always had to stay close to the rice plant. Preharvest time often coincided with pre-election time — there were elections then — and before a crop came in, it was important for the government not to have rice prices rise. Officials had to juggle the interests of rural farmers and urban consumers — trying to obtain for the former a decent return on their produce and for the latter a decent price at the market. President Ferdinand Marcos had good reason to be interested in IR-8. He went to Los Baños to learn more about it on June 3, 1966. Marcos was so impressed that, a few days later, he invited representatives of IRRI to come to Manila and explain their work to his cabinet. The local press was also invited. Chandler gave Marcos a two-kilogram bag as a keepsake. The next day, one Manila newspaper came out with the headline "MARCOS GETS MIRACLE RICE." IR-8 got stuck with that "miracle" tag, which was a shame, because from then on it was supposed to produce miracles. That story and others that ensued also created a demand for IR-8 among Filipino farmers, who thought they could put the miracle to better use than could their president. IRRI promptly announced that any farmer who came by could have his own two-kilograms' worth. IR-8 was formally launched on November 28, 1966, which must have been a cause of some relief at FAO headquarters in Rome; the FAO had already proclaimed 1966 as International Rice Year, and time was running short. (A month earlier, President Lyndon Johnson, who liked to be in on things early, had been introduced to IR-8 by Marcos while touring the Pacific. Whether Johnson also got a two-kilogram souvenir is uncertain; he certainly would have been pleased, if anybody told him, that among IR-8's ancestors there was allegedly a good ol' rice from Texas.) The dean of the College of Agriculture of Louisiana State University said that the new rice was the biggest thing in his line of work since hybrid corn. He went even further. "It is likely to go down in history," he declared, "as the most significant contribution to the welfare of mankind in this century."

IR-8, being only an evolutionary step in the perfectibility of plants, could hardly have been expected to live up to its miracle billing, and it didn't. Its grains had a tendency to break when they were being milled. They had an unattractively chalky color. Some detractors said that that contributed to IR-8's peculiar taste, which was not to their taste. ("They may not like it," Chandler remarked to an acquaintance later on, "but they had full bellies when they said they weren't liking it.") Some Indonesian ideologues thought it to be American — there was, after all, the Rockefeller and Ford aegis — and thus, to them, subversive. (IRRI's relations with Indonesian leaders were unaffected. "We just talk rice to them and let them run their country and everything seems to work out all right," Chandler said in 1964.) Also, part of the Indonesian diet was fish that spawned in canals that irrigated rice paddies; when farmers used pesticides they'd been told would be helpful, if indeed not essential, for the proper propagation of IR-8, the chemicals killed not only rice predators but also the fish. One hidebound South Vietnamese farmer resented IR-8 because, he told an American journalist, President Thieu came around one day with a bunch of soldiers and *ordered* him to plant it. "My father planted our type of rice before me, and his father's father before that, so why should I change?" he said. He ultimately had to change. By 1972, owing to the war, South Vietnam was importing three hundred thousand tons of rice a year, much of it from the United States. The recipients weren't especially fond of its taste, but they had no options.

Notwithstanding, IR-8 had a monumental impact on rice production. The year after it was introduced, rice yields in the Philippines went up by 11 percent. By 1968, IR-8, or its close relatives, occupied more than 60 million Asian acres — one-fifth of all the rice land on the continent. In two years, the value of the entire Asian rice crop had increased by $300 million. (Up to then, IRRI had cost its sponsors $15 million; the return on that investment would surely have gratified John D. Rockefeller and Henry Ford.) Since the end of the Second World War, Burma had remained pretty much aloof from the Western world and its offshoots. A Burmese trade delegation visited IRRI in 1965. By 1968, more than four hundred thousand Burmese acres had been planted to IR-8, and Chandler had been invited to come over and inspect them. Yet there was another hitch. IR-8 was a rice that did best on irrigated — not solely rain-fed — land. As Dana G. Dalrymple, the United States Department of Agriculture's expert on high-yielding varieties of all cereals, once observed, "Man does not live by irrigated wheat and rice alone." Indeed, only one-third of Asia's 338 million rice-growing acres were irrigated. Without irrigation, and without such other recommended inputs as pesticides and fertilizers, the yields of IR-8 fell markedly short of their potential. "The new rices, however," an IRRI publication would later assert in rebuttal to some of the center's adversaries, "continue to outyield traditional rices even where low levels of inputs are used, and to far outyield the traditionals where those inputs are increased. The advantage of the higher yielding new rices is that genetic transfer has given them the disease and insect resistance of the traditional rices, sometimes in an improved form." The statistics continued to be impressive. Many rice eaters in Colombia, who normally get about 14 percent of their calories from rice, thought IR-8 was too glutinous; nevertheless, rice yields in Colombia leapt from fourteen hundred pounds an acre in 1965 to thirty-five hundred in 1975; the gross value of that added production came to $350 million. As for the Philippines, it had long been importing rice; its production doubled between 1960 and 1980, and it became an exporter.

Few varieties of any plant last indefinitely. Three or four years is usually about the best that can be hoped for; by then, their enemies will have mutated and brought them low. IR-8, which, according to Nyle C. Brady, an American agronomist who succeeded Chandler as IRRI's director in 1973 and remained until 1981, "brought about more social change in Asia than all the social sciences combined," was despite that encomium no exception to the rule. For all its exemplary traits, it was no match for rice's indefatigable enemies. IR-8 was moderately resistant, to be sure, to the green leafhopper, but its defenses were weak against three biotypes of the brown planthopper and the gall midge, not to mention bacterial leaf blight. A grim local joke in Pakistan went, "Miracle rice has led to miracle locusts." The scientists at IRRI were not surprised. They could have rested on the laurels they had unarguably accumulated, but instead they went right on breeding, from IR-8 stock, even better rices. They had IR-20 ready in 1969 when Philippine farms were hit by the disease tungro. When IR-20 fell prey in 1973 to grassy stunt virus and the brown planthopper, they were ready with IR-26. In 1973, a new biotype of brown planthopper went after *it*. (IR-26 also kept getting knocked down by winds. IRRI hoped, as a stopgap, to supplant it with a wind-resistant rice indigenous to Taiwan. But there wasn't enough of that available; it seemed that the Taiwanese who'd traditionally cultivated it had largely abandoned it for IR-8.) Then in 1976, seven years in the making, came IR-36. Its multibranched family tree had rice genes on it from China, India, Indonesia, Japan, the Philippines, Taiwan, Vietnam, and the United States. It was quite a rice. It was resistant — at least at first — to blast, tungro, grassy stunt, bacterial blight, green leafhopper, gall midge, stem borer, and brown planthopper. It grew equally well in wetlands both irrigated and rain-fed. It could also withstand droughts. It was not bothered by soil conditions, being able to tolerate salinity, alkalinity, boron toxicity, aluminum toxicity, zinc deficiency, and iron deficiency. It matured, even under ordinary circumstances, in 120 days. It had a long, slender, translucent grain, and it cooked well. IRRI shies away from the use of the word "miracle," but it has been willing to dub IR-36 "the world's most popular rice." The institution that bred and nurtured it has credited IR-36 — which not long after its launching had taken over 65 percent of all rice land in the Philippines and 60 percent of that in Indonesia and had increased production in Asia by five million tons — with contributing a billion dollars in additional income a year to the Southeast Asia rice industry, not to mention a half-billion-dollar saving in insecticides. Indonesia had produced five million tons of rice in 1960. In 1972, there had been riots in Djakarta because rice prices were too high. (The *Far Eastern Economic Review* had said — and it would have applied to many another Asian land — "The price of rice and politics are inseparable in Indonesia.") In 1982, despite a drought, Indonesia produced twenty million tons. Because of the admirable new rices by then available, especially IR-36, some rural Indonesians who'd given up on farming and had migrated to cities went back home. In 1978, two years after IR-36 made its debut, the minister of agriculture of the Philippines had run into Nyle Brady. "IR-36 is giving us a lot of headaches," the minister told the director. He paused. "We have so much rice we do not know where to store it." An unprecedented four whole years went by before a new brown planthopper biotype evolved in north Sumatra against which IR-36 had no defenses. By that time, no longer to anyone's surprise, there was an IR-56 waiting in the wings. The seesaw battle between rice breeders and the pests they seek to neutralize may never end, because although no insects are yet known to have received Ph.D.'s, they can alter themselves nearly as fast as humans can alter the plants the bugs dote on. "The best we can ever hope for with pest management," one rice geneticist said not long ago, "is not to put pressure on the pest to change but to arrive at a state of peaceful co-existence."

In 1962, when whatever words Mao Zedong uttered became instant gospel in China, he said, "Take grain production as the key link and ensure an all-around development in agriculture." China produced, and still produces, more rice each year than any other country — at last count, some 140 million tons of it. For the first couple of years of IRRI's existence, however, the center had no more contact with the People's Republic than did much of the rest of the outside world, although it was pleased through third parties to be kept reasonably up to date about rizocultural practices there — to learn, for instance, that the Chinese were combating brown planthoppers by putting ducks in their paddies. Ducks like planthoppers as much as planthoppers like rice. By 1965, IRRI did have two Taiwanese on its scientific staff: Te-Tzu Chang, a geneticist with a Ph.D. from the University of Minnesota, and Keh-Chi Ling, a plant pathologist who got his doctorate at Wisconsin. (Dr. Ling, who died in 1982, is hallowed in rice annals because of his discovery of a wild Indian rice, *Oryza nivara* — the only rice containing genes resistant to grassy-stunt virus. *O. nivara*'s singular genes have since been incorporated into myriad other varieties.) IRRI had been hoping almost since its inception to establish some sort of relationship with the People's Republic. It seemed foolish for an international rice center to be cut off from the world's largest body of rice eaters. The Chinese themselves were aware of the work being done at Los Baños; as far back as 1964, some of their scientists had met one of IRRI's at a conclave in Bucharest and had heard about the rice that would be called IR-8; later, President Marcos had given some IR-20 seeds to the Chinese. After President Nixon's fence-mending visit to China in 1972, everything, of course, was different. A delegation representing the United States National Academy of Sciences was invited to Peking in 1974. Among its members was Nyle Brady, who had taken over from Robert Chandler at Los Baños the previous year. A Coloradan who had earned his Ph.D. in agronomy at North Carolina State College, Brady had taught that subject for twenty-eight years at Cornell and had, among extracurricular activities, served as director of science and education for the Department of Agriculture and chairman of the Agricultural Board of the National Research Council. That first encounter with the Chinese led to many more. In 1976, Peking sent a delegation to IRRI, headed by its vice-minister for agriculture and forestry; Brady and some of his staff made a reciprocal visit to China. (That was the year — the year of IR-36 — in which, at a Los Baños conference of thirty-nine scientists from all over the globe, one of the participants observed gloomily that "the new technology itself probably requires the world's agricultural scientists to run ever faster in order to stand still.") The bond between IRRI and mainland China became increasingly stronger. China let one of its scientists join the IRRI board of trustees in 1978. The following year, IRRI held an International Rice Testing Program *in* China. In a welcoming address, the head of the Chinese Academy of Agricultural Sciences called the increase of production "a glorious and arduous challenge for rice scientists." (He also managed to get in a crack at Lin Biao and the Gang of Four.) Brady, in a nonpartisan response, called the meeting a "historic occasion." By 1980, IRRI and the Chinese Academy would be jointly publishing *Rice Improvement in China and Other Asian Countries.* By 1981, the two research institutions would be jointly putting on a training course for rice scientists at Changsha, and China would be asking IRRI for advice so it could set up a national rice research institute of its own. Meanwhile, IRRI, which wants to be friends with all who are friendly to rice, kept on amicable terms with Taiwan. (At one Los Baños conference to which both Chinas had been invited, the delegates from each wanted "CHINA" on their name tags. Brady worked out a compromise acceptable to both sides: "PE-KING CHINA" and "TAIWAN CHINA.") By 1982, IRRI and the Chinese Academy had co-published five books (an entire one devoted to the brown planthopper) and had four more in progress. In April 1983, when IRRI was awarded a Third World Prize of $100,000 by the London-based Third World Foundation for Social and Economic Studies — it was the first institution ever so honored — the presentation was made, in Peking, by Zhao Ziyang, the premier of the State Council. Zhao expressed the hope that cooperation between the People's Republic and IRRI would continue forever, and he proposed that IRRI be tendered a standing ovation.

Many of the communist countries are rice-eating countries, and IRRI has got along splendidly with most of them, despite their awareness of its Rockefeller and Ford associations and of the fact that 25 percent of its budget has been regularly funded by the United States Agency for International Development. IRRI scientists have been welcomed in Rangoon, in Hanoi, in Havana. Cuba, which in the pre-Castro era had been far and away the biggest importer of rice in Latin America and a steady customer of the Gulf states' crops, had later come to look upon CGIAR and its affiliate centers as anathematic outposts of capitalistic imperialism. The high-yielding rices of the 1970s softened that hard line. Nyle Brady spent an hour once talking to Fidel Castro about rice. In the course of their chat, Castro — whose agriculturists were then working not only with IRRI but also with CIAT, on the development of herbicides for weed control on rice farms — told Brady that when the first shipment of seeds of IR-8 arrived in Cuba he'd had the privilege of planting them with his own hands.

By 1984, 35 percent of all the rice on earth consisted of high-yielding varieties with IRRI pedigrees. IRRI had not only won a number of prizes — among them one given by the World Bank called the King Baudouin International Agricultural Research Award — but had itself honored some of its special heroes. At Los Baños, there was a Harrar Hall, a

Forrest F. Hill Laboratory, and a Nyle C. Brady Laboratory. Brady had returned to the United States in 1981 to become Senior Assistant Administrator for Science and Technology of the Agency for International Development. (He had nineteen grandchildren and was responsible for, among other things, AID's global programs on family planning and birth control.) He was succeeded at IRRI by the then director general of the Indian Council of Agricultural Research, Monkombu Sambasivan Swaminathan, who understandably prefers the use of initials to that of his given name. The son of a surgeon who had been instrumental in ridding India of elephantiasis-bearing mosquitoes, Swaminathan was a Cambridge Ph.D. who had played a major role in India's adoption of high-yielding varieties of both rice and wheat. He could reflect with satisfaction that over the thirty years dating back to 1950 India's output of food grains had nearly tripled and that its growth rate in food production was slightly ahead of its growth rate in population. The institute over which Swaminathan began presiding had had quite a growth rate itself. It boasted a staff of two thousand, abetted by four hundred indigenous laborers. It had an annual budget of more than $20 million. In twenty years, it had trained three thousand scientists, 95 percent of them from rice-growing countries of the Third World. Its books and publications had been translated into more than eighteen languages and dialects; *Field Problems of Tropical Rice,* for instance, was out in Bengali, Burmese, Hindi, Filipino, Indonesian, Spanish, Tamil, Telegu, and Vietnamese. Along with its International Rice Testing Program, designed to furnish IRRI and other interested parties with accurate data on how various rices fared in various environments, the institute had fostered an International Rice Agro-Economic Network, an Asian Cropping Systems Network, and an International Network on Soil Fertility and Fertilizer Evaluation for Rice. IRRI was also probing the mysteries of blue-green algae, which grow in water and can fix nitrogen, an essential ingredient of fertilizers. To keep chemical-fertilizer plants functioning the world over requires two million barrels of oil a day. About 10 percent of all the nitrogen that goes into fertilizers is used for rice. An FAO pamphlet published in 1981 stated:

Blue-green algae represent a self-supporting system capable of carrying out both photosynthesis and nitrogen fixation, the energy bill for the latter process being paid by the sun. . . . If we could utilize these algae, particularly in rice fields, which form an ideal environment for them, our costly reliance on the energy intensive nitrogen fertilizer input could be substantially reduced. Recent research has shown the feasibility of using these algae as a biological input in rice cultivation and of obtaining additional yields for which the incremental input cost will be low. The use of these regenerative biological sources may also minimize the environmental hazards and maximize the ecological benefits.

In other words, blue-green algae are dandy. So, when it came to substitutes for conventional fertilizers, one of them might be the azolla, a water fern that plucks nitrogen from the atmosphere and tucks it away; some IRRI researchers were working on that. Others were concentrating on high-protein rice, and had pushed that content up from 7 or 8 percent to 9 or 10. Others were searching for salinity-tolerant rices: there are 150 million acres of land in Asia that have soils with a high saline content and are waiting for a rice that can cope with that as yet inhibiting condition. Still others were devoting their time and trouble to the neem tree. The neem tree has an oil in its fruits and leaves that insects find repulsive. Neem-oil cakes scattered around rice paddies might someday give the coup de grace to the brown planthopper — unless, of course, the critter regenerates itself into a mutant that fancies them.

Meanwhile, under the patient supervision of Te-Tzu Chang, the geneticist from Taiwan, IRRI had been collecting samples of all the different varieties of rice it could get its hands on. Chang once guessed that there were perhaps 130,000 of them somewhere or other on earth. After the attack of leaf blight that devastated the corn crop of the United States in 1970 — a horror that resulted from the widespread planting of a single type of that grain — worried rice men flocked to IRRI from all over to assess *their* situation. IRRI already had more than 10,000 varieties safely in its custody, but the visitors were not entirely reassured. "The disappearance of the world's rice germplasm has reached the crisis stage," a group of them reported. "All sources of potentially valuable germplasm must be collected soon; otherwise they may be lost forever." IRRI accelerated its efforts to acquire them; it hoped to have bagged 120,000 by 1987. By 1984, it had more than 70,000 "accessions," as the samples are called — each dried in a special oven for fourteen hours at 38 degrees centigrade, then packed by hand in vacuum-sealed aluminum cans, 60 grams to the receptacle, and stored at 2 degrees centigrade. That's for short-term storage — about ten years. When a variety gets long in the tooth, as it were, it is taken out and planted, and fresh seeds are packaged and stored. (Samples are also cached at minus 10 degrees centigrade, at which temperature they are expected to have a viability of at least fifty years.) Nyle Brady said of this burgeoning trove, in 1981; "IRRI holds this bank in trust for the scientists and agricultural leaders of the rice-producing countries. It is their rices, collected primarily by them, and sent to IRRI for safekeeping."

Currently, IRRI, ever in quest of further improvement of the breed, draws on its vast assortment of rices of old and new to grow half a million rice plants a year, and at last count it had 109,657 rice pedigrees in its records — so many rices that by now they have designations that sound like Social Security numbers: IR5853-118-5, for instance. Every year, the center sends out to be tested and nurtured, by scientists hither and yon, 10,000 samples of seed. In emergencies, IRRI can respond as swiftly as a small-town volunteer rescue squad. In 1981, for example, South Korea's rice was hit by a wave of blast. In November 1980, IRRI had forehandedly obtained 305 kilograms' worth of 28 varieties of Korean rice — offspring of earlier IRRI strains into which had been incorporated blast-resistant genes from Bangladesh, Sri Lanka, the Philippines, and Vietnam. (To sow one acre usually takes 160 pounds of seed, but rice·can multiply even faster than mice. In three generations, 18 pounds can become a million tons.) Seeds from that planting were ready for harvesting in mid-March of 1981. One-hundred-and-five tons' worth of them were rushed to the Manila airport and flown to Seoul. South Korea had a decent rice crop in 1982. One-third of it was the result of that airlift. That same year, when what remained of Cambodia had become Kampuchea, there was another crisis. Many Cambodian peasants had been driven from their villages in 1975, and when they had returned four years later there were no traces of the rices they had traditionally raised. But IRRI had begun collecting these back in 1973, and Chang had no fewer than 800 of them on tap in his imposing inventory. The Oxford Committee for Famine Relief — Oxfam — wanted to get the farmers under way again, and IRRI was ready with enough seeds of several dozen Khmer varieties to mount another lifesaving airlift. "To manage a large germplasm collection is not a very glamorous job," Chang once reflected. "Still, it is imperative for somebody to look after everybody's business."

V

SOYBEANS
The Future of the Planet

This was the goal of the leaf and the root.
For this did the blossom burn its hour.
This little grain is the ultimate fruit.
This is the awesome vessel of power.

— GEORGE STARBUCK GALBRAITH

IN NOVEMBER 1983, a week before the American harvest festival of Thanksgiving, schoolchildren and their elders in the United States were urged to give up their lunch to help some starving child elsewhere have something to eat. It was one more manifestation of the widely held concept that such admirable self-sacrifice will somehow get a peanut-butter-and-jelly sandwich into the lunchbox of some hungry youngster in, say, Mali or Mauritania. The generous American children might perhaps more usefully have been urged by their teachers to ponder a 1981 report of the FAO titled *Agriculture: Toward 2000,* which stated:

If the experience of the 1960's and 1970's drove home one lesson, it was that a sustainable and prosperous agriculture is central to the achievement of many strongly desired objectives. It is central to the elimination of hunger and poverty, to improving equity within developing countries, to boosting their economic growth and industrialization, to preserving the environment — and to helping to reduce imbalances within countries and between them. By the end of the 1970's, in the light of the history of the previous two decades, it was difficult to imagine another sector in which such a massive and needed contribution to the future was possible.

Most people on earth do not eat much peanut butter and jelly, or beef or pork or fowl or fish, though they probably wish they could. They eat rice and wheat and corn and sorghum and millet and cassava and potatoes. These, to them, mean food — the rooted staples without which, for more than half the world's population, life would be unsupportable. Contemporary farmers can readily produce enough grains and tubers to provide every living human being with three thousand calories a day of nourishment — well above the accepted minimum for an adequate diet. But many poor people can't get to what is available — and if they can, they can't afford to buy it, even when, as they often do, they spend three-quarters of their disposable income on food. A barber in India can earn so-and-so much rice for each haircut. If the price of rice climbs more steeply than he can raise his tonsorial rates, he and his family simply eat less. There was a time in 1982 when people in one part of Zimbabwe were lining up for hours to receive a modest dole of cornmeal, while in another part of the same country there was a surplus of that commodity. It took a foreign philanthropic organization to underwrite the cost of moving the meal from the one area to the other. During the Ethiopian famine of 1983, it was determined by concerned outsiders that much as that distressed nation needed food, it was in no less urgent want of 50 trucks and a few light airplanes to deliver what supplies were forthcoming to those most desperate for them. Chad had a famine that same year. The FAO calculated that 109,000 tons of emergency grain supplies were available to relieve the situation, but because of poor transportation and poor storage facilities, the country could only handle 3,500 tons a month. Chad needed 150 trucks to carry grain to its hinterlands. It had only 40 that were serviceable. Nearly one-quarter of the cost of distributing grain anywhere on earth consists of transporting it from one place to another. The problem was not so grave when people lived close to the source of their food. Now, more and more of them dwell in urban settlements, where food has to be delivered and purchased. In an editorial entitled "Distribution: The Fragile Link," the FAO magazine *Ceres* stated not long ago:

By the end of this century, perhaps as much as half of the human race will be removed from direct access to the simplest types of self-sufficient food systems. Inevitably, growing millions will need to find their sustenance at the retail end of massive metropolitan marketing systems. Whether they can afford to feed themselves adequately will depend partly, of course, on employment opportunities. But it will also depend on what sort of incentives and support are required for those who remain on the land to produce in abundant excess of their own needs, and how efficiently that surplus can be moved to those no longer able to grow any significant portion of their food supply.

In *Coriolanus,* Shakespeare had it that "the gods sent not corn for the rich men only." But the poor who subsist largely on plant foods often receive far too small a share of them. The French Revolution was fought in part for bread. Fifty years after what to the commoners who uprose must have seemed a victory, the principal fare of the French peasantry, according to the agricultural historian Arthur Young, was a "detestable bread made from rye, barley, or peas and potatoes; and, to make the matter still worse, without yeast, and being sometimes kept for weeks, it becomes covered with mould, and altogether presents an appearance enough to turn the stomach of a savage." When people in the industrialized, Western world find themselves with an excess of cash over their norm, they allocate only 5 or 10 percent to the purchase of food; in the rest of the world, the figure is more likely to be 50 or 60 percent. In Calcutta, where the very notion of having any extra money would be for most residents bizarre, four out of five people get less than 900 calories' worth of food a day; the minimum adequate intake for an adult at rest, let alone an active one, is 1,600. India as a whole has been nearly self-sufficient in food production since the 1960s; notwithstanding, the director general of the Nutrition Foundation of India told a World Bank seminar in the spring of 1983 that of 23 million children expected to be born in his country that year, because of insufficient nourishment almost 3 million of them would die before they were a year old, another 1 million would never reach adulthood, and fewer than 3 million would ever become truly healthy. (There are ill-fed people, obviously, in the Western world as well, but their plight has rarely achieved monumentality; it was not until that same year of 1983, for instance, that the United States House of Representatives, which has a committee or subcommittee to mull over practically every imaginable issue of national consequence, got around even to contemplating the establishment of a Select Committee on Hunger.) The bleak statistics abound, and proliferate. Brazil is by no means as badly off as several dozen other nations; even so, people there still sell their eyes and their kidneys for food money. Perhaps 40 million human beings are dying every year from lack of a proper diet. In Tanzania alone, 50,000 children succumb to protein deficiencies. In 1974, a World Food Conference held with great fanfare in Rome adopted a Universal Declaration on the Eradication of

Hunger and Malnutrition, which piously pronounced that "every man, woman, and child has the inalienable right to be free from hunger and malnutrition"; and several years later the director general of the FAO, Edouard Saouma, declared unilaterally that "the fact that everyone has a right to enough to eat is now everywhere accepted and more widely proclaimed than ever before. But alongside this goes the fact that more human beings are hungry and malnourished than ever before and that the number is growing all the time." The World Bank thinks the number has reached 1 billion. The FAO is more optimistic: it puts the figure at between 400 million and 500 million. Its most pessimistic view of what the grim statistic will be at the turn of the century is 685 million. Its most optimistic is that it will be only — only! — 260 million. But to bring the latter about would require an additional annual investment in agriculture, above the $5 billion currently allocated to that end, of $13 billion.

The protruding ribs of every emaciated child in the bleak Sahel region of Africa could be sheathed in flesh if anywhere near all the food that is planted reached maturity. Food, of course, is perishable. The FAO has a Prevention of Food Losses program (reduction of rice losses in on-farm marketing in Liberia, rat control in Somalia, construction of small-grain warehouses in The Gambia, storehouses to protect corn from pests in Ethiopia); and the United States has a National Crop Loss Assessment Network. For all that, the extent of the perishability of food is staggering, as indeed it has been since a despairing scribe in ancient Egypt wrote, "Worms have destroyed half the wheat, and the hippopotami have eaten the rest; there are swarms of rats in the fields, the grasshoppers alight there, the cattle devour, the little birds pilfer; and if the farmer loses sight for an instant of what remains on the ground, it is carried off by robbers." The amount of plant food lost nowadays on the ground or in transit or in storage could, if it survived, feed 300 million people for a year. Ten percent of the American corn crop is lost annually because of weeds, 12 percent because of insects, another 12 because of diseases; the respective percentages for wheat are 12, 6, and 14. That translates into about 120 million tons of corn and 85 million of wheat. In the United States alone, the potential output of more than 100 million acres of cropland is never realized owing to insects — a deprivation of some $30-billion worth of produce every year. There is a National Potato Anti-Bruise Commission based in Maine; in its gloomy opinion, bruises are responsible for an annual loss to that sturdy crop of between $100 million and $150 million. It sometimes seems a wonder that anybody has anything to eat at all.

Even when crops manage to get themselves healthily harvested, they face more perils than Pauline. Ten percent of the grain that goes into storage founders there. The United Nations General Assembly, which loves to pass resolutions, passed one in 1975 decreeing that there should be at least a 50-percent reduction in post-harvest losses by 1985. One could almost hear the dread flour beetle — which, given enough sustenance and a hospitable environment, can multiply 76-million-fold in six months — chuckling to itself. The poorest storage facilities on earth, not surprisingly, are in the Third World, which is the part of the world most reliant on grains and roots and tubers. The Third World's post-harvest losses just of grains come to 70 million tons a year. In Latin America, and in Africa, it is routine for close to one-third of all harvested cereals and tubers to vanish, or at any rate to become worthless. When corn is stored in Zambia for as long as twelve months, moths and weevils damage 90 to 100 percent of its kernels. (That situation may have brightened; Australia not long ago contributed $416,000 to a corn-handling-improvement program in Zambia.) The People's Republic of China has, among its many exhortatory slogans, one that goes "Store Grain Everywhere," and the injunction is often qualified by four "withouts" — without insects, without fungi, without birds and rodents, and without accidents such as fire and flood. (Merely by constructing some new godowns at Rangoon, Burma not long ago averted the loss of 28,000 tons of rice a year.) In India, rodents destroy 25 percent of all crops theoretically stored for future consumption. The United States does better: it loses only 7 million tons of stored grain a year to rats. At Kansas State University, researchers have lately been studying the kangaroo rat, because it seems to be able to store grain more efficiently in its cheek pouches than men can in their warehouses. The exemplary rat doesn't get cancer, either.

After a dreadful drought in Africa in 1983, Director General Saouma of the FAO judged that twenty-two sub-Saharan countries urgently needed 700,000 tons of food over and beyond what they had already been receiving to alleviate their considerable plight. Two years earlier, when on an FAO map the color black was used to designate nutritional adversity, more than half that continent was dark. (In 1983, even South Africa, normally an exporter of food to its more disadvantaged neighbors, was stricken: drought reduced its production of corn from 7 million tons to 4.3 million.) To circumvent, if possible, such crises, it has long been argued by people who care that there should at all times be huge reserve stocks of food available for emergencies — at least 17 or 18 percent, according to FAO calculations, of annual consumption. The 1974 World Food Conference set 10 million tons as a reasonable figure for an International Emergency Food Reserve, to be run by the FAO, but it was not until 1981 that even .5 million tons was achieved. The grand scheme could in any event hardly have been expected to succeed without the cooperation of both the Soviet Union and the United States. The U.S.S.R. has never seen fit even to become a member of the FAO, and various U.S. administrations have blown hot and cold about how an international emergency food reserve should be operated.

Quite apart from all that, the FAO has a World Food Program, which has been functioning since 1962 — it was an outgrowth of the Food for Peace program launched in the United States the year before — and which in 1983 released 1.5 million tons of food to 117 countries. Almost 90 percent of that consisted of cereals, mostly from the United States and Canada, although other countries did chip in on a modest scale — some cocoa from Ghana, tea from India, sugar from Cuba, and tinned beef from Botswana. Since 1968 the FAO has also sponsored a food-for-work scheme, under the terms of which more than $1-billion worth of edibles (one-quarter of them, nowadays, from the United States) has gone to countries that allot them in lieu of wages to laborers recruited for such communal projects as schools or public toilets. In Lesotho, for instance, a nation entirely surrounded by South Africa, thousands of women, some with babies strapped to their backs, built more than 600 miles of new roads and paths so that goods could be moved to markets without, as had previously been the case, having to travel into South Africa — where most of the women's husbands, likely as not, were at work because there were no employment opportunities at home. In Bangladesh, over a recently completed four-year stretch, two million laborers at fifteen hundred locations, using hand tools, spaded up enough earth to construct more than 1,500 miles of canals and nearly 2,000 miles of flood-control embankments. They received 5.5 pounds of wheat for every ton of soil they displaced. They moved more earth than was excavated for the Panama Canal. The purpose of their canals and dams was to increase rice production in Bangladesh by 200,000 tons a year, and to that end 480,000 tons of wheat were dispensed as wages — a rare instance of one staff of life contributing directly to the propagation of another.

Food aid, in whatever form it is meted out, is not infrequently tied to politics. Of the 76,427 tons of cereals that the United States contributed to the International Emergency Food Reserve in 1982, for example, 61,317 tons were rather pointedly earmarked for refugees from Afghanistan. By the same token, the trucks that Ethiopia needed the following year, for all known purposes to expedite the transport of food supplies, could have been furnished by the United States, but weren't, on the ground that they also could have been used to transport military supplies. Still, ever since the Second World War, the United States has been unparalleled in succoring the needy. From 1954 to date, much American food aid has been sent abroad under the terms of the Agricultural Trade Development and Assistance Act, generally known for short as P.L. 480. The millions of tons that have thus been shared with the rest of the world have not, to be sure, been outright gifts, but rather have been purchased by governments with whom it is deemed prudent to maintain, or create, friendships; indeed, the text of P.L. 480 defines it as "an act to increase the consumption of United States agricultural commodities in foreign countries, to improve the foreign relations of the United States and for other purposes." Some effects of this consumption on the economics of recipient nations have been questionable. Colombia produced 160,000 tons of wheat in 1955, and imported an additional 50,000. A generation later, with

American-grown wheat readily available at relatively low, Colombian-government-subsidized prices, and with less incentive accordingly for Colombian farmers to grow much of their own, that country was producing less than 50,000 tons and importing 400,000. But where staple foods are involved, nothing ever works perfectly, and uncertainty always prevails. Somebody should have told Henry Kissinger that before he delivered himself of the dubious prediction, in 1978, that "by 1985, no child should go to bed hungry." Of course, most statesmen in well-fed nations simply don't have the time, except in severe crises, to learn much about the dietary predicaments and peculiarities of ill-fed ones. Back in 1946, for instance, the United States government, aware that its Chinese wartime allies had bare larders, bigheartedly sent over to Manchuria a hefty consignment of soybeans, which at least some Americans also knew to be, next to rice, a favorite staple of the Chinese. What the donors did not realize was that at that time, although the Manchurians would indeed have welcomed almost any kind of food, they had such a surplus of soybeans on hand that they were using them for fuel.

In 1946, there were relatively few Americans outside of food-relief agencies who knew much more about the history of the soybean — termed "the miracle bean" by the ancient Chinese and also by such latter-day journals as the Sri Lankan *Soyanews,* which is published in Sinhalese, Tamil, and English, and the merely monolingual *New York Times* — than they did about Manchuria. (At Cornell University, which had long been a bastion of agricultural research, there were plenty of scholars who knew: one of them, in a bulletin published the previous year, had characterized soybeans as "a tremendous reserve food supply that can save great populations from hunger and disease.") Today, the impact of the soybean on the American agricultural and economic scenes is thumping, though as a foodstuff it has not yet made much of a dent on American minds, hearts, and stomachs. On 65 million acres, American farmers now produce more than 2 billion bushels — 70 million tons — of soybeans yearly. The United States, which enjoys 85 percent of the world trade in soybeans, exports half that mountain of beans — a $6-billion cash crop. In the early 1960s, the most lucrative American exports were jet airplanes. Soybeans overtook and passed them and left them laboring behind. Wheat and corn are single items at the Chicago Board of Trade; the soybean is traded, vigorously, as itself, as its oil, and as its meal. The University of Illinois plant geneticist Theodore Hymowitz, who has pursued soybeans all over the planet and is so obsessed with them that he once read through all of Benjamin Franklin's extant letters hoping to find a single mention of them (he finally spotted just one), has acclaimed his favorite plant as "the most important grain legume crop in the world in terms of total production and international trade." When the United States, about 1978, persuaded the shah of Iran to switch to American soybean oil from the sunflower-seed oil his country had been buying from the Soviet Union (which he did even though one of his top-ranking generals was worried that soybeans, already suspect for inducing flatulence, might also be a cause of sterility), that alone represented foreign exchange of $117 million a year. Fortunes have been made and lost trafficking in soybean futures, the prices of which per bushel fluctuated in the 1970s from $3.25 to $12.85. (Soybeans were known in American financial circles as "the Cinderella crop" in 1971, and as "the market's miracle legume" in 1978.) In 1977, almost 8 million soybean contracts — each representing 5,000 bushels — were swapped at the Chicago Board of Trade; every swing of one penny in the bushel price represented a fifty-dollar profit or loss on every contract. That was the year in which the Hunts of Texas — Nelson Bunker, W. Herbert, et al. — tried to corner the soybean market. They acquired control of 23 million bushels of soybeans worth around $300 million (the limit for any person or group of speculators was supposed to be 3 million bushels) before they were forced to cut out their shenanigans and were fined $500,000 by the Commodity Futures Trading Commission. (Brazil, which before 1960 grew hardly any soybeans, has become the second-biggest trader in them. By 1980, soybeans occupied nearly 20 percent of Brazilian cropland, and it was one of the typical and baffling ironies of contemporary agriculture that while countless Brazilians were seriously malnourished that year, 10 million tons of soybeans were shipped out of that country.) It was in 1973 that soybean-futures prices peaked. A poor harvest was predicted; the Soviet Union had begun a large-scale chicken-raising program and couldn't get fish meal to feed the fowl because of a skimpy Peruvian sardine catch; President Nixon's advisers were afraid that if soybeans got any more expensive at home the cost of livestock feed might go uncomfortably high, and with it, inevitably, the cost of meat and milk and butter and eggs and everything else. So the president briefly imposed an embargo on all soybean exports from the United States. That upset the Japanese, who had become dependent on American soybeans to the clanging tune of $100 million a year. The Japanese newspapers reported that many of their countrymen were suffering from a novel ailment — Nixon Soybean Shock.

The soybean — *Glycine max* — is an unusual vegetable. It has two great advantages over most of the staple food plants, and indeed over most foods in any category. For one, it bulges with protein — 38 percent of its edible weight. It has three times the protein of wheat or corn or other cereals, three times that of eggs, more than twice that of lean beef, twelve times that of cow's milk. A pound of protein from beef costs $12.40, from milk $2.52, from medium eggs $6.77, from granulated soybean $.71. Moreover, the soybean plant is blessed with nitrogen-fixing bacteria that form nodules on its roots. American farmers who had no other outlets for what few soybeans they grew once raised them chiefly to plow under as fertilizer for crops that were deemed more valuable. Outside of Manchuria, the soybean fares best in the American Midwest and in southern Brazil. The soybean is sensitive to day length. Different varieties do best at different latitudes. Because Dairen, Manchuria, and Decatur, Illinois, are on about the same latitude, native Manchurian varieties could be successfully nutured in the American Midwest. Northeastern China, just south of Manchuria, is generally conceded to be the birthplace of the soybean — or soy bean, or soya bean, as it is variously known in English. A onetime Chinese name for soy sauce was *chiang-yiu,* which the Japanese pronounced *show-yu,* which got contracted, or so some agri-etymologists contend, to *so-ya* and in turn to *soy-a.* It was Linnaeus who coined "*Glycine max.*" In some forms, the soybean has a strong and, to Occidental palates, unappetizing taste. "*Glycine*" comes from a Greek word meaning "sweet." Linnaeus may never have chewed on what he christened.

The soybean, an important constituent of the regular diet of hundreds of millions of Chinese, Japanese, Koreans, and Indonesians, was one of the five sacred plants mentioned — the date is arguable, but may have been around 2800 B.C. — in the writings of the Chinese emperor Shen-nung, among whose sobriquets were "the Heavenly Father" and "the Father of Chinese Agriculture." (The other four sacred plants were rice, wheat, barley, and millet.) Soybeans are unarguably known to have been cultivated in east-central China as far back as 1100 B.C. One king's cook of that era was a soy-sauce specialist; he kept 120 jars of the stuff, each a bit different from the others, in stock at all times. (Secret recipes for soy sauce were treasured and handed down from Chinese generation to generation like rare porcelains. Sainam, fifty miles southwest of Canton, was generally conceded to be the source of the most admirable sauce; unscrupulous Cantonese shopkeepers were not above labeling their inferior offerings "SAINAM SOY SAUCE.") A Chinese legend about the origin of the soybean has it that some bygone itinerant merchants were besieged by bandits, took refuge on a hilltop, and were running out of food when a servant called their attention to a viny plant with little round beans in its pods. That saved them, and when they introduced their discovery to their compatriots, it was agreed that they'd returned home with a treasure far more valuable than anything the bandits had been after. To those Chinese who wondered how that fruitful plant had got to that hill in the first place, the answer was sometimes given that it was obvious: Hou Tsi, an ancient god of agriculture, had put it there knowing that at some time or another it would be approached and appreciated. (Another yarn featured a king of Wei called Wên, who threatened to kill his brother Ts'ao Chih unless Ts'ao Chih could, while walking precisely seven steps, compose a poem acceptable to the throne. Ts'ao saved his skin by coming up with a four-liner in which the royal family was a beanstalk and he was a bean — probably a soybean — and thus it would be unkind for Wên to do any harm to any part of the family tree.) The Japanese, who became acquainted with the soybean in the first century A.D., soon produced their own version of its arrival on the mundane scene. Once again, five precious plants were involved, though in this instance not exactly the same ones. It seemed that when the god of gods Izanagi came down to earth and created the islands that became Japan, he also created a pantheon of lesser gods and goddesses. The god of the sea didn't fancy being wet all the time, so he came ashore, had a disagreement over alimentary rights with the goddess of food, and slew her. From her buried corpse five plants at once sprang up — first the soybean, then a larger, common bean, and following them rice, millet, and barley.

Wherever all those strange goings-on allegedly took place, Manchuria emerged as the primary source of soybeans, and for centuries it was just about the only source. Manchuria was the locale of *The Good Earth,* and soybeans, which dominated a quarter of its cultivated acreage, gave it that cachet. In *The Soya Bean,* the twentieth-century British author Elizabeth Bowdidge rated her subject "the most remarkable of all legumes," and mused: "One wonders what the people of the Far East would do without the soya bean! . . . Manchuria has gold, iron, coal, and minerals, but surely the real prize is the soya bean." By the nineteenth century, soybeans were prized in Manchuria for all kinds of virtues: their oil, for instance, proved to be repellent to most insects that preyed on silkworms. What little of the Manchurian soybean crop the Chinese permitted to get to Japan passed through the port of Newchwang. The Japanese coveted far more of the beans than they could peacefully obtain, and in 1894 they went to war for them. After defeating the Chinese, and taking over Newchwang, for a while the victors showed their contempt for the losers by using the soybeans to which they now had ample access principally as fertilizer. By the turn of the century, the Russians, eager to get into the combative soybean scene themselves, had taken over the port of Dairen. That led to another war, to another Japanese triumph, and to an increasing awareness in much of the rest of the world of the desirability of the soybean, then highly regarded, for one thing, as a source of cooking oil. Japan sparked that interest. It suddenly found itself with a surplus of the commodity. (The Chinese had a deficit; they had to import coconut oil from Indonesia.) In 1908, Japan began shipping soybeans to Great Britain — a whopping 400,000 tons of them in 1909, destined mainly for oil and soap. By 1910, an English Customs official posted to Dairen, reporting to his superiors on the activity in soybeans over the previous three years, would write that "their rapid emergence from obscurity . . . has been one of the most remarkable commercial events of recent times." And how they did emerge! By 1918, Manchuria was exporting 612,000 tons of whole beans, 151,316 tons of oil, and 1,055,000 tons of cake.

It was chiefly in Asia, however, that soybeans played, and still play, a conspicuous role in human diets. The Japanese quickly subdued their distaste for the soybean as a loser's fare and began to eat it with gusto. Today, there are more than thirty thousand establishments in Japan that make tofu — soybean curd fried in bean oil, which in China is sometimes known, nonpejoratively, as "stinking curd." (The odor of soybean oil, one occidental observer of the oriental scene has written condescendingly, "is not very pleasant, but this is of no consequence to the Chinese people.") The Japanese are no less partial to miso, a soybean paste they gobble up in soups, and they spend $2 billion a year to slake their prodigious thirst for soy sauce. Tempeh, a concoction made by treating soybeans with a fungus, is exceedingly popular in Indonesia, where 41,000 shops employ 128,000 workers who turn out 169,000 tons of it a year. (British soldiers in a Japanese prison camp in 1943 tried boiling some soybeans they acquired. They were indigestible. Dutch prisoners who'd lived in Indonesia suggested trying to convert the beans into tempeh, and contrived to do so by fabricating a suitable fungus out of dried hibiscus petals. According to *Deficiency Diseases in Japanese Prison Camps,* a 1951 report of the Medical Research Council in London, that improvised dish was "successfully used in treating protein and vitamin deficiencies.") The Chinese, especially those in the northeast, have long consumed soybean in so many guises, including cheese analogs, cooked sprouts, and soy milk — the last fashioned from dried beans that have been soaked, ground, and boiled — that *Glycine max,* although it has occasionally been put down as the "poor man's meat" (Buddhist vegetarians, among others, applaud it as a first-rate meat substitute) has also more testimonially been exalted as "the Cow of China." Soy milk has had its special aficionados in India, where some Buddhists are of the opinion that if children drink cow's milk, which should rightfully be reserved for calves, they'll grow horns. (People on kosher diets can combine soy meat-substitutes with genuine cow's milk, and soy milk with beef, without violating any religious laws; in the United States today there are such esoteric eating establishments as kosher macrobiotic vegetarian restaurants. It may well have been after patronizing one of these that an American versifier whose raptness eclipsed his rhyme was inspired to pen "Soybeans can be the cream in your coffee, the dog in your bun, the chow for your cat, and then some.")

Soy milk had been around China for ages, but it served mainly as a hot breakfast soup until an American medical missionary turned up there early in the twentieth century. This was Dr. Harry W. Miller, who before his death at ninety-seven became known as "the China Doctor." An Ohioan born in 1879, Miller got his professional training at the Medical Missionary College, in Battle Creek, Michigan, a Seventh-Day Adventist institution affiliated with Dr. John H. Kellogg's celebrated health-foods sanatorium. Dr. Miller made the first of several trips to China in 1903, and soon elected to live like his hosts — native garb, pigtailed hair, tofu for breakfast, and all that. Among the sanatoria he ultimately founded all over the world was one in Shanghai, in 1928, and to nourish some of the infant orphans who arrived on its doorstep he began to experiment with soy milk. It had an off-putting flavor which was generally described as "beany," but one day a disembodied celestial voice revealed to him, he himself was glad to reveal, that cooking it longer with live steam would enhance its palatability. The China Doctor had a soy dairy in operation by 1936, with deliveries throughout Shanghai, and some to the Chinese Army; but then the Japanese demolished the place. Back in the United States for a spell, he became an indefatigable booster of all soy foods. While continuing to practice medicine (he specialized in goiter surgery), he set up a company at Mount Vernon, Ohio; one of the many accomplishments for which he is revered in soy-foods circles is his having successfully perfected the world's first meatless hot dog. More consequentially, a process he developed led to a soy-milk-based soft drink called Vitasoy, which in the 1970s became so popular in Hong Kong that it actually outsold Coca-Cola. Dr. Miller had another go at Shanghai in 1949, when he was a youthful seventy, but he had barely arrived when the Communists moved in and he had to move out. Four years after that, he went to Taiwan, where Chiang Kai-shek — who was so fond of Dr. Miller's vegetable milk that once, fearful he might run out of it, the generalissimo sent a plane a thousand miles to replenish his supply — received him heartily, and, before the venerable physician departed in 1956 to seek new converts elsewhere (at ninety-four, Dr. Miller traveled to India to help out with a soy-milk plant), invested him with the Order of the Blue Star of China.

A British doctor who gave physical examinations to many of the hundred thousand Asians who served in France during the First World War as members of the Chinese Labour Corps was impressed by the fine condition of their teeth — especially, though it scarcely seemed much of a yardstick, compared to English teeth. He attributed the good dental health to soybeans, as he credited them later, during a visit to China, for the absence of rickets in children at a time when, he said, at least 80 percent of the elementary-school students in London had at least a trace of it. Doctors in Moscow have prescribed soybeans as a cure for rickets. Chinese physicians, for their part, had long had — like Dr. Miller — a high regard for soybeans' restorative powers. They used the beans as a remedy for ailments of the heart, liver, stomach, lungs, liver, kidneys, bladder, bowels, and nerves; and recommended them for improving the complexion and stimulating hair growth. Yellow soybeans were favored to overcome underweight (to soybeans of all colors is attributed the fact that Chinese are on the whole less afflicted than other races by obesity), and for cooling the blood; black soybeans were often fed to horses before a long journey, to augment endurance. In Japan, doctors have urged soy milk, which has more iron and less fat than cow's milk, upon diabetics and arteriosclerotics; and in some circles there the ingestion of at least one bowl of miso soup every day is considered to be a way of averting stomach cancer and ulcers. An American businessman visited a cement factory in Ghana not long ago. Its managers said their productivity was appalling. They had a 40-percent turnover in their labor force, a 33-percent absenteeism rate, and their employees seemed unable to work for more than a couple of hours at a stretch without getting perceptibly weak. The American, whose motives were not entirely selfless because he happened to be a soybean processor, suggested that the factory hands be put on a soy-supplemented regimen. Within eighteen months after that was done, the American claimed he was informed, productivity had tripled, there was a negligible turnover, the absenteeism rate had fallen to 1 percent, and the employees were tossing cement bags around all day long without even flinching.

Jesuit missionaries stationed in China probably were the first voyagers to bring soybeans to Europe, where the plants, like potatoes before them, were considered a horticultural curiosity. They were on exhibit at the Jardin des Plantes in Paris in 1739, and in London's Kew Botanic Gardens — these probably coming from India — in 1790. (Even earlier, in 1712, a German botanist, Engelbert Kaempfer, who had visited Nagasaki in the 1690s, had published a recipe for soy sauce; that may have been the first time any Europeans were informed that the bean was in any respect edible.) Benjamin Franklin has been credited, perhaps apocryphally, with having espied soybeans at the Jardin des Plantes and brought a few home. He would have been a logical courier: He belonged to the Philadelphia Society for Promoting Agriculture, which swapped seeds with Paris, and he was acquainted with the head of the garden there. In any event, there were soybeans in the United States, probably brought over from China by clipper ship, in 1804, at which time an admirer wrote, "The soybean bears the climate of Pennsylvania very well. The bean ought therefore to be cultivated." Whether or not the Society for Promoting Agriculture followed that advice is uncertain; it is known that a botanical garden in Cambridge, Massachusetts, had some soybeans on display — once more merely as a rare exhibit — in 1829. They were called "Japan peas," and they got written up in the *New England Farmer* that October. Soybeans enjoyed another brief flurry of notoriety in 1854, when Commodore Perry brought some back from Japan. In 1879, they were being grown, experimentally, at both Rutgers Agricultural College and Kansas State Agricultural College. They also began to be scrutinized by botanists at Cornell — among them Edward Lewis Sturtevant, who in 1882 appraised soybeans as "of excellent promise as a forage plant"; but he added, as he doubtless would not have when he got to know them better, "even if the beans are not acceptable to the palate."

At the 1893 World's Columbian Exposition in Chicago, soybeans had still made no more headway in the United States than to be displayed yet again as an oddity. A visitor to the exposition would himself have been regarded as very odd indeed had he predicted, accurately, that within ninety years 500,000 American farmers — with Illinois farmers in the van — would be growing them. (Of course, if he had predicted jet airplanes he might have been deemed even more daft.) But soon afterward *Glycine max* began to attract more than sightseers' attention. In 1896, the *American Journal of Pharmacology* ran an article entitled "Soybeans and Soybean Products," and that same year there was another, in the *Pharmaceutical Review,* on how to prepare tofu. In 1898, the U.S. Department of Agriculture began testing soybeans and distributing them to farmers. The reaction was mixed. A bulletin issued in March 1901 by Kansas State Agricultural College quoted 292 Kansans who were known to be raising soybeans. H. C. Whitford, of Garnett, in Anderson County: "Tried to cut with mower, but this broke the clods and we had to resort to hand pulling. Got badly injured in the shock. [Presumably the beans, not himself.] I thought them worthless and fed them to hogs; the hogs were ·very fond of them." William Matthias, of Huron, in Atchison County: "Pigs and poultry got a taste of the ripe beans and they made desperate raids on the field." Joseph Shaw, of Strong, in Chase County: "Pigs were crazy for them, and ate stalks and all." John German, of Hiattville, in Bourbon County, said *his* hogs wouldn't touch the stuff, although his calves and yearlings would; C. O. McLane, another Bourbon County man, from Uniontown, said concurringly that calves and also colts would climb low fences to get at some sorghum he had liberally laced with soybeans. Several farmers grumpily observed that soybeans were mighty attractive to rabbits; nary a grower seemed even to entertain the notion that the crop might ever be food for human beings.

In 1911, there was a crushing plant at Seattle, to produce oil and meal from Manchurian soybeans. The first such plant to process homegrown soybeans was unveiled in 1912 at Elizabeth City, North Carolina — the state that for a decade or so thereafter led the rest of the union in producing the still infant crop. The government's Agricultural Experiment Station at New Haven, Connecticut, where much important research had been done in corn, potatoes, and other vital food plants, looked into soybeans in 1913, but concluded that as far as the United States was concerned they were of little worth except as green manure and hog feed. In 1916, on the eve of war, barely more than three hundred thousand American acres had been allotted to them. But there were intimations of change. By June 1917, in a "Sam Jordan's Corn Talk" — Samuel M. Jordan was a popular Farmers' Institute lecturer sponsored by the Missouri State Board of Agriculture — there were forty questions and answers about soybeans. Did they have uses beyond livestock feed? Yes, they were actually eaten by humans in China, Japan, and parts of the southern United States. "They are very rich in protein, and one learns to like the flavor." Before the First World War was over, American soybean imports from Dairen would more than quadruple, and the secretary of agriculture would be issuing a circular entitled *Use Soy-Bean Flour to Save Wheat, Meat, and Fat,* which contained patriotic recipes for Soy-Bean Meat Loaf, Soy-Bean Mush Croquettes, and Victory Bread. But the going was slow, despite such public encouragement and despite the private efforts of citizens like Hudson Maxim, the gunpowder inventor, who kept chiding his fellow members of the Chemists Club in New York for not eating more soybeans and periodically sent them samples to remind them of their dereliction. Soybeans did not reach the Corn Belt of the Midwest, where they now proliferate, in any appreciable numbers until 1927. They were warmly received. European corn borers had raised havoc with that region's corn, and it turned out that corn borers didn't fancy soybeans. By 1929, United States production of them had exceeded 9 million bushels. Then soybeans began to take off. By 1939, the total was 91 million bushels. By 1942, the United States was outproducing Manchuria.

Around the turn of the century, it was the praiseworthy policy of the Department of Agriculture to mount expeditions that scoured the globe for new varieties of wheat or rice or corn that might benefit American farmers. (It was a time-honored practice: Queen Hatshepsut had dispatched a hunting party out of Egypt in 1570 B.C. to fetch her some agreeably scented frankincense.) The Department of Commerce and Labor, in 1909, had asked United States consulates everywhere to report back on whatever soybean activity they observed in their bailiwicks. (The consul in Newchwang, understandably, was obliged to submit a lengthy response; the consul in Calais got off easily, because nobody there had ever heard of the plant.) That year, there were fewer than two dozen varieties of *Glycine max* known in the United States; by 1947, there would be ten thousand, and the number has been mounting ever since; between 1973 and 1980, for instance, 801 new ones were registered with the Agriculture Department's Plant Variety Protection Office. Many of the superior breeds of soybean that the safaris tracked down were bagged by the agronomist William J. Morse, who has been called "the Father of Soybeans in America," and who had delivered himself back in 1918 of the iconoclastic opinion that the soybean was "a very desirable article of human food." Morse had added, "The large yield of seed, the excellent quality of forage, the ease of growing and harvesting the crop, its freedom from insect enemies and plant diseases, and the possibilities of the seed for the production of oil and meal and as a food all tend to give this crop a high potential importance and assure its greater agricultural development in America." (Two esteemed varieties of soybean in the United States have been named the George Washington and the Morse.) Born in 1884, Morse, like so many other agricultural giants, studied at Cornell (its graduates in the agricultural sciences are sometimes affectionately known around the world today as "the Cornell Mafia"), and on getting a bachelor-of-science degree in 1907 went to work for the Bureau of Plant Industry of the Department of Agriculture. His immediate superior was Charles V. Piper, a pro-soybean man who soon had his apprentice cultivating soybeans on an experimental farm the department ran across the Potomac from the District of Columbia — a site that Agriculture would later reluctantly yield up so the Pentagon could be ponderously enshrined upon it. Morse became the head of the Office of Soybean Investigations, a cofounder, in 1920, of the American Soybean Association, and the coauthor with Piper, in 1923, of *The Soybean,* still regarded as a classic in its field. "There can be little doubt that the soybean is destined to become one of the major American crops," they wrote in it, though at the time that was largely wishful thinking. Morse kept plugging away in what to many others seemed a hopeless cause. "We may keep this work going," he wrote on his own in 1927, "and place the soybean where it belongs — in the King row with King Corn and King Cotton."

In 1929, Morse set off for the Far East, along with Palemon H. Dorsett, an explorer in Agriculture's Office of Foreign Plant Introduction. They spent two years there collecting soybeans of all sizes and shapes and colors. They brought back more than forty-five hundred samples of two thousand varieties of *Glycine max,* among them some used in Asia, when they were green and not fully ripened, as vegetables on the order of peas. Morse had sampled these abroad, and, like Dr. Harry Miller before him, he had been impressed: they tasted not unlike lima beans and were cheaper to produce and contained twice as much protein. Morse persuaded the Department of Agriculture to distribute one-hundred-seed packets of them to home gardeners, and until his death, at seventy-five, in 1959, he was one of their most faithful consumers. One of his favorite dishes, an entrée then as now not very widely served in Massachusetts, was Boston Baked Soybeans.

In 1930, of 110,000 tons of soybean meal processed in the United States, 99,100 tons had been used for animal feed, 10,000 for glue, and only 900 for human food. By 1936, the University of Illinois College of Agriculture would be publishing a pamphlet entitled *The Soybean: A Plant Immigrant Makes Good,* but it had made good, despite the proselytizing of Morse, Miller, and others, mainly because Corn Belt farmers liked to feed it to their livestock. The Department of Agriculture, to be sure, was still putting out publications like the 1938 recipe booklet *Soybeans for the Table* (soybean casserole, soybean soufflé, soybean milk soup), but most American tables were familiar with the bean, if they were aware of it at all, only because its oil was an ingredient of margarine. Nobody seemed to have been paying much attention to a message Rudolf P. Hommel had delivered to the United States in his *China at Work*, published the previous year:

The soy bean and its products supply in a measure to the Chinese diet what milk and dairy products would offer, and one could not well imagine the absence of both in our era or before without serious detriment to the welfare of the people. It was a rare instinct which led the Chinese to the utilization of the legumin or vegetable casein which the soy bean yields so abundantly. Here our food experts should take a hint and inquire why the soy bean is only used for forage in America, while in China its products come next in importance to rice.

That was the sort of no-nonsense talk that would have appealed, if he read it, to Henry Ford. Ford's conception of the utilization of the soybean was immense. Not only was he something of a vegetarian and health-food faddist, but he was fascinated by new products, and new uses for old ones. How grand that his intimate friend Thomas Edison once somehow made a light bulb from bamboo and a tire from goldenrod! And had not another contemporary, the chemist Arthur D. Little, created a silk purse from sows' ears? In 1930, when Ford's automobile business was rattling along on all cylinders, he began to evince a particularly strong interest in agriculture. (One of his pet slogans was "The farm and the shop; each needs what the other produces.") Ford liked to have his photograph taken while at the helm of a tractor. He bought a rubber plantation in Brazil — it could, of course, furnish him with tires — and straightaway christened it Fordlandia. He began eating soy foods. At Dearborn, Michigan, he kept a jug of soy milk in his refrigerator. In 1930, he began to raise some three hundred varieties of soybeans on a nine-thousand-acre tract there. He pledged himself further to buy just about all the soybeans that nearby farmers could bring him. When a visitor stopped by to discuss, say, the purchase of ten thousand trailer trucks or the acquisition of a Grosse Pointe dealership, Ford would, like as not, escort him on a hike around a muddy soybean field, pausing every now and then to bestow a loving pat on a plant that especially appealed to him. Ford spent $1.25 million on soybeans in 1932 and 1933. At the 1933–34 Century of Progress world's fair in Chicago, he served some thirty apprehensive guests a sixteen-course, soy meal, from soup to nuts and a soy-based coffee substitute. Quite beyond the frontiers of edibility, Ford perceived the soybean as an entity of vast industrial potential. (Parts of it have been used in the manufacture of bottle caps, pencils, diesel fuel, dusting powder, enamel, disinfectants, paints, face cream, firefighting foam, linoleum, nitroglycerin, cement, wallboard, oilcloth, and varnish. One constituent, lecithin, is a handy emulsifier for enabling chocolate and cocoa butter to cling together inside candy bars. In addition, as it sometimes pains ardent soybean-eaters to have to reflect, the whey left over when soy milk is curdled makes an excellent detergent for removing grease from pots and pans.) How the soybean could figure in the manufacture of motor vehicles was patently one of Ford's high-priority concerns. Plastics made from soybeans, he was pleased to learn from his engineers, could be — and in due course were — used in gearshift knobs, horn buttons, window frames, accelerator pedals, light-switch assemblies, and ignition-coil casings. For a while, every Ford car had at least two pounds of soybeans somewhere in or on it. But Ford dreamed bigger dreams than that. By the mid-thirties, he had so many soybeans lying around that he didn't know what to do with them; his apple orchard was already all but smothered in soy fertilizer. To utilize his spare beans, he visualized a car upholstered in material made from soybean fibers, and with a tough, soybean-plastic exterior shell. He liked to challenge his house chemists. (George Washington Carver occasionally worked with them.) Ford would wander into their laboratories with bags full of chicken bones, cantaloupes, or watermelons and wonder how aside from their conventional functions they could be used. He showed up one day toting a gunnysack and dumped its contents on the floor at the feet of several men working there. "These things are called soybeans," Ford said. "You guys are supposed to be smart. You ought to be able to do something with them." He mentioned the upholstery and the plastics and departed. Eventually Ford was delighted to be presented with a car sheathed in the plastic. To demonstrate its strength, he invited a cameraman to come around and photograph him pounding a trunk lid with an ax. He was supposed to have at it with the blunt end, but he used the sharp end instead and — while one of his young chemists, William T. Atkinson, looked on aghast — sliced clean through. Fortunately, there was a spare lid available, and the second take came out satisfactorily. (During the Second World War, when all metals were precious, the state of Illinois made some license plates out of fiberboard derived from soybeans; they stood up all right in traffic, but a goat ate one.) As for the textile, it never reached the car-upholstery stage, but enough of it was woven for two men's suits, both of which were made up in Ford's size and added to his wardrobe. He liked to have his picture taken in them, too, but he had to be cautious, because the cloth was fragile. Years later, Atkinson was asked how Ford had looked dressed in soy. "I just didn't want him to cross his legs," Atkinson replied. Then the Second World War came along, and nobody has thought much about soybean auto parts ever since.

Ford, whose grandfather had fled Ireland after the mid-nineteenth-century potato famine, had no great love for the British, but he felt that even they should not be deprived of the benefits that he hoped the soybean could confer on that part of the human race that had so long neglected it. In 1932, he bought two thousand acres of English cropland at Boreham, Essex. He dubbed that realm Fordson Estates. Soybeans had never done too well in England. The Royal Agricultural Society had fooled around with them early in the twentieth century, but had abandoned them, institutionally, in 1914. The curator of the Royal Botanic Gardens, though, James L. North, was not so easily deterred. On his own, he obtained thirteen North Chinese seeds from Germany just before the outbreak of the First World War. He planted them in 1914. The next year, he had four hundred seeds, then four thousand, then twelve thousand. He fought his own grim war with rabbits, for whom the soybean is ambrosia everywhere. By 1932, North had come up with four varieties that seemed to be able, like Hyde Park nannies, to cope with English weather. Sir John T. Davies, a director of the Ford Motor Company, Limited, who believed that "the soya bean could be made the mainstay for feeding a country in time of war," knew about North's accomplishments and recruited him to supervise Fordson Estates. Ford had forty-three soybean varieties shipped over from Michigan that he thought might do well abroad. They were duly planted, along with North's four. Only the latter got by. The ungrateful English populace didn't seem to care much one way or another. "It is unfortunate that the inherent conservatism of English people to anything new," Elizabeth Bowdidge lamented in 1935, "has been the cause of past failures to popularize soya bean food products for consumption in this country. . . . With memories of the convoyed food ships of war-time; of the appalling losses due to enemy submarines, and the anxiety for the safe arrival in our ports of those ships which had escaped the danger, it would be comforting to know that in the soya bean, which provides a green vegetable, flour for bread, and a substitute for meat and milk, we should have an assurance against starvation." If her fellow Englishmen and -women did not enthusiastically concur, the Nazis did. Three or four years before the start of the Second World War, they began hoarding soybeans (along with other staples), until they had a two-million-ton cache. It spilled over the floors of schoolrooms and ballrooms commandeered for storage. Still more of it was hurriedly grown by I. G. Farben in Austria, Rumania, and the Balkan states. During the war, the Nazis produced nearly thirty thousand tons of edible soybean products a year. In his 1942 book *Soybeans: Gold from the Soil,* Edward Jerome Dies wrote that "some commentators have ascribed almost as much significance to the German supply of soybeans as to her supply of airplanes."

Nearly half a century after he stopped worrying about the fit of Henry Ford's trousers, William Atkinson, by then retired from more than forty years of probing the promise of *Glycine max,* told an acquaintance, "The true destiny of the soybean is in food for humans." It is a destiny as yet — in the Western world at least — emphatically unfulfilled. Only 2 percent of the soybeans produced in the United States are used for that purpose. Americans average a paltry annual per-capita consumption of soybean products of just under nine pounds — the equivalent of a couple of small sacks of potatoes. Relatively few as they may be, those Americans who have embraced the soybean as a fundamental part of their diet are an articulate lot, and touchingly unflagging in their zealotry. Sometimes they get a boost from an unexpected source, as when Mimi Sheraton, the *New York Times* restaurant critic, gave a four-star rating — it was surely coincidental that this was one of her last public judgments before she left that job — to a Japanese restaurant whose *carte* included a "sunny and fragrant" soybean soup along with squid tentacles broiled with miso bean paste, iced bean-curd squares, raw fish and aged-soybean paste, and dumplings of bean-curd sheet wrapped around meat. Another writer, Richard Leviton, the ex-editor of the magazine *Soyfoods* — it has a circulation of seven thousand and runs features like "Taking the Soy Venture Seriously" — frequently shares with his readers some of the tribulations they have resignedly accepted as their lot. Leviton attended a World Conference and Exposition on Soya Processing and Utilization held at Acapulco in November 1980. It was sponsored by the American Oil Chemists Society and the American Soybean Association, and it lasted a whole week. He reported gloomily afterward that during fifty-four morning plenary lectures only eight minutes apiece were devoted to tofu and soy sauce, and that of sixty-eight afternoon roundtable papers, only eight dealt with direct human food use. Altogether, tofu, which he identified as the "bellweather [*sic*] of American soyfoods," was allocated only .4 percent of the delegates' attention. And to make matters worse, at two banquets where the assemblage gorged itself on — ugh — meat and potatoes, only two dishes were to his taste: shredded cooked soybeans in a vegetable taco, and white rice with a few green soybeans and carrots. "I detected a core lack of commitment to soyfoods," he reported, "which in our 'generation' of soy enthusiasts is immediately characterized by regular gustatory enjoyment of the gamut of soyfoods." Leviton felt a little better when he visited the simple village of Los Organos, a dozen miles from glittery Acapulco, and got draped with a garland of marigolds and invited to a feast on a schoolhouse porch featuring *picados con soya, donas con soya, salsa con soya, quesadillas de soya, agua de soya, tamales con soya, arroz con soya,* and steamed green soybeans. While the director of the Mexico City branch of the American Soybean Association was to be commended, Leviton went on, for having submitted a report entitled "What's Holding Up the Introduction of Soya into the Human Diet in Latin America?" the sort of thing that appeared to be grievously holding it up was the experience of one philanthropist there who distributed free samples of soy milk to poor farmers, hoping they would give it to their children; instead they gave it to their hogs, and the children drank bottled soda pop. Like many of his readers a die-hard carniphobe, Leviton had to admit, after another professional hegira, to an occasional hankering for forbidden fruits. He visited a soy delicatessen once at Rochester, New York, and was served a stack of barbecued tempeh strips. "Chewing a strip with my eyes closed," he confessed, "I experience a far-off memory galloping wildly into my present consciousness — spareribs with steak sauce."

Among *Soyfoods'* star contributors have been the husband-and-wife team of William Shurtleff and Akiko Aoyagi, who run the Soyfoods Center at Lafayette, California, and are the authors of, among other thick volumes, *The Book of Tofu, The Book of Tempeh,* and *The Book of Miso.* They also put out an occasional newsletter, purveying advice like "Do your own thing related to Soyfoods" and "In this area, your imagination is the limit." When Shurtleff took part in four soy-milk seminars in China in 1983, he was the first Westerner to attend any such assemblage since 1949. A paean to the Shurtleffs that ran in *Soyfoods* said that "by constantly addressing the larger problems of world hunger, human suffering, and liberation, they hope to make their work relevant to people everywhere and a force for planetary renaissance." The Shurtleffs themselves contend modestly that they have done no more for the soybean than George Washington Carver did for the peanut or Johnny Appleseed for the apple.

Most of the American devotees of tofu, tempeh, miso, and their ilk are patrons of health-food stores and the proprietors of mom-and-pop businesses that cater to such establishments, whose menus feature delicacies like tempeh sloppy-joes, strawberry tofu cheesecake, ice bean sandwich, soysage, and soylami. More often nowadays, when the soybean is eaten by people, it is not so boldly labeled. If all the cans and cartons that contain soybeans were removed from most supermarkets, the shelves would look looted. (Dog foods would have to go, too; many of them are 45-proof soybean — 90 percent.) The presence of soybeans in, for instance, Franco-American Beef Ravioli, Quaker Instant Grits, Lipton's Cup-a-Soup, Handy Andy Hot Dog Buns, Chef Boyardee Spaghetti Dinner with Meat Sauce, Birds Eye Swiss Style Vegetables, Nabisco Onion Tuna Twist, Rich's Frozen Coffee Whitener, and A. & P. German Style Potato Salad is rarely advertised and, indeed, is referred to chiefly in the small type that is employed to identify ingredients and is seldom scanned. Soybean boosters can be very defensive. "There's something about the soybean that just seems to put a lot of people off," one of them said not long ago. "You know, if soybeans are in storage along with cereals, rats will always eat the soybeans last. Even the rats don't like us." Many of the human beings in whose diet soybeans does prominently figure are people who have no choice about what they eat — prisoners, soldiers, children at school. The Department of Defense now permits hamburgers served to the armed forces to have a 20-percent soybean content. Federal regulations governing the twenty-three million school lunches served daily in the United States are even more lenient; their meat patties may have a 30-percent slice of soybean. (Ray Kroc, the founder of the McDonald's chain, went to his death, in January 1984, stubbornly refusing to permit even a trace of soybean in any of *his* burgers.) The soybean has made similar, anonymous inroads in the schools of other countries: soy-fortified cornmeal in Bourkina Fasso (né Upper Volta), soy-fortified wheat in Bhutan, soy-fortified milk in Trinidad and Tobago. The Chinese dispense with disguise: children there skip off to school carrying paper bags with whole cooked soybeans in them, and when they feel like a snack nip open the pods and lick off the beans inside.

It has been argued that one reason the soybean hasn't yet caught on with many humans outside Asia is that it has no effective lobby working for it. There is the American Soybean Association, to be sure, with headquarters in Saint Louis, but it is not an especially pushy group, and one reason for that is that although there are a half million farmers growing *Glycine max* in the United States (few of them could tell a tempeh from a tofu), there are not many *soybean* farmers: they also raise corn or wheat or cattle or hogs, and consider those their primary preoccupation. Nor, unlike most of the other staple plant foods, does the soybean have a big center, under the aegis of the Consultative Group on International Agricultural Research devoted to its study and improvement. Inasmuch as CGIAR addresses itself principally to the concerns of underdeveloped nations, and as more than half the American soybean crop is exported, there is little enthusiasm in the United States for encouraging other nations to become potentially competitive. Also, CGIAR wants to ameliorate the production of foods for human consumption, and as Richard Leviton was unhappily reminded at Acapulco, most soybean producers have other priorities. Soybean studies have been a major concern of an independent establishment on Taiwan, the Asian Vegetable Research and Development Center; and across the Formosa Strait, the People's Republic of China has at least two more soybean-research sites — one at Changchun and one at Harbin. Sri Lanka, moreover, to which the Dutch brought soybeans from Southeast Asia in the seventeenth century, has had its own Soybean Foods Research Center since 1975; prison officials have been taking soybean-cooking lessons there, so they can pass on what they learn to their inmates. The commissioner of police runs a salesroom, where the general public can buy prison-baked loaves of bread fashioned from what the local *Soyanews* — which sometimes seems to feel that tempeh and tofu are about the only worthwhile viands extant — refers to as "food of the gods."

One of the principal soybean-research institutions in the United States is the International Soybean Program — known for short as INTSOY — at the Champaign-Urbana campus of the University of Illinois College of Agriculture. The First Annual Corn Belt Soybean Day was held there in 1920. Since 1922, Illinois has almost always led the nation in soybean production, and the U.S. Soybean Germ Plasm Collection there, with close to nine thousand soybean varieties in well-secured custody, is one of the world's largest. More soybeans are processed at Decatur, in the center of the state — sixteen thousand tons of them every working day — than anywhere else on earth. Decatur, accordingly, calls itself "the Soybean Capital of the World," and its precincts harbor a Soy Capital Bank and Trust Company, a Soy City Motel, a Soy City Marina, and Soy City Plumbing and Heating. A national softball championship was held at Decatur in the fall of 1983. There were hot-dog and hamburger stands — serving real hamburgers — to accommodate the spectators. There was also a sloppy-joe stand, with the sloppy-joes made of soybeans. It was presided over by the proprietor of a local breakfast-and-lunch emporium called Just Around the Corner. His sponsor and supplier was Decatur's biggest business, Archer Daniels Midland, a global corporation with annual sales of nearly $4.5 billion. Ninety-eight percent of its income from soybeans comes from oils and animal feed. ADM, as the company is usually known, has soybean-oil production lines that turn out 23 different grades of oil under 434 labels belonging to its customers. It also has a roomful of traders in soybeans and soybean futures, chained to phones day in and out, dealing in such huge quantities of commodities that a change in price of a quarter of a cent a bushel can mean hundreds of thousands of dollars if somebody guesses right or wrong. To ensure a steady flow of all its soybeans — not to mention corn, wheat, and other commodities it handles — ADM has a private fleet of 700 barges, 300 tank and trailer trucks, and 8,000 railroad cars.

The sloppy-joes at the softball championship were made of a soybean extract called "textured vegetable protein," or TVP. William Atkinson, who helped tailor Henry Ford's soybean outfits, was instrumental also in developing TVP. Soybeans thus textured have approximately the chewability of animal meat — or, as ADM executives like to put it, "mouthfeel." TVP is the principal ingredient of ADM's half dozen varieties of "bacon bits." Dog-food trailer trucks can frequently be found in ADM parking lots, waiting to be loaded up with

Alpo beef or Alpo chicken or Alpo lamb or Alpo rib of veal, much of which consist of ADM TVP, chopped and diced and shredded into different textures to appeal to different canine mouthfeels. The sloppy-joes did so well that Dwayne Andreas, the urbane chairman of the board of ADM and cochairman of the U.S.-U.S.S.R. Trade and Economic Council, who sometimes functions as a one-man soybeans-for-humans lobby, offered to provide Just Around the Corner with all the raw materials it needed if it would stay open for dinner and would serve soybean-derived equivalents of chicken a la king, chow mein, and lasagna. All hands involved in the enterprise were aware of the widespread misgivings about eating soy foods; the word "soy" nowhere appeared on the menu. Andreas dropped in at the restaurant shortly after it embarked on its soybean venture and said he liked the mouthfeel of all its offerings except the lasagna. That surprised the proprietor, because it was the lasagna that everybody else had seemed to like best. As Henry Ford treated Century of Progress visitors to a soybean feast in 1934, so do ADM executives similarly regale visitors to their corporate headquarters. Among the soybean-based items on the menu at a lunch over which Andreas presided at Decatur in 1983 were chocolate soy beverage; taco dip; salami rolls; spareribs with barbecue sauce; stir-fried chicken; beef and snow peas; soy-flour bread; margarine; and all-vegetable frozen dessert. That was shortly before Tofutti, the mock-ice-cream soybean hit of the eighties, made its imitative presence widely known.

Dwayne Andreas — who was born in 1918 to a Mennonite wheat-growing family in Iowa, got involved with soybeans in 1938, joined ADM in 1965, and became its chief executive in 1971 — maintains a year-round apartment at the Waldorf Towers in New York. When he entertained there in 1983, he was apt to supplement what room service proffered with items from his own kitchenette — soy-milk drinks in various flavors, and such Archer Daniels Midland experimental soybean products, which it had labeled but not yet marketed, as Uncle Archie's Vegetable Protein Entrées (Chicken Almondine Style, Pepper Steak Style, and Sweet-n-Sour Pork Style). Uncle Archie's Uncle Dwayne would tell a guest heading toward a Waldorf elevator as burdened as if the visitor had just left a supermarket that his Chicken Almondine was all but indistinguishable in taste from, and incomparably superior in nutrition to, chicken almondine made from real chicken. Andreas could afford to eat whatever he liked — he and his family owned a large chunk of ADM stock, and his salary was three-quarters of a million dollars a year — but he has long been partial to statements like "Do you know that filet mignon is 30 percent tallow and the curse of the rich?" In making converts to soybeans, so far he has done better among the poor than the rich. His daughter, who met Mother Teresa in India and became one of her followers, later took charge of the nun's feeding-the-needy activities in Washington, D.C., and its environs. Andreas *père* provided the soybean meat-substitutes that those soup kitchens dispensed. After Andreas *fille* reported back to him that her clientele, although ignorant of what they were ingesting, really seemed to enjoy that fare, her happy father began to furnish soy foods to soup kitchens in Des Moines and Minneapolis. "You could feed the whole world with soy if people would just learn to eat it," he said.

In one of its television commercials, ADM declared that "the newest development in nutrition is one of the oldest foods known to man." (The text of another message included the phrase "That's using the old bean.") ADM marketing executives have been glad that their livelihood does not have to depend on instant public response to such statements. "Edible soy is a very hard sell," one of them says. "One problem is that when our people go out, they keep being told, 'What is this that you are proposing we eat — dog food?' " Andreas does not consider that an unreasonable question. "My dog eats better than I do," he says. He believes, further, that the most practical way of insinuating soy directly into human stomachs, instead of passing it first through cows or pigs or hens, is by means of bread, the universal food; but in his view the big bakeries lack proper motivation. "They want to make bread cheaper, not better," he says. Making bread better — the soybean's abundant proteins are rich in lysine, a highly nutritious amino acid — and making it cheaper — soybeans are relatively inexpensive — has long been a noble humanitarian concern. Making bread out of ingredients other than, or supplementary to, wheat has been a longtime practice. But until recently few bakers turned to the soybean. Venetians blended rice with wheat for their bread in 1589. England had a wheat-and-potato bread in 1832. Some French bread baked during the First World War resembled a tossed, or shipwrecked, salad, containing as it did peanuts, chestnuts, broad beans, chickpeas, potatoes, rice, sorghum, barley, and even cotton. The Cuban government decreed in 1932 that all wheat flour there had to be adulterated by an 18-percent admixture of cassava. Brazilian and Paraguayan bakers are currently required to put a cassava content of at least 5 percent in their bread. Pakistan insists on 10-percent sorghum, and Senegal on 15-percent millet. Since 1964, the FAO has had a small-scale composite-flour program in operation; research on that has been conducted at the Institute for Cereals, Flour, and Bread at Wageningen, in the Netherlands; at the Department of Grain Science and Industry of Kansas State University; and at the Institut de Technologie Alimentaire at Dakar. No leavened bread of any kind can be made, of course, as far as natural substances go, without gluten; and until scientists can insert the DNA genetic codes of gluten into other plants — as they someday may well find a way to do — wheat's haughty possession of gluten will enable it to reign over all other breadstuffs.

"There is no question in my mind," Dwayne Andreas has said, "but that the soybean is the fundamental future of the planet." That may be, but it will probably not come to pass, if it ever does, without difficulty. "The aesthetic and nutritional qualities of a foodstuff are all important," the potato historian Redcliffe Salaman said in 1943, "and the failure to meet the requirements of social man in either respect would damn the future of any newcomer." (The Jerusalem artichoke might readily have become to Ireland what the potato did, and it might have survived the famine that undid the potato there, but it simply had too strong a taste for people to be willing to eat it at every meal every day.) It could be quite some time before the proponents of soybeans no longer have to put up with slights like the closing statement of Mark Nathan Cohen's 1977 book *The Food Crisis in Prehistory:* "Perhaps it will aid us in our economic transition to realize that human populations once faced the notion of eating oysters and later the prospect of eating wheat with much the same enthusiasm that we now face the prospect of eating seaweed, soy protein, and artificial organic molecules." Moderate as the enthusiasm may be for such foods of the future, there are yet others the mere mention of which almost makes saliva stop flowing. Some scientists have cheerfully discussed an edible, protein-rich powder which there is no present reason to believe cannot be fashioned from bacteria, yeast, phosphate compounds, and crude oil. Others are busy coaxing food out of wood pulp, cattle manure, and — Henry Ford would not have been surprised — automobile tires.

Among the six thousand or so plants that have been identified as having edible parts, there are some that, like the soybean, might meaningfully sustain future inhabitants of the planet. Some that once did so and still exist have been largely forgotten — varieties of *Amaranthus,* for one, which has more amino acid than most cereals. The Aztecs grew the amaranth in abundance — twenty thousand tons of it was given to Montezuma, as a tribute, every year. Unfortunately, for their rites the Aztecs mixed its nourishing grains with human blood. That did not set well with Hernán Cortés when he came along and invaded Mexico in 1519. He forbade them to practice their traditional religions and rituals, and while he was at it forbade all further cultivation of the amaranth. The FAO has been fostering its resurrection since 1967, but it has been making a very laggard comeback. Then there is quinua, whose grain is also rich in protein; the Incas grew that one — and some mountain people in Bolivia, Chile, Ecuador, and Peru still do, grinding its seeds for bread and for cake flour, also for breakfast cereals and beer. Grain amaranth and quinua were among thirty-six neglected plants cited in a 1975 publication — *Underexploited Tropical Plants with Promising Economic Value* — of the National Academy of Sciences. Others included a wild Australian cereal grass called *Echinochloa turnerana; Zostera marina,* a grain-producing plant that grows in salt water; and *Arracacia xanthorrhiza,* alias the Peruvian carrot or apio. (*Food from the Veld,* a 1982 volume sponsored by the South African Institute for Medical Research, itemized and described more than one thousand edible wild plants in that part of the world alone.) The National Academy has been especially sanguine about the prospects of a distant relative of the soybean called the winged bean — *Psophocarpus tetragonolobus* — to which it devoted an entire euphoric publication in 1975, with a second edition in 1981. A viny vegetable that reaches heights of thirteen feet, the winged bean has flowers that, when cooked, resemble mushrooms; spinachlike leaves; tubers like those of the cassava and the potato, but with a much higher protein content; and pods and beans that at one stage or another of their development can be consumed in all sorts of fetching ways. Like the soybean, the winged bean lends itself to oil-processing and to conversion into tofu, tempeh, and a milk substitute. Its admirers have called it "a supermarket on a stalk." The soybean does not grow well in humid climates; the winged bean, which thrives in sultry places like Papua New Guinea, has also been called "the soybean for the tropics," and has been subjected to much intense scrutiny by botanists in the Philippines, Indonesia, and Sri Lanka, where an International Winged Bean Center has been established. Beans of any sort are not to be belittled; eleven million tons' worth of common beans are consumed annually — nearly half that total in Latin America. It is fitting that the International Center for Tropical Agriculture — CIAT, for short — which specializes in bean research, is located at Cali, Colombia. Since 1973, the director of the bean program there has been a Dutchman, Arte van Schoonhoven, a Ph.D. from Kansas State. In van Schoonhoven's view, he does not have an easy row to hoe. "Beans have no literature to speak of," he told a recent visitor to Cali, "and you never hear of any fellowships in beans. Maybe that's because beans are just there, like motherhood, and there are no political problems associated with them. [Nicaragua, however, has expressed a predilection for a CIAT-bred bean with the name of Revolucion 8.] The only people who seem genuinely fond of beans, aside from a few specialists here like me, are entomologists, because beans get so beautifully riddled with insects." Van Schoonhoven, who is by most accounts one of the half dozen or so most knowledgeable bean men on earth, thinks that *Psophocarpus tetragonolobus* has been overrated and oversold. He has a one-acre garden at his home, and has therein lovingly nurtured pineapples, mangoes, plantains, bananas, and passion fruits. When the National Academy of Sciences began touting winged beans, he cultivated some of them. He was not impressed. "A stupid plant," he told a houseguest. "I practically had to force my children to eat it. Its seeds are rock-hard, its pods can be eaten only when they're small and fresh, and nobody knows what insects and pests and fungi might do to it if it ever gets widespread." There is no united front in beanland.

Addressing himself in 1981 to the question of what rural families in India would do if they could somehow obtain enough fertilizers and improved seeds to increase their income from agricultural pursuits by 25 percent, Leslie Swindale, director general of the International Crops Research Institute for the Semi-Arid Tropics (ICRISAT), located at Hyderabad, said:

What evidence is available . . . suggests that they would consume more food: more calories and more protein, more sugar and less starch, more protective foods such as milk, vegetables, and fruits. If they could obtain more fuel they would have more cooked meals and fewer intestinal parasites. No doubt they would put more into important social obligations. If their incomes increased sufficiently they would buy more radios — thereby increasing their access to technological information — and bicycles — thereby increasing their access to the market. They might elect to keep their children in school for one more year or improve their homes and household sanitation. Surely rural people can hope for — even expect — such modest improvements in the quality of their lives. . . . Finally, if the farmer cannot find anything else to do with the grain he produces, he and his family can always eat it. The rural people of this country have nutritional deficiencies, the most important in calories. They simply do not get enough to eat.

Indians and others in a similar bleak fix could increase their produce by far more than 25 percent if only the yields of crops as they exist today could somehow come close to their potential. Agricultural practices in the United States are far more sophisticated and efficient than they are in India and the rest of the less developed world; but even so, there is an enormous gap between average American yields and what world-record yields suggest could be produced under ideal conditions — for corn, 2.16 as against 8.48 tons per acre; for wheat, .84 and 5.8; for soybeans, .76 and 2.96; for potatoes, 10.64 and 37.68.

At least the danger has abated that many of the varieties of food plants crucial to human survival will simply become extinct. Of the forty-five hundred soybean specimens that Morse and Dorsett painstakingly brought back to the United States in 1931 after their two-year hunt in Asia, more than three-quarters either got thrown away or lost, because there were inadequate facilities for storing them. As late as 1974, there was no collection anywhere on earth of all the known varieties of *any* major crop. That year, CGIAR established, with its seat of operations at FAO headquarters in Rome, the International Board for Plant Genetic Resources, and ever since, the IBPGR has been exhorting geneticists the world over to collect and secure every specimen of plant germ plasm they find in the wild or they breed. "Genes should be available like books in a library," the head of the IBPGR, J. Trevor Williams, said recently. Williams does not object to drives by concerned citizens who want to save the whale, the condor, the giant panda, or the spotted

lynx; but he sometimes wishes that he could muster equal support for such IBPGR endeavors as its 1981 expeditions to collect wild-potato germ plasm in Uruguay, rare corn lines in
South Korea, and some of the more inaccessible sorghums and
millets of Bourkina Fasso. By 1983, there were more than
eighty plant-gene banks scattered around the globe. The largest
is at Fort Collins, Colorado: the National Seed Storage Laboratory, where nearly a quarter of a million specimens have been
assembled and stored since it opened for business in 1958.
(Some of its seeds are in cryogenic storage — immersed in liquid nitrogen and chilled to a temperature of minus 321 degrees
Fahrenheit.) The enormous variety of genes in custody there
and in other vaults constitutes, according to a 1981 report to
the General Accounting Office, America's congressional
watchdog agency, "the basis for future intentional or evolutionary crop improvement and development, and the fundamental defense against natural and manmade threats to crop
survival." (Jack Harlan, the University of Illinois plant geneticist, has put it even more strongly: "These resources stand between us and catastrophic starvation on a scale we cannot
imagine. In a very real sense, the future of the human race rides
on these materials.") Some agronomists fear that the survival
of the Seed Storage Laboratory itself may be threatened by a
couple of manmade neighbors: it is flanked by a munitions factory and a nuclear reactor.

Food scientists who have seen the Green Revolution come
and go have been more lately talking about a Gene Revolution.
What — to cite just one of many breathtaking examples — if
nitrogen-fixing genes like those of the soybean could be introduced into corn? That could revolutionize — would reduce by
billions of dollars — the sums now spent on chemical fertilizers. Great strides have already been made in tissue-cell cul-

ture — breeding plant varieties from a single cell in laboratory test-tubes. Microbiologists have already come up with a rice comparatively rich in lysine; with its added protein, that kind of rice should be more nutritious than traditional rices. (One problem is that as protein increases, yields usually decrease; scientists are working now to try to uncouple that negative correlation.) If a photosensitivity-gene could be put into winter wheat, which ripens according to the amount of daylight it is exposed to, that crop could be successfully planted in latitudes so far inhospitable to its propagation. To try to protect crops against the brutal onslaughts of insects, entomologists are studying ways of changing the pests' biological rhythms — addling their tiny brains, so they'll mature not when they usually do but in the winter, when their customary food supplies are scarce. Four-fifths of all the fresh water in the world, moreover, is now used, in one way or another, to grow food, and water tables are dropping everywhere, from the North China plain to Arizona to the Aral Sea; if more plants could be bred that would grow in salt water, or if desalinization could be cheaply realized on a massive scale, the effects would obviously be consequential. Considerable headway has been made in the breeding of plants that can make a go of it in heavily acidic soil, and in Brazil alone there are 600 million acres of such land that are now of little agricultural value. And someday geneticists — who have already produced triticale by crossbreeding wheat and rye — may conceivably mate such totally unrelated species as wheat and corn. (China is rumored to have crossbred rice and sorghum, but no persuasive evidence of that has yet crossed its borders.) Science has done much for agriculture up to now, and will certainly do much more, but there is a quantum leap from the laboratory to the field, as even the most respected and successful researchers are aware. Norman Borlaug said not long ago, "Don't look for a genetic solution to our problems."

For the immediate future, most of the human race will have to expect to be fed, as it is today, by the handful of familiar, reliable, indispensable old plants that have sustained it since it began to breed itself. But as these food plants will no doubt change in the next hundred years, so have they already, for better or worse, been profoundly altered. "In the process of domestication, food plants have quite literally crossed a threshold," the geneticist Garrison Wilkes has written. "Their survival is keyed to human beings preparing the ground for them; to human beings guaranteeing them decreased competition with other plants; to human sowing of their seed in the proper season; to human protection during their growth period; and, finally, to human beings collecting their seed. The process of domestication has made these plants our captives." It has been a two-way evolutionary process, for we in turn have become their captives, too. In the succinct words of M. S. Swaminathan, "We live in this world as guests of green plants."

INDEX

Bartlett, John S., 52-53
Bates, Katharine Lee, 172
Beadle, George W., 25-28, 30-31, 35
beans, 4; winged, 293-295. *See also* soybeans
bears, 76-77
Beaven, E. S., 31
beetles, 78, 105-106, 162, 258
beriberi, 212
Berkeley, Sir William, 221
billbugs, 78
birds, 49-50, 161-162, 237
black cutworms, 77
blackleg, 104
black rot, 104
black scurf, 104
Black Tartarian (oats), 144
blight, 12, 78, 79, 98, 104, 119, 125-127, 180, 242, 249
Bloody Butcher (corn), 68
Boerma, Addeke H., 151, 190
Bogle, George, 102
Bogorad, Lawrence, 36
Book of Wheat, The, 151
Borlaug, Norman E., 59, 85, 183-194, 196, 210, 298
Boston Potatoes, 128
Bowdidge, Elizabeth, 267, 281-282
Bradfield, Richard, 182
Bradford, William, 47
Brady, Nyle C., 241, 243, 244-245, 246, 247, 249
Brazil: corn in, 33-34, 39; hunger in, 256; soybeans in, 264; wheat in, 39, 158
bread, 150-151, 165-170, 255-256; GMS-made, 167; myths about, 168; rye, 168, 172; soybeans in, 291; unleavened, 167; white, 169, 171, 172. *See also* wheat
Bread and Wine, 166
Brevor (wheat), 182
Brontë, Patrick, 121
broomcorn, 160
Brown, Lester, 164
Brown, William L., 70-71
Browning, Elizabeth Barrett, 128
brown rot, 104
Bryan, William Jennings, 60
Bukasov, Serge Mikhailovich, 107
Burbank, Luther, 24, 69, 134

Burma: rice in, 214, 220, 240, 259; wheat in, 155
Burns, Robert, 141, 142
Burton, W. Glynn, 107

Canada, wheat in, 175-178, 199
Candies Good for Children, 13
Candolle, Alphonse de, 17, 149
Candy Stick (corn), 28
Capote, Truman, 103
Capp, Al, 8
Capron, Horace, 181
Carleton, Mark Alfred, 179-180
Carlton, Steve, 224
Carver, George Washington, 66, 280
cassava, 4, 37, 38, 95-99
Castro, Fidel, 246
Catherine the Great, 178
Central America, corn in, 14, 42
cereal, origin of word, 151
Ceres, 206-207, 255
certificates of protection, 74-75
CGIAR (Consultative Group on International Agricultural Research), 208-210, 228, 246, 286-287, 296
Chad, famine in, 254-255
Chandler, Robert F., Jr., 229, 234, 236, 238, 239, 240, 241, 244
Chang, Te-Tzu, 244, 249, 250
chapatties, 167
Charles I (king of Spain), 38
Charles II (king of England), 117, 118
Chiang Kai-shek, 156
China: corn in, 9-10, 11, 12; potatoes in, 91, 92; rice in, 89, 211, 215, 219, 220, 229, 230, 243-246; soybeans in, 262, 265-266, 278, 286; wheat in, 156-157
CIAT (International Center for Tropical Agriculture), 209, 294
CIMMYT (International Center for the Improvement of Maize and Wheat), 194-196, 209, 210
CIP (International Potato Center), 99, 100, 101-109, 126, 209
Civil War, 88
club wheat, 154
Clusius, Carolus, 110
Cobb, Irvin S., 16
Cobbett, William, 51-52, 118
coconuts, 4, 224-228

Kalm, Peter, 49
Kalyan Sona (wheat), 189
Kanred (wheat), 179
Kansas Morgage Lifter (wheat), 179
Kaunda, Kenneth, 171
Kellogg, John Harvey, 130–131, 269
Kellogg, Will Keith, 131
Kendrick, James B., Jr., 80, 81
Kennedy, Patrick, 128
Kenya: potatoes in, 91; sorghum in,
    162; wheat in, 164
Kharkov (wheat), 180
Khrushchev, Nikita, 72
Kipling, Rudyard, 54
Kissinger, Henry, 109, 195, 262
Klippart, John H., 152
Knapp, Seaman A., 222
Korea: rice in, 215, 216, 224, 250;
    wheat in, 155
Kraho Indians, 36
Kroc, Ray, 286
Kubanka (wheat), 180
kwashiorkor, 81

Lampton, William James, 16
late blight, 104, 125–126
Latrobe, Benjamin, 12
leafhoppers, 105, 241, 242
leaf roll virus, 104
Lecknovitch, Vadin, 107
Lenin, Vladimir, 202
leprosy, 213
Lever, Sir William H., 226
Leverett, John, 129
Lévi-Strauss, Claude, 33
Leviton, Richard, 283–284, 287
Ling, Keh-Chi, 244
Linnaeus, Carolus, 5, 8, 49, 265
Little, Arthur D., 278
locusts, 162, 242
Logan, James, 73
Longfellow, Henry Wadsworth, 44
Long Fellow (oats), 143
Louis XVI (king of France), 113, 114
lysine, 81–82

MacArthur, Douglas, 180–182
McClintock, Barbara, 23, 81
Macdonell, Alexander, 175
McKay, Robert, 121
McLane, C. O., 274

MacNeish, Richard S., 27
Madison, James, 175
maize, 4, 6–7. See also corn
Maize, or Indian Corn, 52
Maize in the Great Herbals, 70
maizolith, 14
malaria, 213, 214
malnutrition, 256–257. See also famine
Mammoth Johnson (corn), 61
Manchuria, 267, 268
Mangelsdorf, Paul Christoph, 5, 18–25,
    26, 27, 28, 29, 31–32, 34–36, 48, 73,
    74, 75, 182
Manihot esculenta, 96. See also cassava
Manioc in Africa, 99
Mankind at the Crossroads, 19
Manual of Corn Judging, A, 62
Mao Zedong, 89, 156, 195, 243
Marcos, Ferdinand, 238–239, 244
Marie Antoinette, 113, 114
Mark, Joan, 46
Marquis (wheat), 176, 177
Matthias, William, 273
Matzner, Dieter, 114–115
matzoth, 167
Maxim, Hudson, 275
Mayans, 41–43
Mayer, André, 194
Mayer, Jean, 194
Mencken, H. L., 144
Mennonites, 178–180
Merry Wives of Windsor, The, 112
Mexico: corn in , 18, 24, 34, 35, 38,
    39–41, 63–64; wheat in, 185, 188,
    191, 194
mice, 76–77
Micronesia, coconuts in, 226–227
Miller, Harry W., 269–270, 271
Millet, Jean-François, 114
millet, 4, 9, 87, 159, 160, 162, 164, 167
milo maize, 160
Miracle (wheat), 179
mites, 78, 105
Montgomery, Alfred, 69
Morse, William J., 276–277
moths, 105, 162
Muhammed, Amir, 205–206
Mundurucú Indians, 37

Napoleon, 85, 86
National Academy of Sciences, 4, 80

National Corn Growers Association, 200–201
National Crop Loss Assessment Network, 257
National Potato Anti-Bruise Commission, 258
National Seed Storage Laboratory, 297
National Sweet Corn Breeders Association, 21
neem tree oil, 248
nematodes, 104–105
Niederhauser, John S., 186
Nigeria: sorghum in, 161; wheat in, 164–165
Nixon, Richard, 264
Nobel Prize, 85, 183, 184, 191
Norin 10 (wheat), 181, 186
Norris, Frank, 198
North, James L., 281
Nutrition Foundation of India, 256

oats, 4, 7, 143–145
Oats and Oat Improvement, 145
Ochoa, Carlos, 106–107, 109
Octopus, The, 198
Odyssey, The, 149
Oldenburg, Claes, 115
Omaha Indians, 46
Opaque-2 gene, 82
Oregon Wheat Growers League, 158
Origin of Corn Conference, 31
Origin of Cultivated Plants, 17, 149
Oryza nivara, 244
Oryza sativa, 211, 212, 215, 221. *See also* rice
Ovid, 151
Oxfam (Oxford Committee for Famine Relief), 250

Pakistan: rice in, 215, 216; wheat in, 205–206
Pamet Indians, 47
panic grass, 6
Panis sordidus, 150, 172
Parker, Arthur C., 48
Parker, John H., 19
Parmentier, Antoine-Augustin, 112–114
patents, 74–75, 76
Paterson, William, 119
Paul, Saint, 144–145
peanuts, 4

peanut butter, 154
Peel, Sir Robert, 122, 123–124
Peelings, 137
pellagra, 52, 81
Penone, Giuseppe, 115
Peru: corn in, 43–44; potatoes in, 93, 94, 99, 100–101, 103
pests: corn, 49–50, 76–78, 80, 258; potatoes, 104–106; rice, 80, 216, 237, 241–242, 243, 244, 248; sorghum, 161–162; wheat, 173–175, 258
Peta (rice), 237
Peter the Great, 109
Pfister, Lester, 68
Philippines: rice in, 155, 212, 215, 216, 217, 219, 232–242; wheat in, 154–155
Phytophaga destructor, 173–175
Phytophthora infestans, 125–126
Pilgrims, 46–48, 173
pink eye, 104
pink rot, 104
Pioneer Hi-Bred Corn Company, 68, 70, 71, 72–73, 78
Piper, Charles V., 276
Pit, The, 198
Pitt, William, 118
planthopper, 80, 242, 243, 244, 248
Plants, Man, and Life, 20, 29
Plant Variety Protection Act, 74
Pliny, 145, 149, 151
Plymouth Indians, 48
Poats, Susan V., 102
Poland, potatoes in, 92
Ponnamperuma, Felix N., 217
popcorn, 26
Porcupine, Peter. *See* William Cobbett
Post, Charles W., 131
potato(es), 4, 43, 51–52, 83–138; amounts grown, 91–92; business of, 134–138; diseases of, 98, 104, 119, 123, 125–128; in history, 110–132; insect pests and, 104–106; myths about, 111, 112; nutritional value of, 92–93, 102, 110–111, 131, 133–134; propagation of, 94–95; religions and, 101; research on, 101–109; scurvy and, 92; TPS (true potato seed), 95
Potato and Its Wild Relatives, The, 107
Potato Book, The, 103–104
Potato Chip Cookbook, 136
Potato Eaters, The, 115